ST

E

F

A

B

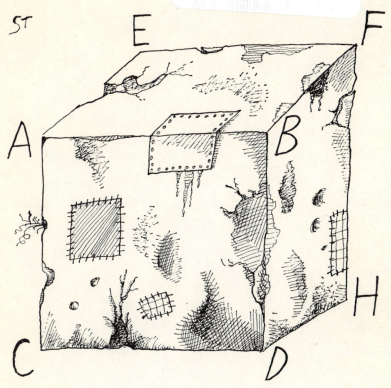

H

C

D

KANT'S ANALYTIC

BY

JONATHAN BENNETT

PROFESSOR OF PHILOSOPHY AT THE
UNIVERSITY OF BRITISH COLUMBIA

CAMBRIDGE UNIVERSITY PRESS

Published by the Syndics of the Cambridge University Press
Bentley House, 200 Euston Road, London, NW1 2DB
American Branch: 32 East 57th Street, New York, N.Y.10022

© Cambridge University Press 1966

Library of Congress Catalogue Card Number: 66–15281

ISBNS
0 521 04157 0 hard covers
0 521 09389 9 paperback

First published 1966
Reprinted 1975

First printed in Great Britain
at the University Printing House, Cambridge
Reprinted in Malta by
St Paul's Press Ltd

CONTENTS

CONTENTS

ANALYTIC OF CONCEPTS

ANALYTIC OF PRINCIPLES

CONTENTS

PREFACE

This book concerns the first half of Kant's *Critique of Pure Reason*; a treatment of the second half, under the title *Kant's Dialectic*, is in preparation. The present work ought to be readable by those who know nothing of the *Critique*. It is in some sense an 'introduction', but a selective one which does not expound all the *Critique*'s most important themes. What I hope it provides is one fairly unified way of viewing a good part of Kant's achievement.

To this end I have freely criticized, clarified, interpolated and revised. I make no apology for adopting this approach, for fighting Kant tooth and nail. Had I instead indulged him, or even given him the benefit of every doubt, I could neither have learned from his opaque masterpiece nor reported intelligibly on what it says.

Like all great pioneering works in philosophy, the *Critique* is full of mistakes and confusions. It is a misunderstanding to think that a supreme philosopher cannot have erred badly and often: the *Critique* still has much to teach us, but it is wrong on nearly every page.

I have no feelings about the man Immanuel Kant; and in my exploration of his work I have no room for notions like those of charity, sympathy, deference, or hostility.

Because I aim to be clear yet fairly brief, I devote little space to acknowledging debts and pursuing disagreements with previous writers on the *Critique*. I am indeed somewhat out of sympathy with such of these as I have read; but I have learned from the works of Bird, Ewing, Kemp Smith, Körner, Walsh, Weldon and Wolff, more than my comparative silence about them might suggest.

I have, with difficulty, checked Kemp Smith's translation of every passage quoted from the *Critique*. I do not italicize the phrases 'a priori' and 'a posteriori'; my few other departures from Kemp Smith are noted as they occur.

Following standard practice, I refer to the first edition of the *Critique* as 'A' and the second as 'B'.

The present work was written in three large Parts and then, early in the re-writing, divided into fifty-four sections. At the last minute, I have imposed a division into chapters. This was not part of my original plan, and I have not adjusted the text to accommodate it. Still, the chapter-titles are roughly accurate, and could help a reader who wishes to find whether and where I have discussed this or that large Kantian theme.

The Analytical Table of Contents, read in conjunction with the text, may help readers to grasp the book's main lines of argument and exposition.

The Notes at the end place every passage quoted or mentioned in the text, and refer to backing for assertions in the text about the views of Kant and others. The Notes contain nothing of any other kind. The few page-references given in the text are repeated in the Notes, so that the latter provide a complete list of passages referred to.

Drafts of some or all of the work have been read and helpfully criticized by A. J. Ayer, Malcolm Budd, N. Buder, A. C. Ewing, John Kenyon, M. J. Scott-Taggart, P. F. Strawson, W. H. Walsh and R. Ziedins; and for thorough criticisms of late drafts I owe a special debt to Gillian Bennett, Ian Hacking and Michael Tanner. I am also grateful to Saul Steinberg for his commentary on the uneasy relationship between the a priori and the empirical, which appears as the frontispiece.

J.F.B.

Cambridge
March 1966

ANALYTICAL TABLE OF CONTENTS

Aesthetic

§1. The Aesthetic is supposed to concern the senses, as the Logic does the intellect; but it is better seen as a treatment of some problems about space and time.

§2. In his account of the analytic/synthetic distinction, Kant overlooks sentence-ambiguity; explains the distinction in psychologistic terms; and sometimes seems to count as analytic only the elementarily analytic or true by definition. §3. An a priori judgment is 'necessary' in a very strong sense. Kant's view that Euclid's theorems are a priori but not analytic appears false unless 'analytic' means 'true by definition'. §4. However, Kant seems to think that Euclid's theorems are necessary not because they are (unelementarily) analytic but for some reason which does not rest on conceptual considerations. I shall construe him thus through §§5–8, but shall later re-interpret his conclusions in terms of what is analytic though not elementarily so.

§5. The outer-sense theory: the outer world as I experience it is Euclidean not because of uniformities in outer things but because of the uniform operation of my outer sense. §6. If this theory is a posteriori, so is Euclid's geometry; if it is elementarily analytic, it begs the question; and to call it synthetic and a priori is obscure. I shall argue that something like it is analytic, but not elementarily so (§§11–13). §7. Because he thinks it is synthetic and a priori, and because he offers it as a philosophical theory of great generality, Kant cannot take the outer-sense theory to be concerned with sense-organs or with anything phenomenal. §8. Kant's transcendental idealism (phenomenalism) says that what we can meaningfully say about phenomena, i.e. things which can be known through the senses, is restricted to what experience could teach us about them. He also thinks we have no concepts except phenomenal ones: so we cannot even speculatively apply concepts to the non-phenomenal, i.e. the noumenal. Yet he says there must be noumena, or at least that we must be able to 'think' noumena. The outer-sense theory seems to demand a noumenal subject-matter; but this would not be so if the theory did not have to be construed as synthetic and so did not have to reify outer sense.

§9. A spatial world must obey a geometry, and Kant may have thought that Euclid's is, although synthetic, the only consistent geometry. But a spatial world might obey a geometry only usually and approximately; so why should Kant think that there can be *no* exceptions to Euclid's theorems? §10. He probably assumed, wrongly, that what we say about space must be based on what could in principle be seen at a glance.

ANALYTICAL TABLE OF CONTENTS

§11. A case can be made for the suppressed premiss in §§9–10, namely that what is outer (objective, other-than-oneself) must be spatial. Strawson presents an auditory chaos which has no place for objectivity concepts and so contains nothing outer. §12. An ordering of the chaos which lets in objectivity concepts also introduces a spatial dimension. This is based on a 'master-sound', but a 'travel-based' ordering would be better. §13. The auditory world would be more objective still if there were movement and qualitative change in it, though if these were unrestricted the world would collapse back into chaos. §14. Each development in §§11–13 increases the grip of objectivity concepts on the auditory world. A Quinean theory explains why: each development increases those concepts' abbreviating power.

§15. Strawson's theory, that what is outer must be spatial, may be analytic; but unlike Kant's examples of the analytic it is (a) unobvious, and (b) concerned with the preconditions for a concept's having any—even negative—work to do. It is useful to pretend that this is what Kant means by 'synthetic and a priori'. Like most worthwhile analytic results, Strawson's is not conclusively provable; and although its analyticity is important its apriority is not.

§16. The inner-sense theory: temporality is imposed on all experience by inner sense. Kant seems to be right that all our concepts presuppose temporality, and that it is nevertheless not analytic that the only reality is temporal; but this does not make the inner-sense theory acceptable. Kant's transcendental idealism about time is also unsatisfactory: applied to objective time it is uncomprehensive; applied to time in general it is trivial.

§17. Kant is sometimes psychologistic, and sometimes Wittgensteinian, in his talk about concepts. He aligns the concept/intuition distinction with the understanding/sensibility and active/passive distinctions, saying that there could be an active (non-sensible, intellectual) intuition, but not for humans. This is too obscure to be assessed. §18. Despite the criticisms of §8, Kant's negative use of 'noumenon' makes a valid point: that our world is temporal is a contingent fact, yet we cannot entertain the possibility of its not being a fact. But he is wrong to equate 'noumenal' with 'knowable by a non-sensible intuition' and to assume that such an intuition would confront us with things as they are in themselves. The equation of intellectual or active intuition with intuitive understanding is also wrong: it exploits an ambiguity in 'intellectual'.

§19. Kant regards intuitions of space and time as somehow basic to concepts of them. This seems to come down to a claim about the logic of such phrases as 'a space' and 'a time'—a claim which Kant wrongly thinks will explain why space and time are necessarily singular. §20. Anyway, Kant's assumption that space is necessarily singular (and infinite) is false; his corresponding assumption about time may be true but does not prove his conclusion that time is 'an a priori intuition, not a concept'.

xi

Analytic of Concepts

§21. In defensible uses of 'concept', e.g. Kant's, concepts correspond to *functional kinds* of judgment. To have the concept of cause, say, is to be able to handle judgments which work like those we express in sentences using 'cause'. So Kant can speak of concepts of totality (associated with universal judgments), negation (negative judgments) etc. §22. Kant lists twelve functional kinds of judgment. He thinks they are the basic 'forms' a judgment may have: all its other features either pertain to its 'content' or, if formal, are definable in terms of Kant's twelve. §23. He thinks that his twelve judgment-kinds—and thus the corresponding concepts—are indispensable just because they are the basic 'forms' of judgments. Apart from the shakiness of the form/content distinction, this argument fails. Kant's twelve fall into four trios, and the most he can claim is the indispensability of one from each trio. This is too weak for his purposes; and if it is true it must be true by definition. To get untrivial results of the sort Kant wants, we must analyse 'judging' or 'employing concepts' or the like; we cannot argue from a list, as Kant tries to do.

§24. 'Concept' is useful only in describing a language in which general and past-tense judgments can be expressed. Kant seems to think that judgments require language, and that all languages must be concept-exercising. Thus, doubly wrongly, he equates 'x makes judgments' with 'x has concepts'. Still, his views about self-consciousness (§§28–31) entitle him to focus on the special case of judgments expressed in a concept-exercising language. §25. Some of Kant's favoured dozen—his 'categories'—are arguably indispensable to any concept-exercising language; others are not. §26. Although Kant purports here to prove the indispensability of all twelve categories, he later re-argues the case for just the relational ones—perhaps because these do not correspond as they should to the relational judgment-kinds.

§27. Our concern has been with what it is to have concepts, not with how they are acquired. There may be interesting analytic truths about the species concept-learning, but not about the genus concept-acquisition. The debate over 'innate ideas' has been fed by neglect of the difference between acquisition and learning.

§28. The Transcendental Deduction seeks to show—roughly speaking—that there cannot be experience which is not brought under concepts. Kant's premises are that every sensory state must be (a) a state of a unified mind and (b) accompanied by self-consciousness. (b) is true at least of the kinds of experience which concern Kant, viz. those of which one can intelligibly ask: 'What would it be like, "on the inside", to be like that?' §29. In an 'empirical' act of 'synthesis', one reasons one's way to an awareness that a unity—e.g. of different properties of a single thing—obtains. Awareness that one's own mental

A by-product of the 'solution': we apply to empirical things not the category but its schema. This involves images, and therefore sensibility, and therefore time. E.g. the schema of cause (= conditionality) is the concept of conditionality-in-time, which Kant takes to be the ordinary concept of cause.

§38. Kant thinks that Hume's analysis of cause must omit a non-empirical notion of necessity. He rightly does not attack Hume through counter-examples: *known* counter-examples could not discredit the programme for an *empiricist* analysis of cause. What does Kant mean by causal 'necessity'? Four possible answers, including:– (a) Perhaps he moves from 'There must be causal laws [if there is to be graspable experience]' through 'Causal laws are necessary' to 'Each causal law involves necessity'; but the lemma is ambiguous, and the whole move invalid. (b) According to a genetic version of the trans-cendental-synthesis doctrine (§30), causal laws are necessary because imposed a priori on experience by the understanding. This, which is part of Kant's 'Copernican revolution', is worthless. §39. A fifth possible answer: he misleadingly uses necessitarian language to make the claim—which Hume could not have accepted—that causal laws must be 'strictly universal', i.e. that a law which failed in even a single instance could not be used in genuine explanations.

§40. The 'Principles' chapter offers: (a) a single principle about 'quantity' in a different sense from that introduced in the Metaphysical Deduction (§41); (b) a single principle about reality and negation, with nothing said about limitation (§§42–3); (c) three principles about substance (§§45–50), cause (§§53–4) and community; and (d) three explanations of the modal categories in their empirical employment. The 'community' part of (c), and the whole of (d), will not be discussed further.

§41. An extensive magnitude is one which something has by virtue of having parts: size and duration seem to be the only extensive magnitudes. Kant tends wrongly to subordinate size to duration. The Aesthetic implies that all intuitions have extensive magnitude; but this does not, as Kant thinks, guarantee that 'pure mathematics, in its complete precision' must apply to the empirical world. §42. 'Intensive magnitude' is definable only as 'non-extensive magnitude'. Kant fails to prove that sensations must have continuous degrees of intensity; but successfully uses the general notion of intensive magnitude to correct some old mistakes about 'the real in space', by distinguishing 'How much of this region is occupied?' from 'In what degree is [the whole of] this region occupied?' This refutes 'If there is motion there is empty space', but Kant denies that anything could count as evidence for the existence of empty space (wrong) or of eventless time (right). §43. Kant uses 'intensive magnitude' against Mendelssohn's argument for the soul's immortality. His rebuttal is correct, but he accepts Mendelssohn's false premiss that change must be continuous if time is.

that every objective process must be governed by causal laws. §54. His 'ordering argument' is better: to recollect the order of occurrence of two past events—even purely inner events—one must appeal to causal considerations bearing directly and specifically upon that temporal ordering. Subject to certain qualifications, this is true; but it does not establish the second Analogy in its full strength.

AESTHETIC

1

SYNTHETIC A PRIORI JUDGMENTS

1 The place of the Aesthetic in the Critique

The *Critique* has two parts of unequal size and merit: the 'Transcendental Doctrine of Elements' and, less than a quarter as long, the 'Transcendental Doctrine of Method'. The former is our main concern.

The main division within the Elements is into the Aesthetic and the Logic. For Kant, aesthetic considerations are ones pertaining to our senses—to what we see, hear, feel, taste and smell—and have nothing to do with the artistic questions which would now be called aesthetic. Logic, for Kant, comprises all matters which might be called 'intellectual', such as the assessing of evidence, the drawing of conclusions and the spotting of inconsistencies.

The Aesthetic is a tiny fragment of the Elements, and has no important divisions within it. The Logic divides into the Analytic and the Dialectic. In the Analytic, Kant undertakes to describe how the intellect works when it is on its best behaviour; in the Dialectic he treats of certain misuses of the intellect and of the bad metaphysics arising therefrom. The two are related somewhat as physiology to clinical medicine. The Analytic in turn divides into the Analytic of Concepts and the Analytic of Principles, a division which I shall explain later. The over-all picture, then, is like this:

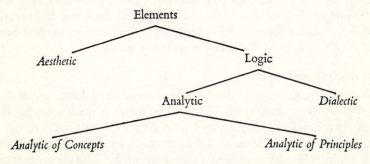

Three of the italicized items on this chart correspond to the three parts of the present work; the fourth, *Dialectic*, will be the topic of a further book.

3

The chart puts the Aesthetic on a level with the Logic, and this is misleading. Not only is the Aesthetic vastly the smaller, but also it relates in a quite different way to its nominal subject-matter. The Logic is a direct assault on various philosophical problems concerning the intellect, while the Aesthetic centres on problems not about the senses but about space and time. The Aesthetic and the Logic are nevertheless put on a par by Kant because he thinks that in solving his problems about space and time he can prove something about the senses analogous to something which, he thinks, the Logic proves about the intellect.

Considered as a source of cogent, detailed argument from true premisses to interesting conclusions, the Aesthetic is not impressive; and yet I would make a case for discussing it at length. Kant has a natural, subliminal sensitivity to philosophical problems, so that even where he argues badly his writing is rich in hints and suggestions which can lead one to insights which Kant himself did not have. Moreover, attention to Kant's treatment of his problems about space and time is required for an understanding of the more mature and fruitful parts of the *Critique*.

The 'Transcendental Doctrine of Method' consists in rambling repetitions of material in the Elements; plus an exposition of Kant's views about geometrical method[1]—views which, though ingenious, have been revealed by later work on the philosophy and logic of mathematics as thoroughly and tiresomely wrong. This part of the *Critique* clearly owes its existence to Kant's belief that it ought to exist rather than to the intellectual pressure of anything he has to say in it. It is announced ambitiously: '...we shall have to treat of a *discipline*, a *canon*, an *architectonic*, and finally a *history* of pure reason'[2]— and sure enough there are four chapters, whose respective lengths are 86, 37, 20 and 5 pages! I shall sometimes quote from the Method part of the *Critique*, but I shall not discuss it as a whole.

2 Analytic and synthetic

The central arguments of the Aesthetic depend upon Kant's use of the terms 'analytic' and 'synthetic'. He uses them to mark off what he calls two kinds of judgment and what I shall call two ways of construing declarative sentences. If we construe a sentence as analytic, we are taking it 'as adding nothing through the predicate to the concept of the subject, but merely breaking it up into those constituent concepts that have all along been thought in it, although confusedly'.[3] For example, 'All bodies are extended' is taken by Kant as analytic because

I do not require to go beyond the concept which I connect with 'body' in order to find extension as bound up with it. To meet with this predicate, I have merely to analyse the concept [of body], that is, to become conscious to myself of the manifold which I always think in that concept.

A sentence is taken as synthetic if it is taken to 'add to the concept of the subject a predicate which has not been in any wise thought in it, and which no analysis could possibly extract from it'; for example:

When I say, 'All bodies are heavy', the predicate is something quite different from anything that I think in the mere concept of body in general; and the addition of such a predicate therefore yields a synthetic judgment.

Kant seems to overlook the possibility that a sentence might properly be taken either as analytic or as synthetic, depending on which of two equally standard meanings is attached to one of its terms. His analytic/synthetic distinction between two kinds of 'judgment' amounts, in fact, to an uneasy mixture of (a) a distinction between two ways of construing declarative sentences and (b) a distinction between two sorts of declarative sentence. I shall try to explain this.

The distinction between left-handed and right-handed uses of tennis-racquets does not divide tennis-racquets themselves, for any racquet can be used in either way. As against this, the line between left- and right-handed uses of golf-clubs is also a line between left- and right-handed golf-clubs. Kant seems to intend the analytic/synthetic distinction to divide sentences, as the left/right distinction divides golf-clubs. Presumably he does not think it impossible that there should be a sentence which is sometimes construed as analytic and sometimes construed as synthetic; but he seems to think that there are in fact no such sentences, or none worth mentioning. A sentence can be called 'analytic', then, in the way in which a racquet could be called 'right-handed' if it were our custom never to permit any racquet to be used sometimes right-handedly and sometimes left-handedly.

Kant would no doubt reply that what he calls 'analytic' are not sentences but judgments, and that a judgment is indeed either always analytic or always synthetic. 'If a sentence can be construed either analytically or synthetically,' he would say, 'this just means that it can express more than one judgment. There is no condemnation of my procedures in this.' But there is. If 'judgment' is to be used like that, then expressions of the form 'The judgment that . . .' will refer unambiguously to a single judgment only if the sentence in the blank admits of only one normal construction. Just as questions of the form

'Is the sentence "..." analytic?' may have to be answered by 'Sometimes yes, sometimes no', so questions of the form 'Is the judgment that...analytic?' may have to be answered by 'For one of the judgments to which you have referred, yes; for the other, no.' Kant shows no awareness of this possibility.

I shall sometimes follow Kant in speaking of judgments as analytic or synthetic. When I say 'The judgment that all bodies are extended is analytic' I shall mean 'The sentence "All bodies are extended" is, when construed in any normal way, analytic'. But I shall not assume, as Kant seems to, that every sentence can be described either as analytic, i.e. always construed analytically in ordinary discourse, or as synthetic, i.e. always construed synthetically in ordinary discourse. This will limit my use of 'the judgment that...'. For example, I may not use the expression 'the judgment that what a man does voluntarily is always what he wants to do', because I think that 'want' is in ordinary parlance ambiguous in such a way that the sentence 'What a man does voluntarily is always what he wants to do' can properly be used to say something which is true by virtue of the meanings attached to the words, and can equally properly be used to say something which is simply false. Thus the phrase 'the judgment that what a man voluntarily does is always what he wants to do' does not uniquely refer to a single judgment.

There is another snag in Kant's account of the analytic/synthetic distinction. He says, in effect, that a judgment is analytic if and only if it is true solely by virtue of the concepts it involves; which I take as short-hand for: A sentence is analytic if and only if on its normal construction it says something true solely by virtue of the meanings of its constituent terms. It follows that self-contradictory judgments are not analytic, for they are not true by virtue of concepts or of anything else. Are they then synthetic? If we take Kant literally, they are: in its normal meaning, the sentence 'All squares are circular' is taken to 'add to the concept of the subject a predicate which has not been in any wise thought in it, and which no analysis could possibly extract from it', which is Kant's formula for a synthetic judgment. This is just an oversight, for Kant certainly intends analytic judgments to comprise only those which are true solely because of the concepts they involve, and synthetic judgments to comprise only those which cannot be determined by purely conceptual considerations either as true or as false. He thus needs a third class of judgments, namely those which are false by virtue of the concepts they contain. This third class is squeezed out of

6

Kant's account because he wants a classification of judgments which might be judged or thought to be true, and he tends, I think, to assume that no-one could think to be true something which was in fact false by virtue of the concepts involved. This mistake, though unimportant in itself, is a symptom of a major and very insidious defect in Kant's account of the analytic/synthetic distinction, namely the psychological terms in which he states it.

Kant implies that the way to discover whether one construes a sentence of the form 'All *F*s are *G*' analytically is to 'think the concept' associated with the subject and to note whether in so doing one also 'thinks the concept' associated with the predicate. This introspectionist account of the examination of meanings encourages Kant to restrict the label 'analytic' to such sentences as are obviously, trivially, self-evidently analytic. For example, he says of a certain theorem about triangles that it is not analytic because to discover that it is true

I must not restrict my attention to what I am actually thinking in my concept of a triangle (this is nothing more than the mere definition); I must pass beyond it to properties which are not contained in this concept, but yet belong to it.[1]

The references here to 'the mere definition', to what is 'contained' in a concept, and to 'what I am actually thinking', all suggest a restriction to what one would first think of when asked what 'triangle' means, or to what one might first say when asked to explain what it means: a theorem about triangles, it seems, is to count as analytic only if it is true by definition, true in such a way that someone could not doubt it if he knew the meanings of the relevant words. Also:

The concept of the sum of 7 and 5 contains nothing save the union of the two numbers into one, and in this no thought is being taken as to what that single number may be which combines both. The concept of 12 is by no means already thought in merely thinking this union of 7 and 5; and I may analyse my concept of such a possible sum as long as I please, still I shall never find the 12 in it.[2]

That the straight line between two points is the shortest, is a synthetic pro-position. For my concept of *straight* contains nothing of quantity, but only of quality. The concept of the shortest is wholly an addition, and cannot be derived, through any process of analysis, from the concept of the straight line.[3]

In each of these passages, Kant concludes from the most casual of premises that analytic procedures cannot yield a certain result. Given the complexity which such procedures may have, and the novelty of the results which may be proved by them, is this not rash? It is, unless we take 'any process of analysis' to refer only to the scrutiny of what goes on in one's mind when one 'thinks' a concept.

This narrowing of 'analytic' to something like 'true by definition' is—like the introspectionist account of meaning which helps to generate it—contrary to Kant's own considered intentions. He takes the analytic/synthetic distinction to divide two radically different ways in which judgments can be shown to be true. In his paradigmatic picture of what it is to show that a judgment is analytic, the judgment's truth is shown to stem from the definitions of the words which express it or from facts about what first comes to mind when we consider what those words mean. But from a judgment which is in this way self-evidently true or true by definition, we may derive, by steps whose validity is warranted by elementary facts about meanings, a conclusion which is not self-evident or true by definition. In proving such a conclusion we use the same means as in showing that something expresses a self-evident or definitional or 'merely verbal' truth; for in each case we merely attend to the meanings of words. Kant nowhere suggests that he gives any theoretical weight to the difference between simple and complex, or short and long, investigations of meanings. On the contrary, he repeatedly says that a synthetic judgment is one whose truth cannot be derived 'from concepts', or whose predicate 'no analysis could possibly extract from' the subject because it is not contained even 'covertly' in the subject. Consider this passage:

No doubt the concept of 'right', in its common-sense usage, contains all that the subtlest speculation can develop out of it, though in its ordinary and practical use we are not conscious of the manifold representations comprised in this thought.[1]

Here the concept is described as a 'thought', but it is allowed to contain more than we are 'conscious' of its containing. There is no room here for an equation of the analytic with the trivial.

So we have a problem. Kant denies that the theorems of Euclid's geometry are analytic: do we take this as saying that they cannot be verified by purely conceptual means, or only that they are not true by definition in a quite narrow way? To see what makes this problem important, we must examine two more of Kant's technical terms.

3 A priori and a posteriori

'A priori' and 'a posteriori' are among Kant's hardest-worked technical terms. His use of them is complex and many-layered, but all we need

8

at this stage is the division of judgments into a priori and a posteriori on the basis of what risk a judgment runs of being falsified by experience.

'Necessity and strict universality', says Kant, 'are...sure criteria of a priori knowledge.'¹ The context clearly implies that necessity and universality are entailed by apriority as well as entailing it. Thus, if the judgment that all Fs are G is a priori, then experience *cannot* render it false by yielding even a single F which is not G. If it is a posteriori, then it *could* be falsified by experience.

The exegesis of the Aesthetic is largely an inquiry into the role which the words 'cannot' and 'could' and their cognates play in Kant's account of apriority and aposteriority. It may be noted at once, however, that Kant counts as a posteriori many judgments for which we have never found, and are confident we never shall find, a counter-instance. For example, the judgment that every human body is larger than any ant would be described by Kant as a posteriori. The 'cannot' through which 'a priori' is explained has to be stronger than that arising from 'flatly against what we have so far discovered about how the world works'.

Analytic judgments are all a priori, and for them at least a suitably strong sense of 'cannot' is available. If 'All bodies are extended' is analytic, then we may say 'There cannot be a body which is not extended' on the grounds that the meanings of the relevant terms do not allow 'a body which is not extended' as a consistent phrase whose realization can be expected, feared, hoped for or theorized about. While 'body' and 'extended' have the meanings which render 'All bodies are extended' analytic, the impossibility of there being a body which is not extended is guaranteed by conceptual considerations and is, on the face of it, of a quite different kind from the impossibility of an occurrence which, though consistently describable, is ruled out by well-tested scientific hypotheses.

Of course, an analytic sentence may come to express something false, for one or more of the words in it may change in meaning; but in that case the judgment (or proposition) expressed by the sentence will not be the one now expressed by it; and it is this judgment or proposition which is declared to be a priori, i.e. incapable of refutation at the hands of experience. Powerful arguments have been adduced by Quine,² and can be extracted from Wittgenstein,³ for saying that there is no sharp distinction between what a word means and what it in fact applies to; and from this two consequences follow. (a) The analytic/synthetic distinction is not sharp either: for analytic sentences are defined as ones which say something true solely by virtue of what their words mean and not at all by virtue of the facts about the things their words apply to. (b) The a priori/a posteriori distinction is not sharp either: for a priori judgments are defined as ones which cannot turn out to be false; so that an a priori judgment must be expressed by a sentence which cannot come to say something false except by coming to express a judgment other than the one it now expresses, i.e. except by changing its meaning. The view of Quine and Wittgenstein, however, is that there is no sharp line between the case where we move from saying 'It is the case that S' to saying 'It is not the case that S' because we have come to mean something different by S, and the case where we make this move because we have changed our minds as to the facts. There is much force in this, but it does not dissolve the problem which Kant creates for us when he says that *some judgments are at once synthetic and a priori*. (I take this to mean that a sentence may express a judgment (i) whose truth does not derive solely from the meanings of the words in the sentence, but (ii) which cannot be rendered false by experience.) Even if there is little point in saying that a sentence is analytic or that it expresses an a priori judgment—a matter to which I shall return at the end of § 15—I think Quine would agree that, in so far as 'analytic' and 'expressing an a priori judgment' have any intelligible use, they *go together*. It is just this which Kant denies.

In saying that every analytic judgment is a priori, Kant would presumably have the agreement of everyone who has any use for the expressions 'analytic' and 'a priori'. If every synthetic judgment were a posteriori, then the two ways of classifying judgments would coincide. I believe that they do coincide, in so far as one can see how they work at all; but Kant thinks that some judgments are at once synthetic and a priori, i.e. that some sentences can be construed both as synthetic and, on that same construction, as expressing something whose refutation by experience is, in a suitably strong sense, impossible. This commits him to finding for 'impossible' a sense which is (a) stronger than that of 'flatly against what we have so far discovered about how the world works', and (b) other than that of 'ruled out by the meanings of the words involved'. For a judgment is a priori only if its refutation is 'impossible' in a sense which satisfies (a), and is synthetic only if its refutation is 'impossible' in a sense which satisfies (b).

It is because I cannot find for 'impossible' a sense satisfying both (a) and (b) that I deny that any judgment can be both synthetic and a priori. Kant is acutely conscious of the attractiveness of the view that one cannot say something synthetic except at the price of saying something which could be refuted by experience. He therefore sees it as a major problem to show how it is possible for a judgment to be at once synthetic and a priori. He asks '*How* is it possible...?' because he does not doubt that some judgments, including those expressed by Euclid's theorems, *are* both synthetic and a priori. His most famous formulation of the problem first appeared in his *Prolegomena*,[1] and was then incorporated in the second edition of the *Critique*; but the problem itself dominates the Aesthetic in both editions.

As well as asking what risk of refutation a judgment runs, we may ask what grounds there can be for thinking it to be true. In addition to 'Might you be wrong?' there is 'How do you know?' Kant raises the question of the grounds for a judgment by putting with great force the case against synthetic a priori judgments.[2] When we make a judgment 'in which the relation of a subject to the predicate is thought', we assert a connection between two concepts. Kant implies that we can fairly ask of any such judgment 'What connects those two concepts in the way the judgment says they are connected?' If the judgment is analytic, the answer is easy: triangularity is linked with straight-sidedness as required by the judgment that all triangles are straight-sided, because the latter concept is a part of the former. Strictly speaking, we should not ask 'What links this concept with this other concept?'; for straight-sidedness, although it is not the same concept as triangularity but only part of it, is not *another* concept than triangularity. Here, in Kant's words, 'the connection of the predicate with the subject is thought through identity'.[3] With synthetic a posteriori judgments there is also a straightforward answer: when we judge that all sugar-cubes are soluble in water, we assert a connection between two concepts because our past experience has connected *instances* of them—we have found many soluble sugar-cubes and no insoluble ones. This connects the two concepts by a brute-force link, so to speak, which is known to hold for instances which we have put to the test and is conjectured to hold for all instances whatsoever. When Kant calls such a judgment a posteriori he means that it is based upon individual items of past experience and—what he rightly takes to be a consequence of this—that it is vulnerable to individual items of future experience.

The problem of how a judgment can be synthetic and a priori, then, presents itself to Kant as the problem of how two concepts, neither of which includes the other, can be connected in a way which does not rest upon past experience and is not vulnerable to future experience.

This talk of a concept which includes another, and of judgments in which 'the connection of the predicate with the subject is thought through identity', echoes ominously Kant's 'narrowing' approach to analyticity. It suggests that he is asking how a judgment can be a priori without being true by definition, or trivially or elementarily analytic. But we have an answer to *that* question: a judgment can be a priori although not definitionally true, just so long as its truth is guaranteed by purely conceptual considerations.

I do not think that this is Kant's problem, however: the solution which he offers looks like an attempt to show of certain judgments that they are a priori although their truth is not guaranteed by conceptual considerations of any sort whatever. An example may help to make this clear.

4 A geometrical experiment

Consider the case of someone who undertakes to test Pythagoras' theorem. He cuts out of a sheet of three-ply wood a triangular piece, one of whose angles is a right-angle. He tests this for triangularity by counting its sides and testing them for straightness, and for rectangularity by cutting out three congruent pieces and seeing that the four together exactly fill 360°. He next cuts out three cardboard squares of different sizes, each one with sides of the same length as one side of his triangle. Pythagoras' theorem tells him that if his triangle is right-angled then the square on its longest side is equal to the sum of the squares on its other two sides; he proceeds to test this, and finds that the two smaller squares, when dismembered and reassembled, cover the largest square with some to spare.

He will probably take it that he has made some mistake. But suppose that he re-tests his piece of wood for triangularity and rectangularity, and re-tests his cardboard pieces for squareness and for equality of side with the sides of the triangle; suppose also that other people conduct these tests as well, with the same result, and that the careful use of witnesses and of a cine-camera yields no evidence that any of the experimental materials have changed in size or shape during the relevant times. Logically, this supposition is unexceptionable: each successive action and result is logically possible, and a sequence of logically possible sub-stories which have no temporal overlaps constitutes a logically possible story.

Our experimenter, then, has to face the fact that a triangle was carefully tested for rectangularity and for the Pythagorean property; that it passed the first test and failed the second; and that all attempts to find a specific mistake in either test have failed. Should he then claim to have found a counter-instance to Pythagoras' theorem?

This conclusion seems to be right if the theorem is construed as a posteriori, i.e. as being in principle vulnerable to refutation. The experimenter may construe the theorem in this way and fend off the conclusion that he has refuted it, by insisting that *something* must have been wrong with the techniques or materials of the experiment, and attributing to abnormally bad luck his failure to discover what. But if he puts too much strain on 'bad luck', he will cease to be a scientist. If the experiment has the same result every time it is performed, however nicely, and if he can find no viable hypothesis as to what has gone wrong, the time will come when it is more reasonable to say 'This is a right-angled triangle which is not Pythagorean' than to persist stubbornly in saying 'It is only because of mistaken techniques, or some subtle instability in the materials, that these tests seem to show that the thing is a right-angled triangle and is non-Pythagorean; I still think that it is not both'.

There is, however, a way in which the experimenter can save the theorem without postulating a lurking defect in the conduct or materials of the experiment; for he may construe the theorem as elementarily analytic, or true by definition. In that case he will say that his tests, even if flawlessly conducted, were not sufficient to show conclusively that an angle is a right-angle, that something is square, that two lines are of equal length etc. He will regard the question of whether he has constructed a right-angled triangle with squares on its sides as necessarily an open one until he discovers whether two of the squares are equal to the third. 'It is part of what I mean by "right-angled triangle"', he will say, 'that a right-angled triangle has the Pythagorean property. To think that a test could refute the theorem is like thinking that a test could show that a triangle need not have three sides.'

Kant is surely right in rejecting *this* account of a theorem like that of Pythagoras; but when he says that such theorems are 'synthetic' is this all that he is rejecting? If it were, then his claim that there are synthetic and a priori truths would amount only to saying that the experimenter has a third option open to him, namely taking the theorem to be true, despite the outcome of the test, because it is analytic though not elementarily so. If the experimenter had a set of definitions from which the theorem followed, by steps whose validity was elementarily analytic, then he would have grounds for maintaining that his experiment could not have refuted the theorem. (He might also have grounds for changing some of his definitions; but that leads into Quinean areas which are not relevant to my present point.) He would be wrong, or at least eccentric, if his use of geometrical terms were such as to justify him in taking this option, i.e. in declaring the theorem to be analytic though not elementarily so, but at least his position would be an intelligible one.

Unfortunately, Kant's treatment of the alleged apriority of Euclidean geometry seems not to admit of this interpretation. His explanation of how there can be judgments which are both synthetic and a priori is offered as an account of certain limits upon what can be sensorily encountered in the physical world: rather than saying that the theorem could be saved from the experiment without being taken as true by definition, Kant seems to say that the experiment simply *could not happen*. This 'could not' is to have a warrant stronger than could be supplied by empirical science, but is not to arise from conceptual considerations of any kind. Thus, we are back with our problem.

Through most of my next four sections, I shall construe Kant's account of synthetic and a priori judgments in that spirit, steering clear of any interpretation of it as an attempt to show how a judgment can be—or, to show that certain specific judgments are—a priori without being elementarily analytic.

Nevertheless, the 'narrowing' approach to analyticity must not be forgotten, for from it stems Kant's perfect confidence that some judgments are synthetic and a priori. It is also the root of the once-popular belief that if there were no synthetic a priori judgments the sciences of logic and mathematics would be either trivial or empirical. More important, I shall show in §§11–15 that Kant's solution can be so interpreted as to constitute, after all, an argument for saying of certain judgments that they are true because of certain very complex and unobvious conceptual facts. I doubt if this interpretation is true to Kant's conscious intentions; and this is one good reason for suppressing it until we have explored the other interpretation, which takes Kant to be arguing that certain judgments are a priori although they are not supported by conceptual facts of any kind.

truth based upon knowledge of the workings of th[e] ... could count as knowledge of the workings of oute[r] ... not take outer sense to be some part of the nervou[s] ... [bas]e his theory upon neurophysiology, for he is emphatic ... human bodies could yield only a posteriori results. He ... [thi]nk that apriority is in a peculiar way involved in true ... [hypot]heses, but he denies that empirical inquiries can show us ... [partic]ular scientific hypothesis is a priori. Yet he demands of ... [th]e theory that 'it should not obtain favour merely as a ... [hypo]thesis, but should have that certainty and freedom from ... is required of any theory that is to serve as an organon',[1] ... [sh]ould be 'not merely possible or probable, but indubitably ... [th]e piano analogy is at best a sparsely formal one, then. ... not discuss the status of the outer-sense theory, and his only ... [argu]ment for its truth goes so wide of the mark that it gives no ... of how he might have tackled the status problem: 'Since ... [defini]tions of geometry are synthetic a priori..., I raise the ... whence do you obtain such propositions, and upon what ... [un]derstanding rely in its endeavour to achieve such absolutely ... [a]nd universally valid truths?'[3] The only possible answer, he ... [th]at the understanding relies on the facts to which the outer- ... [theo]ry draws attention. This argument is without value. Even if ... but the outer-sense theory could explain Euclidean geo- ... [h]aving the status Kant thinks it has, it does not follow that the ... [i]s true unless we have the further premise that Euclidean ... [theor]y is synthetic and a priori. This premise is indeed among Kant's ... [share]d assumptions, and motivates his search for an explanation of ... [th]ere can be synthetic a priori truths. But he is not entitled to ... [fr]om it until he argues for it. ... [wh]y is Kant so confident that there are synthetic a priori truths? ... [o]f the answer, no doubt, lies in his tendency to equate 'synthetic' ... [with] not true-by-definition'; but there is an ambiguity in 'a priori' ... [that] may also be relevant. Kant says: 'If we have a proposition which ... [in bein]g thought is thought as *necessary*, it is an a priori judgment'.[4] This ... [sugge]sts that an a priori judgment is simply one which the judger ... [belie]ves to be invulnerable to experience: in this non-committal sense, ... [one ca]n describe a judgment made by someone else as 'a priori' without ... [onese]lf asserting its invulnerability. Now, Kant is apparently not aware ... [of t]he distinction between the weak and strong senses of 'a priori'. In ... [the] following passage he moves from the weak sense to the strong

18

2

THE OUTER-SENSE THEORY

5 The form of outer sense

Kant uses the word 'sensibility' for one's capacity for being in any sort of sensory state. He says that this capacity is exercised in two ways: as *outer sense*, it permits one to have sensory states which are seeings, hearings, feelings etc. of things other than oneself; as *inner sense*, it permits one to have sensory states which may relate to one's environment but may be *just* states of oneself. Thus, all sensory states are mediated by inner sense, and some by outer sense as well: notwithstanding one queer remark suggesting the contrary,[1] the proper contrast is not between 'outer' and 'inner' but between 'outer (and also inner)' and 'only inner'. As Kant says:

Whatever the origin of our [sensory states], whether they are due to the influence of outer things, or are produced through inner causes,...they must all, as modifications of the mind, belong to inner sense.[2]

Our present concern is with outer sense.

In all the variety of my sensory awareness of the world there is, according to Kant, the constant factor that every one of these states of awareness is the end-product of a transaction between my sensibility and some part of the world outside me. Wherever and whenever it occurs, whatever fragment of the varied world it confronts me with, any 'outer' sensory state is given to me by my sensibility in its function as outer sense. This suggests that there might be some features which characterize all my experiences of the world, not because of any uniformity in the world but rather because my outer sense imposes these features upon its entire output. Kant says that this is indeed the case. Specifically, the outer sense of every human is such as to guarantee that the outer world which he experiences will always conform to the theorems of Euclidean geometry—these being construed, we must add, synthetically. Regarding the geometrical experiment described in the preceding section, Kant would presumably say that, although such a sequence of observations can be described without logical inconsistency, its occurrence is ruled out by the *modus operandi* of the human outer sense.

15

Here is an analogue of Kant's doctrine of outer sense: I do not know who is going to play my piano this evening—whether it will be played by someone skilled or unskilled, with good or bad musical taste, aiming to please or to annoy; nevertheless I do know that the piano is built in such a way that it can make only sounds which have the timbre characteristic of pianos, and not the timbre of flutes, pneumatic drills or crying babies. Here, potential pianists correspond to the world, and the piano corresponds to outer sense. In each case, the end-product arises from a transaction between a varying world or pianist and a constant sensibility or piano, and so it has variety and also certain constant and absolutely dependable features. Those features of outer experience which vary with the world are described by Kant as the 'matter' of experience; the invariant features which outer sense imposes upon experience are the latter's 'form'. Analogously, we might say that a recital had the formal property of consisting entirely of piano-sounds and the material property of including a Beethoven sonata.

6 The status of Kant's theory

We now have the outlines of a theory which invites us to place unqualified reliance on Euclid's axioms on the grounds that outer sense will not permit our experience of the outer world to reach us in such a form that the outer world is perceived to be non-Euclidean. The question now arises: 'What does Kant think the logical and epistemological status of his theory to be?' On his own showing, there are just three possible answers.

(1) The theory is synthetic and a posteriori, which is to say that it has the force of 'Outer sense has until now imposed a Euclid-confirming form on all its output, and we may reasonably expect it to continue to do so'. This answer is not available to Kant. If outer sense could cease to impose a Euclid-confirming form on our outer experience, then Euclid's geometry could cease to be true of the experienced outer world, which is just to say that it is not a priori after all. If Kant renders his theory vulnerable to experience, then this vulnerability is transmitted to Euclidean geometry, and that he cannot allow.

(2) The theory is a priori because it is analytic. If the theory is taken to be elementarily analytic or true by definition, then it has the force of 'To qualify for the title "outer sense", a mode of sensibility must impose a Euclid-confirming form upon its output'; and this is un-

acceptable, for the
judgment that all out
other than oneself'—
defines 'outer sense' t
Euclid-confirming, th
experience' from that
outer experience need n
case the outer-sense theo

Alternatively, the theo
true by definition. To dem
trace a conceptual route fro
attempt to do so. I shall arg
analytic though not elemen
'What is spatial is Euclidean
about this, and were therefo
Euclidean' to be analytic, hov
geometry's supposed status as a

Kant does just once seem to ta
definition, that what is outer is sp
'referred to something outside m
region of space from that in which
represent his considered view, and
over the status of the outer-sense th

(3) The remaining option is to s
synthetic and a priori. Where (1) and
prejudicial to the status Kant claims f
option preserves that status, perhaps, bu
seen the difficulty about synthetic a prio
to show that there can be such judgmen
explained by an underlying theory of out
that this theory is itself synthetic and a p
now arises at a new level: the outer-sense th
status as synthetic and a priori, and so this s
some further theory which relates to the
latter allegedly does to Euclidean geometry.
ask, what this further theory might be.

I press this question of the theory's status
whether the theory is to be taken as analytic
a posteriori, we do not know what sorts of
relevant to its truth. That the piano will make sou

is an a posteriori
piano; but wha
sense? Kant can
system, and bas
that a science o
does in fact th
scientific hypo
that any parti
the outer-sens
plausible hyp
doubt which
and that it sh
certain'.² Th

Kant does
serious argu
intimation
the propos
question,
does the u
necessary
says, is th
sense the
nothing
metry's
theory
geomet
unargu
how t
argue

Part o
with
which
in be
sugg
beli

I ca
my
of
th

through an expression which is ambiguous as between them (the italics are mine):

> If, then, a judgment is *thought* with strict universality, that is, in such manner that no exception is *allowed* as possible, it is not derived from experience, but *is valid* absolutely a priori.[1]

Also, he has one explicit argument for the existence of synthetic a priori judgments which seems to rest directly on the weak sense of 'a priori'. Of a priori mathematics and physics he says:

> Since these sciences actually exist, it is quite proper to ask *how* they are possible; for that they must be possible is proved by the fact that they exist.[2]

He defends the claim that a priori physics exists, in a footnote:

> Many may still have doubts as regards pure [= a priori] natural science. We have only, however, to consider the various propositions that are to be found at the beginning of (empirical) physics, properly so called, those, for instance, relating to the permanence in the quantity of matter, to inertia, to the equality of action and reaction, etc., in order to be soon convinced that they constitute a *physica pura*...

It is not clear what we are here invited to 'consider', but Kant seems to be appealing to the way in which physics is done, to the assumptions which physicists do in fact make and do not regard as open to experimental refutation. If this is how he is arguing, then he is using 'a priori' in the non-committal sense. Nevertheless, he does not usually take 'a priori' in this way, and if he did the outer-sense theory would be nugatory. In the weak sense of 'a priori' it is true enough that for many people Euclid's theorems are synthetic and a priori; but this means only that such people have made a mistake—it need not and cannot be explained by a theory of outer sense.

7 Sensibility and sense-organs

We have seen that Kant is debarred from identifying outer sense and what I have called 'the world' with any such empirical items as sense-organs and the world. What blocks him is not just his need for an a priori theory of outer sense, but also something else which I shall now explain.

Consider the sentence 'All our perceptions of objects are caused by the objects perceived'. I shall call this the causal theory of perception, and I offer it not as a version of the outer-sense theory but merely as an explanatory analogue of it.

The causal theory of perception might be defended as a barely legitimate way of saying something which is probably true. If someone stands open-eyed before an elephant and says that he sees an elephant, we shall probably not think of this as requiring causal explanation; but an explanation is called for if he reports seeing an elephant when there is none there, and we can explain the non-standard case only if we could, on demand, explain the standard case also. The tactual incapacities of the leper, the distortions arising from selective deafness, colour-blindness—these and their like can already in some measure be causally explained; and it may well be that every such sensory failure, and every sensory success, could in principle be explained through well-established scientific hypotheses which connect sensory states with the physical conditions of human bodies and their environments. Since the explanation of any sensory success must refer to the thing seen, the sound heard, the surface touched etc., this could be summed up loosely in the sentence 'All our perceptions of objects are caused by the objects perceived'. The causal theory of perception, then, may merely express a worthy optimism about such sciences as optics and neurophysiology.

Of several other ways in which the causal theory of perception might be construed,[1] I shall consider only the one which Locke adopted. Locke noted that most of our experience does, though some does not, fall into certain kinds of complex patterns without which we should have no reason to take any of our sensory states to be perceptions of objects. This very general fact seemed to Locke to need explanation:

If I turn my eyes at noon towards the sun, I cannot avoid the ideas which the light or sun then produces in me. So that there is a manifest difference between the ideas laid up in my memory. . .and those which force themselves upon me, and I cannot avoid having. And therefore it must needs be some exterior cause, and the brisk acting of some objects without me, whose efficacy I cannot resist, that produces those ideas in my mind, whether I will or no.[2]

This too might be summed up by 'All our perceptions of objects are caused by the objects perceived'. But, so taken, the causal theory of perception pretends to explain a certain general fact by pointing to facts which are just parts of the one to be explained.

An example may help to make this clear. In explaining the fact that *Smith has at this moment a heterogeneous visual field*, we may properly refer to the fact that things have various colours. Just because the explanation *might have been* 'Smith has glass eyes which are stimulating his optic nerves in such a way that. . .etc.', or 'Smith is in darkness but radiation is affecting his eyes in such a way that...etc.', it is significant and informative to say that the explanation *is* 'Smith has normal eyes which are now open, he is in daylight, and he is confronted by things which have various colours'. But in explaining the fact that *People sometimes have heterogeneous visual fields*, we cannot refer to the fact that the world is varicoloured, for this is part of the explicandum: if there were no heterogeneous visual fields, there would be no reason to say that things have various colours. One may explain the heterogeneity in terms of lengths of light-waves; and perhaps someone might use his own eyes to establish that the world is varicoloured, and then use this to explain the heterogeneity of the visual fields of others. But the former explanation avoids circularity only because it does not appeal to the world's being varicoloured; and the latter is legitimate—if at all—only because its explicandum omits one set of facts about visual heterogeneity.

The causal theory of perception is similarly defective if it purports to explain why there is order in our experience by appealing to how objects act upon us. It might explain why there is order in the experience of all children, or of all scientists, or—more dubiously—of everyone but him who offers the explanation; but it cannot explain the perfectly general fact that there is ordered experience, because that includes as a special case everything that might be said about objects in the supposed explanation. One can no more move from physics and neurophysiology to the order in our experience than one can move from the world's colour-variety to the heterogeneity of our visual fields: in neither case is there a *move*. (The two cases also differ: while visual heterogeneity may be explained by reference to light-waves, experiential order cannot be explained by *any* facts about objects since *all* these are part of the explicandum.)

Taken only as expressing scientific optimism, the causal theory of perception escapes this attack by speaking of the whole of human experience only in a piecemeal way. It calls attention to the possibility of subjecting any given perception to experimental inquiry; and it need not deny that in such an inquiry some perceptions must be *used* and therefore cannot themselves be inquired into at that time by those experimenters. The theory becomes objectionable only when, as in Locke's hands, it invites us to stand back from all the individual inquiries and to generalize *en bloc* about the relation between the two items: human experience and the world of objects.

Kant intends the outer-sense theory to be like this, which is the ultimate reason why he cannot construe it as a theory about empirical things of any sort whatever. Had it been put to him that outer sense might be an array of sense-organs and nerves, Kant would certainly have replied that since empirical things are given to us only through outer sense it would be absurd to identify any of them with outer sense.

8 Phenomena and noumena

Kant, then, will not have it that the outer-sense theory is about empirical things. Probably, he thinks it is about *noumena*.

'Noumenon' is best understood through the opposed term 'phenomenon'. Kant applies this, and the word 'appearance', to all those objective things, processes and events which we can know about by means of our senses—but not to our sensory states themselves. Physical objects are typical phenomena, but Kant would take phenomena to include battles, victories, rivers, genuine ghosts, and the sky. I shall find it convenient to apply the adjective 'phenomenal' to sensory states as well as to phenomena.

We describe phenomena under such headings as taste, colour, shape, size, position, texture, viscosity, temperature, smell, density, strength, edibility, audibility, solubility, biological classification, commercial utility, rarity, and thousands of others; and the basis for these descriptions is what we know by means of our senses. This does not imply that something can be described as a typewriter, say, on the basis of how it looks and regardless of how it functions; for the question of how it functions is also one which can be answered only on the basis of our senses.

Kant thinks that statements about phenomena are not merely supported by, but are equivalent to, statements about actual and possible sensory states. Something might be the case although no-one had any sensory evidence for it; but it is bad logic to say that something might be the case although there was nothing anyone *could* do which would yield sensory evidence for it. If someone says seriously 'There is no moon', we may think he has some fancy about a permanent visual hallucination or a trick by the Martians. If he is not shaken by close-up photographs of the moon, it becomes harder to know what to make of him. Suppose, however, that after walking on the moon he says: 'I grant that the evidence so far—and perhaps all the evidence there could be—supports the lunar hypothesis; but there is no moon.' We can no longer regard him as fanciful or sceptical, for now we do not understand what he says. We understood him just as long as we could guess at what sorts of evidence he believed could be found to support *(or) investigation into the possibility of a priori knowledge*

his position; now that he admits that his thesis is not answerable to evidence at all, we do not even know what his thesis is.

Kant calls this account of statements about phenomena 'transcendental idealism'—*transcendental* because it is a thesis about meanings, and *idealism* because of the primacy which it gives to sensory states. It must be sharply distinguished from empirical idealism which, without reducing statements about non-mental items to ones about mental items, says that there are in fact only mental items. Whereas transcendental idealism offers an analysis of statements about tables and chairs, empirical idealism denies that there are any tables and chairs. Realisms, too, divide into transcendental and empirical. Transcendental realism, which denies that non-mental statements reduce to mental ones, is 'realism' because it gives to the concept of a non-mental item an irreducible place in our conceptual scheme; while empirical realism says tritely that there are non-mental items in the world—such as G. E. Moore's hands.[1]

The empirical/transcendental distinction may be seen at work in Kant's argument that a transcendental realist is not entitled to be an empirical realist as well.[2] The transcendental realist, for whom there is always a logical gap between statements about non-mental things and statements about actual and possible experiences, cannot know for sure that there are any non-mental things. Nor can he even reasonably believe that there are, for, as Kant says in a different connection:

> I must never presume to *opine*, without *knowing at least something* by means of which the judgment, in itself merely problematic, secures connection with truth, a connection which, although not complete, is yet more than arbitrary fiction. Moreover, the law of such a connection must be certain. For if, in respect of this law also, I have nothing but opinion, it is all merely a play of the imagination, without the least relation to truth.[3]

The transcendental realist may 'presume to *opine*' that there are non-mental things on the grounds that if there were not his experience would *probably* not be as it is. But he cannot know for sure that this is probable, and if he merely opines that it is then he is well on the way to 'a play of the imagination, without the least relation to truth'. His 'empirical' view—his view about what in fact there is in the world—ought to be not empirical realism but the more cautious empirical idealism:

the higher the degree that the connection' thing (ext. obj. → statement is problematic & the (assertion is our knowledge of) external things or b) near influence ... (the more problematic)

It is...this transcendental realist who afterwards plays the part of empirical idealist. After wrongly supposing that objects of the senses, if they are to be

therefore the less certain, the more ... realism tends to depend upon empir. idealism

one on our mental states, and so the less certain we are in a position to speak of the existence of ext. obj.

23

The question [concerning transc. realism & empirical realism] is not between something and its expression in linguistic form, but between (objects and experiences) between objects (which receive linguistic expression) & experiences (which do so do) external, must have an existence by themselves, and independently of the senses, he finds that, judged from this point of view, all our sensuous representations are inadequate to establish their reality.[1]

The transcendental idealist, on the other hand, takes 'There are non-mental things' to say something about actual and possible experiences, and we know for sure that what it says, so taken, is true. 'The transcendental idealist', Kant says, 'may be an empirical realist.'[2] In other words: if we have idealism as our conceptual background, we may have realism as our view of what there is.

We now turn to noumena. A noumenon is anything which is not phenomenal, i.e. which is not a sensory state and which cannot be known about through the senses. The 'things in themselves' of which Kant also speaks can for present purposes be equated with noumena: the relationship between them will be touched upon in §18.

Kant must say that the sentence 'There is a square noumenon' is without sense, because the only sort of meaning allowed by the definition of 'noumenon' is forbidden by the transcendental idealist account of the meaning of 'square'. Indeed, he thinks that there is almost nothing which can be meaningfully said about noumena. The definition of 'noumenon' entitles us to assert 'Noumena are not possible subjects of sensory encounter' and the like; but apart from those licensed by its definition, every sentence containing 'noumenon' is unintelligible. This is because Kant ties meaning so closely to evidence: to know what a sentence means I must know something of what it would be like to have evidence for its truth. The notion of having evidence, for Kant, is essentially the notion of encountering a datum, of running up against a brute fact or, as Kant would say, of being 'given' something. But whatever is 'given' to us is given through our senses and so cannot be relevant to any question about noumena. It follows that no synthetic sentence about noumena can be meaningful to us:

A question as to the constitution of that something which cannot be thought through any determinate predicate—inasmuch as it is completely outside the sphere of those objects which can be given to us—is entirely null and void.[3]

Since we may not use 'noumenon', even conjecturally or sceptically, in any sentences except the analytic ones which define it, what use does Kant have for the term? Well, there are four answers to this.

(1) Kant's thesis is that 'noumenon' cannot occur in meaningful sentences of a theoretical or descriptive or fact-stating kind. There are, however, ways of talking and thinking about *oneself* which are not of

24

this kind: I may describe what I do, but I also *do* what I do; I sometimes predict my future actions, but I can also *decide* what they are to be; I am 'given' to myself as an object of study, but I also *am* myself. Kant uses 'noumenon' in connection with these ways in which I alone can regard myself. In *Kant's Dialectic* I shall discuss how far he is entitled to do so.

(2) In a chapter on the distinction between phenomena and noumena,[1] Kant speaks of the 'negative' use of 'noumenon'. I shall discuss this, his most interesting use of the word in §18.

(3) Kant sometimes implies that 'noumena' occurs in one sentence which is not just meaningful but true, namely 'There are noumena'; as when he argues that since there are phenomena or appearances we cannot deny that there are also noumena without being 'landed in the absurd conclusion that there can be appearance without anything that appears'.[2] This argument is specious: in the sense in which empirical things are 'appearances', namely that statements about them can be wholly analysed in experiential terms, it is not true that there must be something *of which* they are appearances.

In fact, Kant's ostensible thesis in that passage is 'We can think noumena', which he takes, obscurely, to be weaker than 'Noumena are possible' and so weaker than 'Noumena exist'. But if this is all he seeks to prove, then the allegedly absurd conclusion that (a) 'there can be appearance without anything that appears' ought to read (b) 'there can be appearance without its being thinkable that there is something which appears'. Apart from the fact that this is not what Kant says, why should anyone think that (b) is absurd except as a corollary of the alleged absurdity of (a)? To be discussable at all, the argument must be taken as an attempt to show that there are noumena; and, so taken, it is invalid.

Similar lapses occur elsewhere: 'The true correlate of sensibility, the thing in itself, is not known';[3] and 'A priori knowledge...has to do only with appearances, and must leave the thing in itself as indeed real *per se*, but as not known by us';[4] and there are some others.

Kant has been said to argue that since our sensory states come to us unbidden there must be some noumenal cause of them distinct from ourselves.[5] So much the worse if he does, for 'The given must be given by something' is no better than 'Appearances must be appearances of something'. I cannot find this argument in the *Critique*, however. Kant does sanction a certain kind of talk about the 'intelligible [= noumenal] cause of appearances'[6]—'but merely in order to have something corresponding to sensibility viewed as a receptivity'. But this offers us a picture only, not an argument.

(4) Although Kant does not say so, it looks as though outer sense, and that with which it collaborates to produce outer experience, cannot be phenomenal. Kant allows that there can be synthetic a priori truths about phenomena or appearances—indeed I have just quoted him as saying that synthetic a priori truths cannot be about anything else— but when he says that, he is assuming that the outer-sense theory, and certain similar theories, are true and raise no problems as to their own status. Until he has some such theory actually established, Kant must say that there can be only a posteriori knowledge about phenomena. Also, there is the argument of §7,[1] which might be summed up as follows: Kant rightly thinks that statements about phenomena are analysable into statements about what experiences are had or would be had if appropriate moves were made; and the outer-sense theory cannot be embodied in statements of this sort, since it is supposed to show that certain kinds of experience are *impossible*. Presumably, then, it must be about noumena. This, for the outer-sense theory, is the last straw.

The theory's troubles began with the insistence that it be synthetic as well as a priori. I introduced outer sense in §5 as a *capacity* for being sensorily affected in a certain way, but in §§6–8 I have asked what sort of *thing* outer sense might be, and have been assuming that it must be something in the nature of a mechanism with a mode of operation and an intake and output. This looks like a violent change of subject, for one does not ask of a mental capacity what sort of thing it is, or whether it can be identified with this or that, or what its mode of operation is. Nevertheless, this reifying of outer sense was not mere caprice, for it was required if Kant's attempt to explain the synthetic and a priori status of geometry was to be given a run for its money.

Someone who has news for us about outer experience may be offering an *analysis* of 'outer'. That is, he may have arguments to show that experience which is to count as 'experience of things other than oneself' must satisfy certain conditions. The conclusion of such arguments might be called a theory of outer sense, i.e. a theory about one's capacity for having experience of things other than oneself. But if someone says something about outer experience—such as that it must be of something Euclidean—and offers this as 'synthetic', then we must choose. By 'synthetic' he means either (a) 'not true by definition, not elementarily analytic', or (b) 'not to be established by investigating meanings'. Having set aside interpretation (a), I have persisted with (b), and this is why I have had to demand that the outer-sense theory be something other than an analysis of 'outer'. If justice is to be done to the claim that the outer-sense theory is not based upon conceptual considerations, however subtle and complex, then we must take it to be saying something about how outer experience comes into being. Such a genetic theory of outer experience requires a reified outer sense and this, inevitably, must be noumenal.

Let us stop these troubles at their source by supposing Kant's theory to be 'synthetic' not in the strong sense but only in the sense of 'not true by definition'. This preserves us from the question 'What sort of thing is outer sense?' with its inevitable answer 'A noumenal sort of thing'. After some preliminaries in §§9-10, I shall defend part of the outer-sense theory by arguing that it is analytic but untrivial.

This is not the only case where something which Kant offers as 'synthetic' can be partly salvaged if it is reinterpreted as unobviously analytic. Such an interpretation is justified by its fruitfulness in leading us to philosophical insights rather than by its fidelity to Kant's conscious intentions. There probably is no final answer to the question of whether Kant takes 'synthetic' to mean merely 'not true by definition, not elementarily analytic', though I incline to think that he does not.

9 Spatiality and geometry

Why does Kant find it so obvious that Euclid's theorems, construed synthetically, cannot turn out false?

I take it that Euclidean geometry is true if and only if there are physical interpretations of 'straight line', 'congruent' and so on under which Euclid's theorems constitute a true physical theory. It might be said that the failure to find such interpretations would not show that Euclid's theorems are untrue of straight lines, right-angles etc., but would merely suggest that the physical world does not contain any straight lines, right-angles etc. This approach, however, is not open to Kant. For one thing, it involves *defining* 'straight line', 'right-angle' and so on as items of which Euclid's axioms and postulates are true: this equates the truth of Euclidean geometry with its consistency, and so renders it either inconsistent or analytic. Also, since Kant explains the alleged apriority of Euclid's theorems in terms of how things are given to us, he must think that the theorems describe outer things. The relationship between geometry and physics involves complexities of which Kant was not aware, but we must take him to be concerned with *applied* geometry. He cannot drive a wedge between 'Euclid's theorems are false' and 'There is no physical interpretation of Euclid's terms under which his theorems are true'.

It is prima facie possible that there should be no physical interpretation under which Euclidean geometry is true, and none under which any other geometry is true either. The bare denial of a geometry is not a geometry, any more than the placing of an 'It is not the case that' in front of Newton's *Principia* yields a non-Newtonian physics. The experiment of §4 might reflect the fact, not that the world obeys some non-Euclidean geometry, but rather that it does not exactly obey any geometry. In such a case, it might obey some geometry approximately, or usually; but it might be such that no geometry gave anything like a true account of it, and if this were so the world would not be in any plain sense a 'spatial' one.

Kant says that Euclidean geometry is synthetic, which implies that its falsity is logically possible. It has been taken to imply further that the truth of some non-Euclidean geometry is possible, and Kant has been congratulated on this supposed insight.[1] This is very odd. Hume, after all, went so far as to say that the received truths of geometry might be empirically falsified;[2] but it is not usual, nor would it be sensible, to credit *him* with anticipating the mathematical discovery that non-Euclidean geometries are possible. The truth of the matter is that before that discovery was made, an intelligent person could concede that Euclidean geometry might be false while thinking that if that were so then no geometry could be precisely true. Even now, it is hard for the un-mathematical to see what the next move could be after the conclusion of the Pythagoras-refuting experiment: 'If Pythagoras' theorem is false, then we must relinquish at least one of the premises from which we can derive it—obvious, simple premises such as that no two straight lines intersect twice—and what is going to happen then? If we still persist in trying to develop an absolutely general theory about lines and points and the rest, are we not bound to contradict ourselves somewhere?' The answer, as the mathematicians have shown, is 'No'; but this is extremely unobvious, and is not equivalent to the fact that Euclidean geometry might be false.

Someone who, like Kant, did not know that there can be consistent total geometries other than Euclid's would be confronted by a dilemma: either (a) the outer world is Euclidean, or (b) the outer world does not conform to any geometry at all and is therefore not spatial. I shall argue in §§ 11–13 that (b), although not elementarily self-contradictory, is ruled out on complex conceptual grounds. If Kant too regarded (b) as impossible, he would have been left with (a). I suggest that this may have been one source of his confidence in the apriority of Euclidean geometry.

It cannot have been the only source, however. Even if it is true that the outer world must be spatial, and so must obey a geometry, there are no grounds for insisting that it must obey a geometry *exactly* and *always*. Yet Kant is sure that we cannot meet with even a single failure of Euclid's theorems to describe the outer world accurately. As well as his excusable ignorance of the possibility of non-Euclidean geometries, therefore, some additional mistake must be involved. I now suggest what mistake it is and why Kant makes it.

10 Euclidean geometry and eyesight

Kant shares that preoccupation with the visual which has weakened and narrowed epistemology for centuries: throughout the Aesthetic he virtually equates outer sense with eyesight. This prevents him from considering such possible spaces as the purely auditory one which I shall discuss in §§ 12–13; and it militates against his seeing that even the space in which we live—to which eyesight *is* relevant—may not be perfectly Euclidean.

The obsession with eyesight often goes with the belief that visual fields, unlike other sensory states, are themselves spatial; as though they were, in Wisdom's phrase, '*extremely* thin coloured pictures'.[1] The propensity for reifying sense-data and describing them in terms appropriate to physical things—'The stick is straight but the onlooker's sense-datum is bent'—involves depths of error which I need not plumb now. It is relevant, however, to consider the less absurd belief that visual fields have a specially intimate connection with the spatiality of the physical world. I stand on a hill-top and see that the stream is to the left of the thicket, that the farm-house is beyond the road, and so on; and I may think that my visual field, even if not itself spatially organized, does at least constitute evidence of a peculiarly direct kind as to the spatial organization of the things in the valley. In what sense, if any, is this true?

I do not need eyesight to discover how the things in the valley are disposed: a man blindfold could find out by stumbling down into the valley, feeling the road under his feet, then colliding with the farm-house, and so on. He would steer primarily by touch and by his so-called kinaesthetic sense, i.e. his ability to know whether and how he is

29

moving. So I too could check the evidence of my eyes by procedures involving movement and touch.

Now, it could happen that my eyes told me a quite different story about the disposition of the valley's contents from that told me by my hands and feet. If such discrepancies occurred frequently and unpredictably, we could not give our spatial terminology a visual *and* a tactual-kinaesthetic basis. Which basis should be choose? We are not conceptually forearmed for every possible eventuality, but we are for this one. If we had to choose between a visual and a tactual-kinaesthetic basis for our spatial concepts, we should choose the latter. The reason for this is also the reason why tactual-kinaesthetic considerations *are now* more central to our spatial concepts than are visual considerations, even though the two roughly coincide: since physical contact is involved in all the main ways in which things can hurt, soothe, nourish or protect us, the 'Where?' which matters most is the tactual-kinaesthetic 'Where?' which asks how to achieve or avoid physical contact. Visual fields are quick, reliable and fairly comprehensive guides to the spatial relations amongst physical things; but they have this virtue only because they correlate with those tactual and kinaesthetic facts which lie at the heart of our concept of physical space. As Hume says: 'Our sight informs us not of distance...immediately and without a certain reasoning and experience, as is acknowledged by the most rational philosophers.'[1] The most rational philosopher on this topic is Berkeley,[2] whose *New Theory of Vision* presents in cogent detail the argument of this paragraph.

There is, then, no reason for letting eyesight dominate our inquiries into spatial concepts; but I shall argue further that such a domination, in the form which it usually takes in philosophical writing, is positively dangerous.

Sight is favoured because it alone can give us, within a single moment, an impression of the spatial ordering of a sizeable part of the world. The obsession with sight is especially an obsession with what can be seen 'at a glance'. This is implicit in what I have said already, for 'Visual fields have a specially intimate connection with the spatiality of the physical world' is plausible only if it means that a single visual field, i.e. a visual state at some one time, relates to the world's spatiality more directly than do other individual sensory states. Whereas I see at a glance that the thicket is to the left of the stream, the blindfolded man must attend to his changing sensory states as he gropes across the valley.

Immoderate respect for the single visual field has led some writers

30

to insist that 'visual space' at least must be perfectly Euclidean. Ewing, for example, finds in Kant's position the residual truth that we have a 'total inability to see or imagine any except certain kinds of spatial constructions', *viz.* Euclidean ones. He explicitly acknowledges the point I have been making (the italics are mine):

I must admit that in considering these questions I have confined myself to visual space. None of the other senses give me a sufficiently definite perception of any considerable extent of space *at the same moment* to enable me to answer the question in their case.[1]

If we restricted ourselves to what could be 'imagined' or seen at a glance, then perhaps we should be bound to regard space as Euclidean. The experiment of §4 took time, and perhaps we cannot imagine seeing at a glance that something was, or probably was, a non-Pythagorean right-angled triangle. Again, we could discover the falsity of 'Two straight lines intersect at most once' taken in any normal sense which renders it synthetic, perhaps by finding two routes from *A* to *B*, each passing every test for straightness. But it is not clear how one could see at a glance that two straight lines intersected twice: it seems that if both intersections are seen at once then at least one of the lines must look curved.

I am not sure that this is right, perhaps because I am not sure what I mean by 'must look curved'. The main point, however, is this: even if it is true that nothing could 'look non-Euclidean', this is irrelevant to the serious examination of spatial concepts, because single visual fields are only clues, by good luck rather reliable ones, to the spatial relations amongst things. *measuring is another clue utterly unlike seeing*.

If it were found that the wave-lengths of light associated with various colours were such as to put blue closer to green than to purple, we might well say that this was a discovery not about colours but only about the wave-lengths associated with them—or, perhaps, not about visual colours but only about physical colours. This would have a point because one can talk sensibly about colours without knowing anything about wave-lengths: the language of colours, or of 'visual colours', has a life of its own. I think that some of Kant's defenders have wanted to say similarly that the scientists' hypotheses regarding physical geometry may be valid as science but do not touch the 'visual space' which is the only one the layman needs to attend to. This assumes that what can be seen at a glance provides for our spatial concepts an adequate basis, logically independent of other bases in the way that seen colours are logically independent of wave-lengths. I have argued that this is a mistake: single visual fields would be entirely irrelevant to ordinary spatial concepts if they were not correlated with what can be learned about space by movement and touch, i.e. by the time-taking procedures which Kant's defenders too often ignore.

This argument, if it is valid, tells against all who try to isolate something called 'visual space', whether or not they say that Kant told the truth about it. For example, one who says that Kant was wrong even about visual space reports:

In very recent years, experimental mathematico-optical researches by R. K. Luneburg and A. A. Blank have even led these authors to contend that although the *physical* space in which sensory depth perception by binocular vision is effective is Euclidean, the binocular *visual* space resulting from psycho-metric coordination possesses a Lobatchevskian *hyperbolic* geometry of constant curvature. This contention suggests several questions.[1]

It does indeed.

3

SPACE AND OBJECTS

11 Chaotic experience

I have discussed two attempts to derive from the premiss that the outer
world must be spatial the conclusion that it must be perfectly Euclidean.
In one of these, 'spatial' is equated with 'exactly geometrizable', and
Euclid's is assumed to be the only possible geometry; while in the other,
only our actual physical space is considered, and what is said about that
is restricted to what could be learned about it from single glances.
I want to turn now from the over-discussed conclusion of these two
derivations to their common premiss, namely that outer experience
must pertain to things in space—in *a* space, not necessarily in our space
or even our kind of space.

I accept this premiss, and shall support it with arguments which
I draw not from Kant but from the chapter 'Sounds' in Strawson's
Individuals.[1] My debt to this chapter is great. If I supply details which
Strawson omits, or take his argument in directions which he does not
explore, this is because my central concerns are not his.

If we ask, say, what makes a glimpse of a horse-race 'outer' and a
certain buzzing sound 'only inner', we shall have to handle too many
differences at once. We must therefore simplify, e.g. by considering
one sense only. Smell, taste and sensitivity to temperature are too ill-
organized; and sight and touch are too closely linked to physicality,
and thus to the familiar contingencies of our kind of space, to be safely
used. Strawson therefore adopts the heuristic fiction of a creature—
I shall call him 'the hearer'—whose sensory intake is all auditory.

Suppose that the hearer's sensory history consists in a chaos about
which nothing general can be said except that it is auditory and chaotic.
Can he find work for the distinction between 'only inner' and 'outer',
i.e. between experiences which are just his auditory states and ones
which are hearings of sounds that, independently of him, are there to
be heard? Strawson's negative answer is right, of course, but I want to
show in detail why.

For the hearer to have a use for 'I hear an objective sound', he must
have a use for 'A sound now exists unheard by me'. We can speak of
unheard sounds because we can have indirect evidence for a sound's

existing; but this relies upon causal order, and the hearer's experience is *ex hypothesi* chaotic. Let us suppose, then, that the hearer tries to force the notion of an unheard sound upon his 'world' in the following manner. He takes each of his auditory states to be the hearing of a short segment of a continuous, repetitive sound: if the segment is uniform, then so is the unending sound-sequence of which it is a part; if the segment consists in a snatch of melody, say, then the sequence of which it is a part is an endless repetition of that snatch of melody. Equipped with a *Weltanschauung* in which these continuous sound-sequences—'auditory particulars' as Strawson calls them—have a role, the hearer can say 'I now hear a sound-sequence which existed earlier but which was not heard by me because I was in the presence of other sequences altogether'.

Now, the hearer's notion of an auditory particular is vacuous unless any such particular could in principle be heard more than once; so he must have criteria for the truth of 'I have heard this sequence before'. The only criterion available in a chaos would be indiscernibility or similarity: two auditory states count as hearings of the same objective sound-sequence if and only if they are exactly alike, or alike at least to some specified degree. Let us suppose the hearer to adopt a weakish criterion of this kind. Has he now a concept of an objective auditory particular?

Perhaps he has, but his concept is idle, and so his distinction between 'outer' and 'only inner' is idle too. The only grounds he could have for calling an experience 'only inner' or hallucinatory would be that he had never before had one sufficiently like it. But to identify the hallucinatory with the unfamiliar is to abuse the ordinary sense of 'hallucinatory' and is not to employ the 'outer'/'only inner' distinction as I have explained it.

Nor can the hearer have a working notion of a mis-hearing, i.e. of a non-standard or potentially misleading hearing of an objective sound-sequence. To know that one mis-heard X is to be in a position to say 'If all I had had to go by was the way X sounded, I should not have said it was X I was hearing'. Our hearer can never say this, for all he ever has to go by is the way X sounds.

Nor can the hearer make sense of 'two objective sound-sequences which are exactly alike'. He defines identity as an extreme case of similarity, and for him the identity of indiscernibles is therefore analytic.

Our ordinary objectivity concepts serve (a) to mark off sensory states which are not perceptions of anything objective, (b) to distinguish good from bad views, standard from non-standard hearings etc., and (c) to separate the question of what a thing is like from the question of what thing it is. The hearer's concept of an auditory particular is a fraud, because it performs none of these central tasks of our ordinary objectivity concepts.

12 An ordered world

The hearer cannot distinguish identity from extreme similarity because that distinction would require a tension—or at least the possibility of one—between what he can say about an auditory state on the basis of what it is like in itself, i.e. its monadic properties, and what he can say about it on other grounds, i.e. its relations with other auditory states. But an auditory state's relational properties cannot provide reasons for or against any claim as to its identity unless there are some true general statements about the relations amongst the hearer's auditory states; and this is contrary to the hypothesis of chaos.

To give the hearer a working concept of an objective sound-sequence, therefore, we must introduce a degree of order into his experience. To this end, Strawson makes the following proposal. The hearer's sensory states all include the hearing of a 'master-sound'— a continuous sound of unvarying timbre and loudness, ranging in pitch over the whole audible scale. There is a correlation between the master-sound aspects and the other aspects of his auditory states: whenever he hears the master-sound at middle C, he also hears 'Greensleeves'; whenever he hears the master-sound at high G, he also hears 'Finlandia'; and so on.

The auditory chaos does not support a working concept of an objective sound-sequence, says Strawson, because it contains nothing analogous to the feature of our world with which 'the idea of re-identifiable particulars, existing continuously while unobserved, [is] most intimately, naturally and generally connected'. For us, he says,

the crucial idea...is that of a spatial system of objects, through which oneself, another object, moves, but which extends beyond the limits of one's observation at any moment....This idea obviously supplies the necessary non-temporal dimension for, so to speak, the housing of the objects which are held to exist continuously, though unobserved...[1]

This condition is satisfied now that there is a regular relationship between positions on the master-scale and the other aspects of the hearer's auditory states. The master-scale, in short, is 'the necessary non-temporal dimension...'. If the hearer is asked 'Where was X when you were hearing Y?', he can now answer 'X was at middle C as always, and I did not hear it because I was at E above middle C, where Y always is'. So, concludes Strawson, the hearer can now have a working concept of an auditory particular.

I accept this conclusion for other reasons too. Firstly, the hearer can now treat some of his auditory states as hallucinatory and others as not so. If at middle C on the master-scale he normally hears major arpeggios, but just once hears tritones instead, he can say that on that isolated occasion he had an hallucination. Secondly, he can have the concept of a mis-hearing: 'One time when I was at low F it was as though I were hearing a phrase from "Greensleeves" in the major; but that must have been a mis-hearing, for every other time I have been there I have heard that phrase in the minor.' The fact that mis-hearings and hallucinations must be rare if the hearer's world is not to relapse into chaos only strengthens the analogy between his concepts and ours. Thirdly, the hearer can now say 'There are two exactly similar sound-sequences, three octaves apart': for him the identity of indiscernibles is no longer analytic.

Strawson invents an opponent who protests that it is misleading to call the auditory world 'spatial' when it contains nothing like our paradigm of spatiality, viz. a seen spatial array.[1] Strawson meets this objection, which depends on the obsession with single visual fields, much too tolerantly. His imagined opponent does, however, make one pertinent remark to which Strawson does not reply, namely that when we visually sort out a scene into its spatially related parts 'we need no changing master-patch to give us the idea of' the dimensions which provide the spatial ordering. Now it is indeed a flaw in Strawson's story that the spatial ordering of the auditory particulars is created by their relations not with one another but with a further particular, namely the omnipresent master-sound. One consequence of this, pointed out to me by Strawson, is that the hearer cannot get lost; the only sense he can give to 'Where am I?' is that of 'Where am I on the scale of the master-sound?', and he can always learn the answer to this just by listening. This feature of Strawson's auditory world has no analogue in our own; so I want to show how he could dispense with it.

First, a preliminary point: Strawson's hearer gets from one place to another on the master-scale only by passing through each intermediate place; but the spatial order would survive if the hearer could switch instantaneously from place to place on the master-scale. Strawson compares the hearing of non-master sounds with what can be heard by rotating the tuning-knob of a radio; in the radio analogy which I propose, wave-lengths are selected by pressing buttons.

If we do *not* weaken Strawson's story in this way we can weaken it in another, namely by silencing the master-sound. All the master-sound does is to give the hearer a definition of 'between' for non-master sounds, in terms of 'between in respect of pitch' for the associated master-sounds: 'X is between Y and Z' is defined as

'The master-sound which accompanies X is between-in-respect-of-pitch that which accompanies Y and that which accompanies Z.'

It is this betweenness relation which enables the hearer to string all the non-master sounds on a single dimension. But he could as well define 'X is between Y and Z' as

'X is heard at some time between any time at which Y is heard and any time at which Z is heard.'

In Strawson's account, the spatial betweenness of non-master sounds is defined out of pitch-relations amongst master-sounds; in my proposed revision it is defined instead out of ordinary temporal relations, and there is no work left for the master-sound to do.

In my version of the auditory world, the hearer can get lost; for now his question 'Where am I?' is a question about how he is 'travel-related' to this or that sound with which he is familiar, and finding the answer to this requires not just listening but memory. If he travelled in his sleep far enough along the dimension of his world, he might wake up knowing neither how far away, nor in what direction, were the sounds with which he was familiar. This could not happen to Strawson's hearer.

A spatial auditory world, then, does not need an audible dimension. I shall find it convenient to concentrate on auditory worlds ordered by a master-sound rather than by the 'travel-based' betweenness relation which I have introduced; but everything I say will apply *mutatis mutandis* to the latter as well.

13 An ordered, changing world

Strawson allows that a sound-sequence may go out of existence and be replaced, at the same point on the master-scale, by another: there is birth and death in his auditory world.[1] It is clear that if that world is not to lose its objectivity a high proportion of sound-sequences must have fairly long histories—a fact which has its analogue in our world.

Strawson's auditory world is static: there is birth and death in it, but no movement. Let us remedy this by supposing that the associations between sound-sequences and places on the master-scale are subject to change. Such changes must normally occur fairly slowly—not faster than a semitone an hour, say. If at noon 'Greensleeves' is at middle C on the master-scale, then at 3 p.m. it must be somewhere in the three-tone interval A–D♯ around middle C; of course, it may still—or again—be at middle C. Further details can be filled in as one pleases: in the auditory world nature does, or does not, abhor a vacuum; two sound-sequences can, or cannot, occur in the same place at the same time; and so on.

I have imposed a speed-limit upon the sound-sequences because without it there would be chaos again. The spatial order of the auditory world consists in (a) an omnipresent master-sound, and (b) associations between the master-sound pitch and the non-master sounds. To allow the latter to move, subject to a general speed-limit, is to modify (b); but to allow them to move with no restrictions on speed is to abolish (b) and thus to revert to chaos. For (a), unaided by (b), has no power to resolve the chaos into order.

The necessity for a speed-limit can be shown in another way which does not depend upon the details of how this particular auditory world has been constructed. If there were no speed-limit, then any position of a sound-sequence at one time would be consistent with any positions of sound-sequences at other times. In that case, the hearer's decision about what to make of his auditory state at a given time could not be affected by what his auditory states were at other times: all his criteria would have to concern the nature of the single auditory state he was trying to classify or interpret; and thus he would be no better off than he was in the chaos.

A speed-limit is also needed in our world. We identify physical things largely by their locations: it is no accident that discussions of the identity of indiscernibles often work around to considering whether a pair of objects could be qualitatively exactly alike although spatially separate; nor is it an accident—as Kant knew—that Leibniz, who did think the identity of indiscernibles to be necessary, also thought that a spatial separation of two objects *is* a qualitative difference between them.[1] But if physical things could and often did move unlimitedly fast, no facts about spatial positions could have the slightest bearing on any problem about re-identification.

We could develop the auditory world still further by permitting sound-sequences to change qualitatively as well as to move. Here again, objectivity is lost unless there is a limit on the rapidity of alteration. This, like the speed-limit on movement, has its analogy in our own world.

Objectivity concepts sit loose to the chaos, but do get some grip on the static world ordered by the master-sound. I think it would be generally agreed that their security of tenure increases as the ordered complexity of the auditory world increases—through the introduction of a travel-based order, of movement, or of qualitative change. An auditory world with a travel-based order, containing sound-sequences which move and alter, is one in which the concept of an objective auditory particular would be intuitively felt to have a very secure place indeed. This could be justified by showing that with each development of the auditory story the distinction between identity and similarity becomes richer, the concepts of hallucination and mishearing more complex and subtle, and so on. But now I am going to justify it in another way.

14 A theory of concept-utility

Our findings fit nicely a certain general theory about what makes it permissible or mandatory to apply a given concept to a given subject-matter. This theory is consonant with Kant's views about the nature of rational activity, but I have arrived at it as a corollary of Quine's 'Two Dogmas of Empiricism'.[1] Quine's view that questions about truth always involve questions about conceptual efficiency—that in the last resort the true theory is the one which copes most economically with the facts—has the following consequence:— If one has a language L in which to describe a subject-matter S, it is legitimate to add a new concept C to the stock of concepts in L in proportion as L-with-C can describe S more simply than can L-without-C. Concepts are simplifiers; in particular, they are abbreviators.

I shall not try to prove this sub-theory; but I shall test it by bringing it to bear upon the inquiry into auditory worlds—and again, in §51, upon a problem about private languages.

Let us take two objectivity statements which can be made, though idly, in the auditory chaos, and see how they come out in a subjective language, i.e. one in which objectivity concepts play no part. 'At t

I heard an objective sound' is equivalent to 'At t I had an auditory experience'. 'I heard the same objective sound at t_1 as I heard at t_2' is equivalent to 'My auditory state was [nearly] the same at t_1 as at t_2'. In neither case, nor in any others we might take, is the hearer's reporting of his experience any more compact in the objective than in the subjective language.

But now consider 'At t I heard an objective sound' as said in the static world ordered by a master-sound. This is equivalent to something like

> 'My auditory state at t had a master and a non-master component, and over a period of time including t almost every auditory experience I have had whose master component has been exactly like that one has also had a non-master component exactly or nearly like that one'.

(The word 'almost' allows for hallucinations at times other than t, 'nearly' allows for mis-hearings at t or at other times, and 'over a period of time including t' allows that the objective sound heard at t may not be sempiternal.) Here, a statement in the purely sensory language is about eight times as long as its equivalent in the objective language. The statement 'I heard the same objective sound at t_1 as at t_2', if spelled out similarly in the subjective language, gives a result which is some six times as long. However, in these two cases and in those that follow, the abbreviating power of objectivity concepts is really much greater than is shown by my rather simplified expansions of objective into subjective statements.

In the world where sound-sequences move, objectivity concepts save more words still. In that world, the statement 'At t I heard an objective sound' spells out into something like

> 'At t my auditory state had a master component M and a non-master component N such that over a period of time including t every auditory state whose non-master component was very like N has had a master-component differing in pitch from M by not more units of pitch than there were units of time between t and the time of the auditory state in question'

plus a complex condition to allow for there being another non-master sound very like N. The whole tedious thing, oversimplified as it is, would be some twenty times as long as its objective equivalent. The spelling out in subjective terms of 'I heard the same objective sound at t_1 as at t_2' would take about a page and a half.

40

Objectivity concepts have even more abbreviating power in a world where things alter as well as move, and in one with a travel-based ordering. In a world with both these features, such concepts would be more powerful still. For example, many pages would be required to give the sensory cash-value of the objective statement 'I think I am lost'.

The Quinean theory of concept-utility has passed its test. Each judgment as to a concept's legitimacy which was reached in §§ 11–13 by considering the specific jobs which it does has also been reached by considering its abbreviating powers. Why the two sets of results have coincided is plain enough: to say that a concept does a certain job *is* to say that it effects a certain kind of abbreviation.

There are questions not only about when we may, but also about when we must, apply a given concept to a given subject-matter. In our world, it is often said, it is not just permissible but mandatory to use the concept of a physical object. There is one simple reason for saying this—ignoring sophisticated worries about whether there could be a purely subjective language—namely that the concept of a physical object does the job of abbreviation so well that without it we should get almost nothing thought or said; it would all take too long. I suggest that when Strawson asks what the auditory world would have to be like for the hearer to be forced into using the concept of 'I',[1] he obscures the move from objectivity to self-consciousness by combining it with this other move from 'What concepts may he have?' to 'What concepts must he have?'

+ this concept relies
upon spacio-temporality to
identify its physical object

15   The status of Strawson's theory

The argument of §§ 11–12 tends to show that outer experience must be of a spatial world. Every auditory world I have described has had an ordering analogous to that of points on a straight line, but this was not necessary: for example a travel-based betweenness relation could yield a circular world; and many other variations are possible too. But objectivity concepts have work to do, it seems, only in worlds which are 'spatial' in a fairly strong sense—though there is no privileged number of dimensions, nor a privilege for Euclid's or any other geometry.

This, which I shall call 'Strawson's theory', is roughly equivalent to Kant's theory that outer experience must be of things in space. Let us see how the two theories compare as to status.

It is hard to avoid the conclusion that Strawson's theory is analytic if it is true at all. I have not defended the theory by including 'spatial' in the definition of 'outer'; on the contrary, I have defined 'outer' as 'of something other than oneself' and have then explored the implications of it as thus defined. The exploration turned on meaning-relationships between 'other than oneself' and 'existing unperceived', 'having a history', 're-identifiable' and so on. Strawson's theory is far from self-evident, but this is just because it arises in such a complex way out of those elementary facts about meanings which constitute the whole grounds for accepting it. When we recall the problems which beset Kant's theory if it is taken to be synthetic and a priori, we may well feel some relief at being able to classify Strawson's theory as unobvious but analytic.

There is little to be said for restricting 'analytic' to conceptual truths which are obvious, or true by definition; but Strawson's theory, as well as being unobvious, has another feature which might be urged as a reason for not calling it analytic. Compare (a) 'Anything square is rectangular' with (b) 'Anything square belongs to a world in which objective angular measurements can be made'. (a) says what a thing must be like to count as square; (b) seems to do this too, but the condition which it lays down is also a condition on anything's being in a plain sense not-square. While (a) concerns the applicability of 'square', (b) concerns the utility of the 'square'/'not-square' distinction. Strawson's theory is like (b) rather than (a): it says that only in a spatial world is work done by the *distinction between* 'outer' and 'only inner'. We might reserve the title 'analytic' for statements like (a), and describe as 'conceptual' but not as 'analytic' such statements as (b) and Strawson's theory.

By thus dividing conceptual truths into the analytic and the others, and putting Strawson's theory among the latter, we do not involve Strawson in Kant's difficulties over the questions 'What risk of refutation does it run?' and 'How do you know it to be true?' Nor do we commit Strawson's theory to treating 'What sort of thing is outer sense?' as an intelligible question which invites an answer in terms of noumena.

The most interesting truths which Kant calls synthetic and a priori have something like the status I have claimed for Strawson's theory: they are unobvious analytic truths about the conditions under which certain distinctions can be made, or under which certain concepts can have a significant use, affirmative or negative. We shall see, furthermore, that Kant's arguments are appropriate to his conclusions' having

42

this status. So I offer this heuristic rule: 'When Kant calls something synthetic and a priori, proceed as though he had said that it is a truth about conceptual inter-relations of the same general sort as Strawson's theory.' Whatever Kant's conscious intentions were, whatever he 'really meant', this rule is an aid to deriving philosophical insights from what he wrote.

Mention should be made of one specific similarity, and one specific dissimilarity, between Strawson's theory and the judgments which Kant calls synthetic and a priori.

(1) It may be noted that the argument of §§ 11–12 proves only that spatiality is sufficient for objectivity: in relation to the converse of this, i.e. in relation to Strawson's theory, the argument is inconclusive. I suggest that Strawson's theory is of a kind which cannot be proved conclusively. It is sometimes the case that, in arguing that condition C must obtain if distinction D is to have work to do, one must rest content with showing that C does obtain in certain situations where D does have work to do, and urging that one's examples have covered all the relevant territory. In such a case, one is inevitably at the mercy of the overlooked possibility, and one's conclusion must be of the form 'It looks as though D cannot be used unless C obtains'. This is reminiscent of some of Kant's remarks about synthetic a priori judgments. I shall later discuss certain judgments whose truth is supposed to stem from certain a priori brute facts about the nature of the human understanding. The notion of an a priori brute fact about the understanding,[1] unattractive as it is, has similarities with the notion of a conceptual fact which can be reported in such words as 'It looks as though we have no way of utilizing D unless C obtains'.

(2) Analytic judgments are all a priori; but what use is this fact in connection with Strawson's theory, of which we can say only that *if* it is true it is analytic? None; but then apriority as such is never of much interest anyway. We can say that the judgment expressed by a given sentence is a priori or unfalsifiable, only because we can say that the sentence could come to say something false only by coming to express a judgment other than the one it now expresses. This is a harmless manœuvre, but it yields a hollow victory. This sort of apriority does not offer intellectual security of a significant kind: we cannot peel the judgment or proposition off from the sentence and have the comfort of knowing that *it*—'never mind how it is expressed'— cannot be falsified. 'Strawson's theory is analytic if it is true at all'— the point of this is not that if the theory is true then it is necessarily,

43

invulnerably true, but rather that the arguments which can be adduced in support of the theory are of a certain kind. Specifically, they consist in certain ways of assembling facts about meanings: it is not always clear when a fact is about meanings, but this is one of the cases in which it is clear. So we ought not to share Kant's passion for the a priori, even if we can represent his results as analytic. It is often convenient to express his questions and answers in terms of certainties and necessities; but the virtue of his answers does not lie in the limits they set to what our experience could be like, but lies rather in the light they throw on our handling of the experience we do have. The impossibility that there should be an objective but non-spatial world does not matter. What matters is a fact, if it is a fact, about the way in which objectivity and spatiality are connected in our conceptual scheme.

4

THE INNER-SENSE THEORY

16 The form of inner sense

Kant says that time is the form of inner sense, as space is the form of outer sense: all experienced things outside oneself must be spatially ordered, and all experience whatsoever must be temporally ordered.[1]

Here is an analogue. A submarine captain wears sun-glasses all the time and sees beyond his submarine only through a slightly defective periscope: everything he sees looks green, and everything he sees outside his vessel looks blurred as well. This analogue, like the piano one in §5, is inadequate and dangerous. Still, it illustrates Kant's view of the formal relationship between inner and outer sense; and its very defects serve to remind us that Kant, in offering his doctrine of inner sense as synthetic, may have to construe inner sense as a noumenal mechanism which stamps temporality upon its products.

A preliminary point:– I have not spoken of outer experience as itself being spatial or Euclidean, because I do not think that spatial terms can be applied in their ordinary meanings to experience, i.e. to sensory states or sense-data. Those who think that spatial concepts are rooted in visual considerations, and who treat visual sense-data as though they were thin coloured pictures, will cheerfully apply spatial terms to visual sense-data: 'The green patch is to the left of the red patch and a little larger than it.' Wishing to avoid this kind of talk, I have spoken of outer experience not as Euclidean but as Euclid-confirming, or as *of something* Euclidean—or, in the weaker version, *of something* spatial. The situation changes, however, when we come to the inner-sense theory. It is not satisfactory to express Kant's thesis in the form 'All inner experience must be of something which is temporal', for some inner experience is not in any plain sense 'of' anything at all. (I here reject Kant's unhappy notion that, just as outer experience is one's encounter with an objective realm, inner experience is one's encounter with oneself.) But we can speak of experience as being itself temporal in a way in which we cannot speak of it as being itself spatial. My outer experience is experience of a world which is both spatial and temporal; but all my sensory states, whether or not they are perceptions of an outer world, do themselves occur in a temporal order, do

45

themselves have durations, and so on. So we can legitimately express Kant's thesis in the form 'All inner experience is temporal'.

What are we to make of this thesis? Can we find an analytic version of it, analogous to the Strawsonian version of the outer-sense theory? The omens are inauspicious. Strawson's theory states necessary conditions for experience to count as outer, but there are no tests which experience must pass in order to count as inner: inner experience is just experience.

Perhaps, then, we can say that temporality is a feature which any-thing must have in order to count as experience at all. If this were right, it would depend upon facts about the meaning of 'experience', and that would not be relevant to Kant's central thesis. What he wants to say is that it is at once synthetic and a priori that all our data, every-thing we are given, every brute fact with which we are confronted, the whole reality we know, is temporal. This, vague as it admittedly is, confronts us with the following question. Can we say anything about what it would be for a being to have data, know facts, be confronted with a reality, to which temporal concepts did not apply?

I do not think that we can. It seems that we cannot describe any possible state of affairs, whether 'outer' or 'only inner', except in terms which proclaim its temporality. My auditory fictions, for example, including the story about the auditory chaos, all concerned possible courses of experience whose normal temporal order was never called into question; and it seems impossible that the stories should have got under way at all without that basic assumption.

That point concerns whether we can describe what it might be like from the inside, so to speak, to be in receipt of atemporal data. But even if we cannot see or say or envisage or imagine what this would be like on the inside, perhaps we can say what would be involved in knowing that some other being had atemporal data (cf. knowing that someone else can see a fourth primary colour). This suggestion comes to nothing, though. To discover what another is experiencing, I must go by his linguistic and other behaviour; and I cannot suppose myself to observe behaviour which is atemporal. Any story I could tell about another's experience would, therefore, have a subject-matter which was correlated with a temporal stream of behaviour. So the subject-matter, the man's experience, would itself have to be temporal, unless some-one's behaviour could express his experience without endowing it with temporality. I do not believe that there could be a behaviour/experience correlation such that *both* the behaviour expressed or was evidence for the experience *and* the behaviour was temporal and the experience not.

It may be said that we do already have atemporal data, or at any rate atemporal topics of discourse, namely propositions and numbers. In §24 I shall argue that propositions are abstractions from our handling of sentences. This is not to deny that there are propositions, but it is to take a certain view of what kind of thing a proposition is, i.e. of what kind of utility the 'proposition' terminology has. From this view it follows that our talking and thinking about propositions is rooted in, and dependent upon, temporal facts about how languages are used: 'proposition' is a theoretical term whose proper function, if it has one, is to facilitate our theorizing about linguistic behaviour.[1] If this is right, then propositions do not constitute an atemporal subject of discourse in any way which contradicts the thesis I have been defending. To suppose that a being might have knowledge of propositions but not of anything temporal would be like supposing that a being might have knowledge of physical forces but not of anything which was subject to any such force. Similarly with numbers: there are no tenses or dates in arithmetic, but that does not free it from its essential connections with operations of identifying, discriminating and counting.

If we cannot develop the supposition that a being might have atemporal data or knowledge of an atemporal reality, is this because the supposition is self-contradictory? If this were so, then 'All data are temporal' would be analytic and so we should, after all, be able to handle Kant's inner-sense theory in a way analogous with the Strawsonian salvage of part of the outer-sense theory. But I do not think that it is so. There seem to be only three ways in which it might be, and none of them apply.

(1) There is the kind of analytic truth expressed by Strawson's theory: 'All Fs are G' is analytic because all our ways of bringing something under the concept of F require its falling under the concept of G—'All our ways of bringing experience under objectivity concepts require its being experience of something spatial'. It cannot be analytic in *that* way that all data are temporal: Kant's thesis does not allege the impossibility of bringing data under one concept but not another, but alleges the impossibility of not bringing experience under one concept. The Strawsonian kind of analytic truth reports a connection between two aspects of our conceptual scheme, two aspects of our way of handling whatever data we have to handle: it says something of the form 'Our data must be handled in *this* way [brought under spatial

47

concepts] if it is to be handled in *that* way [brought under objectivity concepts]'. But if 'All data are temporal' is analytic then it says, unconditionally, 'Our data must be handled in *this* way [brought under temporal concepts]—the only alternative is having no data to handle'.

(2) Still, it might be analytic that all data are temporal because of facts about the meaning of 'data' and related terms. Our attempts to describe a being whose data are atemporal are not obstructed, I have argued in (1), by any kind of meaning-relationship between 'atemporal' and any other terms which the being is supposed to apply to his data. But the obstacle might be a meaning-relationship all the same: perhaps the stipulation of atemporality is inconsistent with the claim that what we are describing are *data*. I use 'data'—and 'experience', 'sensory states' and all the rest—to point to the very general notion of a basis for knowledge of what is the case; and there are analytic truths about all 'data' in this sense. For example, it is analytic that only a conscious being has data. I cannot tell a story about a being who has no conscious states yet does have data; and if someone announced that he was going to do just that, and still explained 'data' in terms of 'basis for knowledge' and the like, we should have to conclude that he did not understand 'knowledge' or 'conscious' or some other relevant word in its ordinary meaning.

Well, the suggestion is that (a) 'I am going to describe atemporal data' is like (b) 'I am going to describe data of a being without consciousness'. This suggestion seems to be wrong. Whereas (b) announces a flatly self-contradictory programme, (a) announces rather a hopeless programme. Those who have credited God with atemporal knowledge of reality have surely not been contradicting themselves, as though they had said that God knows the fraction which is equal to $\sqrt{2}$. Their claim is rather one which we do not understand: we cannot see what it comes to, or see how to fill in any details.

It is satisfactory to describe (b) as self-contradictory partly because we can say 'If your story is going to banish consciousness it will have to banish data', and this need not mean '...there will have to be no story'. A story about a world in which there is no consciousness, for example about our planet before there was life on it, can be presented as the story which would be told by a conscious being if there were one there. A world without consciousness may be presented as knowable, i.e. so described that we can say 'That is how we should observe it to be if it were left all dead like that except for the introduction of us as observers'. But (a) offers no analogue to this. To the person who

48

proposes to describe atemporal data, we cannot say: 'If time is to be banished from your story, you will have to leave *data* out. By all means describe an atemporal world, giving the story which would be told by a being with data if there were one there; but don't put any such being into the story or you will have temporality back in the story after all.' This programme is as impossible as (a) itself. I conclude that we are not helped to understand the status of 'All data are temporal' by comparing it with 'All data are had by conscious beings'.

(3) Perhaps 'atemporal' is a self-contradictory predicate. It seems that there is some obstacle to our describing any subject-matter without using temporal concepts, as though atemporality were inconsistent with *everything*. A predicate which for routine analytic reasons cannot consistently figure in any story must be an internally inconsistent predicate. This would solve our problem, by putting 'We cannot describe an atemporal reality' on a par with 'We cannot describe a reality in which things are red and not coloured'. If that were the solution, though, 'temporal' would be a tautological predicate, i.e. one which is universally applicable for the same sort of reason that 'either coloured or not red' is universally applicable. That seems hopelessly wrong. It does not look at all as though 'temporal' is tautological, or 'atemporal' self-contradictory; it seems rather that, although there is no logical trouble within 'atemporal', everything we have to say nevertheless involves temporality and so won't square with atemporality.

For these reasons, I agree with Kant's view that the temporality of the given is a fact which, although contingent, cannot be thought away. Nor does it seem plausible to say that we could envisage or describe atemporal data if only our imaginations were more limber or our vocabularies larger. It is here that one feels most sympathy with Kant's belief that there are extremely basic, not-quite-empirical statements which can be known to hold true for all humans.[1]

But this is not to allow that such statements can be neatly classed as synthetic and a priori, still less is it to accept Kant's kind of theory about how they are possible. The minimal objection to 'Temporality is stamped upon experience by inner sense' is that it speaks of what is *done* by inner sense and it therefore presupposes temporality.

Without appealing to anything like a noumenal inner sense we can alleviate, and perhaps remove, the discomfort of having to admit that there is a fact whose contingency cannot be shown by describing a contrary possibility. I can envisage being satisfied that someone could see a new primary colour, only because my evidence for this could consist in data which did not themselves include the seeing of such a colour. But I could not believe that someone was in touch with an atemporal reality, on the basis of data, *my* data, which were temporally organized. Or again, I can imagine myself encountering an invisible physical object, because if I set aside all my visual experience there remains an adequate basis for a notion of physicality. But no *part* of my experience relates to the world's temporality as my visual experience does to its visibility. If I were to imagine being confronted by an atemporal reality, I should have to build on parts of my experience which are not time-infected, but there are no such parts. Our experience is, so to speak, saturated with temporality; and this is why we cannot talk or think about what it would be like to be confronted with a reality which was atemporal.

Kant's view that the temporality of the given is a *fact* about it is embodied, in a somewhat unhappy fashion, in his transcendental idealism about time:

We deny to time all claim to absolute reality; that is to say, we deny that it belongs to things absolutely, as their condition or property, independently of any reference to the form of our sensible intuition; properties that belong to things in themselves can never be given to us through the senses. This, then, is what constitutes the *transcendental ideality* of time...[1]

In so far as this expresses the claim that it is not analytic that all our data are temporal, it is acceptable. But there is a difficulty here all the same. It can be approached through an objection which Kant apparently found both popular and irritating:

Against [my] theory, which admits the empirical reality of time, but denies its absolute and transcendental reality, I have heard men of intelligence so unanimously voicing an objection, that I must suppose it to occur spontaneously to every reader to whom this way of thinking is unfamiliar. The objection is this. Alterations are real, this being proved by change of our own representations [= inner states]—even if all outer appearances, together with their alterations, be denied. Now alterations are possible only in time, and time is therefore something real.[2]

This objection concerns scepticism about time. His opponents, Kant says, allow that space is transcendentally ideal because they think it possible that there may really be nothing spatial at all, that space may be an illusion; and they object that time is not transcendentally ideal because it is certainly not an illusion since the reality of some changes is 'immediately evident through consciousness'.[1] Kant replies, in effect, that scepticism is beside the point. The issue is not about whether time is real, he says, but about what it means to say that time is real.

This rebuttal is correct: here, as almost always in serious philosophy, scepticism *is* beside the point. Still, Kant invites such misunderstandings when he says things like 'We deny to time all claim to absolute reality', rather than using the more sober formulation he gives to his transcendental idealism about space:

It is. . .solely from the human standpoint that we can speak of space, of extended things, etc. If we depart from the subjective condition under which alone we can have outer intuition. . .the representation of space stands for nothing whatsoever. This predicate can be ascribed to things only in so far as they appear to us, that is, only to objects of sensibility.[2]

This is better. Properly expressed, transcendental idealism about any concept C says that it is only because of the way our experience is that we have any use for the concept C. If C is the concept of objective time, or of the temporal order of objective events and processes, then transcendental idealism about it says that it is only because of the way our experience is that we can place objective events and processes in an objective temporal order. This seems to be what Kant means when he says that time does not belong to 'things' absolutely. This, however, is just an aspect of Kant's transcendental idealism about objectivity concepts generally; it is not a controversial addition to it. The position is not 'Transcendental idealism applies to the objective world and also—surprising as it may seem—to objective time', but rather 'Transcendental idealism applies to the objective world and therefore, as a trivial consequence, to objective time'.

Yet Kant's opponents can be excused for finding his transcendental idealism about time controversial. For Kant claims to be a transcendental idealist about time, not just about objective time; time is the form of *inner* sense. In showing how our experience makes it possible for us to have objectivity concepts, including the concept of an objective temporal order, Kant must tell a story which *assumes* that our inner states can be set in a temporal order; and this will show up, embarrassingly, the extent to which he has fallen short of giving a transcendental idealist account of the concept of *time*. So, even if Kant's opponents were wrong to say 'You can't be sceptical about time, because even our inner states are in time', they might justly have said 'What you call the experiential basis for the concept of time is only the experiential basis for the concept of objective time.' Kant would have to reply that he does mean to assert transcendental idealism about time generally, and thus that our ability to bring even our sensory states under temporal concepts depends upon the way our experience is, the way our sensory states are. So indeed it does: it depends on the fact that they occur in a temporal order; but this is not transcendental idealism, but merely the trivial claim that what concepts something falls under depends upon what it is like. Transcendental idealism about subjective time is not false but trivial. In general, I suggest, it is not informative to say of any concept which applies to sensory states themselves that we could have no use for it if it were not for the way our sensory states are: phenomenalisms are designed to operate *across* the subjective/objective borderline. So it would be fair for Kant's opponents to claim that transcendental idealism about time cannot be expressed in such a way as to be both non-trivial and comprehensive. This would deflate Kant's position a little, but would not refute it.

It may be noted in passing that Kant usually addresses himself not to the statement that all experience is temporally ordered but rather to certain more specific statements about time such as that it is one-dimensional. (He also thinks that arithmetic relates to time as geometry does to space, so that the apriority of '$5+7 = 12$' is secured by the form of inner sense.[1] This part of Kant's theory is wrong in a thoroughly boring way. I shall ignore it.) 'Time must be one-dimensional' presents, I think, fewer problems than 'All experience must be temporal'. There is no way of satisfying the conditions for temporality without satisfying the conditions for one-dimensional temporality; so that 'Time is one-dimensional' is, although not elementarily analytic, a conceptual truth of the same unobvious kind as 'All outer experience is spatial'. We can, then, understand Kant's calling it synthetic and a priori.

Illustrating his 'axioms of time', Kant says (according to Kemp Smith's translation): 'Time has only one dimension; different times are not simultaneous but successive...'.[2] This looks like a pair of 'axioms', and it is puzzling that Kant should regard the second of them as synthetic rather than as elementarily analytic: surely the statement that t_1 is simultaneous with t_2 *is* just the statement that t_1 is t_2. The fact is, though, that in the quoted passage Kant thinks he is propounding not two 'axioms' but one. Where Kemp Smith has a semi-colon, Kant uses a colon, so that the passage has the force of 'Time has only one dimension; in other words, different times are not simultaneous but successive'. It is therefore natural for Kant to regard the second clause as synthetic, since he thinks it is equivalent to the first.

The two clauses do not make the same point. The rather persistent belief that they do may be based on the assumption that if times were ordered two-dimensionally—in columns and rows, as it were—then two times could be distinct because occupying different columns, and yet be simultaneous because occupying the same row. This, however, assumes that there is one obviously right way of fitting the notion of simultaneity into the barely coherent supposition that time might be two-dimensional; and that is just false. Kant's own reason for thinking that 'Time has only one dimension' makes the same point as 'Different times are not simultaneous but successive' is even more certainly wrong. Here is his whole sentence:

Time has only one dimension: different times are not simultaneous but successive (just as different spaces are not successive but simultaneous).

The antithesis which follows the colon is clearly supposed to express the difference of dimensionality between space and time, but it does no such thing. When Kant says that different spaces are simultaneous, he means that different parts of space exist at the same time; and this would be no less true if space had only one dimension. In short: in the sense in which it is true that different spaces may be simultaneous while different times cannot, this is not because of a difference of dimensionality but because spaces last through time while times do not.

17 Concepts and intuitions

I remarked in §1 that the boundary between the Aesthetic and the Logic is based upon a distinction between sense and intellect. Now 'intellect' is not one of Kant's technical terms, but many aspects of the human condition usually covered by that vague word are classified by Kant as activities of the *understanding*.

Kant says: 'There are two stems of human knowledge, namely, sensibility and understanding...Through the former, objects are given to us; through the latter, they are thought.'[1] Through the sensibility, that is, we are presented with all our factual raw material: it would be a fair gloss on 'through sensibility, objects are given to us' to say that it is through sensibility that we establish truths about what there is. The understanding, on the other hand, enables us to organize intellectually our raw material by classifying, discriminating, judging, comparing...

Some more technical terminology: 'Sensibility alone yields us *intuitions*...from the understanding arise *concepts*.'[1] For Kant, an intuition is just a sensory state: to 'have an intuition' is to be in a sensory state, and to 'have an intuition of' something is to be sensorily aware of it. One way of having an intuition of a man, for example, is to see a man. To 'have the concept of' a man—or of humanity—is not to be in any kind of sensory state; it is just to be able to recognize men as men, to distinguish men from apes, to know that a man cannot be a vegetable, and so on. To have a concept is to be able to do certain things, particularly linguistic things such as answering questions like 'Is this a man?' and 'Why is that not a man?'

The claim that to have a concept is to have an ability, and the related claim that to analyse a concept is to clarify the proper use of certain expressions and thus to describe the ability to use them properly, might be condensed into the statement that *a concept is an ability*. This is an ellipsis, for it does not carry over literally into our talk of 'applying' concepts, or of concepts as being 'imprecise', 'general' and the like. Still, it is a convenient ellipsis, and I shall avail myself of it.

In crediting Kant with the view that a concept is an ability or skill, I may have flattered him, for his position may be rather that having a concept is being in a mental state which endows one with certain abilities. Wittgenstein has given excellent reasons for classifying concepts as abilities,[2] and for denying that there is any distinguishable mental state which *is* the concept and which *leads to* the abilities. Kant may not want to go as far as this. As I noted in § 2, his explanation of analyticity suggests that the concept of body can be found to include that of extension by the act of 'thinking' or conjuring up the former concept and introspecting it. Also, Kant uses the one word 'representation' to cover both intuitions and concepts, and thus suggests that concepts, like intuitions, are discrete, datable mental items of some kind.[3]

Yet whether or not Kant thinks that concepts are the causes of, rather than identical with, certain capacities, his actual working use of 'concept' is, except when he is explaining analyticity, rather thoroughly Wittgensteinian.[4] For him, as for Wittgenstein, the interest of concepts lies in the abilities with which they are somehow associated.

Kant's mild tendency to think of concepts as introspectible particulars does not, at any rate, take the pernicious form of identifying concepts with something in the nature of sensory states. Some philosophers have said that intellectual activity is the manipulation of 'ideas' which are mental particulars pretty much like sense-data. Descartes and Locke used the word 'idea' to stand indifferently for sense-data and for whatever one 'has in mind' when one thinks or understands. Spinoza assimilated sensing to thinking: seeing something happen is, in his view, a mental operation which does not differ in kind from drawing a conclusion. Hume assimilated thinking to sensing: according to his theory of belief, to judge that the sun is shining is 'vividly' to picture the shining sun.[1] Not only Spinoza versus Hume, but also Leibniz versus Locke, as Kant saw: 'Leibniz *intellectualized* appearances, just as Locke...*sensualized* all concepts of the understanding.'[2] With the possible exception of the chapter on schematism, the *Critique* is completely free of both rationalist and empiricist forms of the conflation of the sensory with the intellectual. It is not hard to see that being in a sensory state differs from having certain linguistic and other skills; but the insight that the distinction between sensory states and concepts is of this sort was an achievement which cannot be truly appreciated until one has read Kant's predecessors. In them we can see how beguiling and, up to a point, how astonishingly serviceable is the view that concepts and sensory states are species of a single genus, differing from one another not at all (Berkeley)[3] or differing only in degree of clarity (Descartes), or reliability (Spinoza), or detailedness (Locke), or vividness (Hume).

Like Berkeley before him,[4] Kant thinks it important to say that thinking is something we do while sensing is something which happens to us. His simple alignment of the active/passive dichotomy[5] with the understanding/sensibility dichotomy underlies a crucial aspect of his use of the word 'intuition'. He applies 'intuition' not only to any individual sensory state but also to the capacity for being in such states. In the latter use, 'intuition' looks interchangeable with 'sensibility', but this is not quite so. By 'intuition' Kant means 'capacity for being confronted by individual items of reality'; and by 'sensibility' he means 'passive intuition'. Since the only intuition humans have is, Kant thinks, a passive or 'sensible' one, the words 'intuition' and 'sensibility' are interchangeable in the human context, the former referring to confrontation with data, the latter adding a reference to passivity. Kant allows that there could be beings with non-sensible intuition, i.e. with a faculty (a) which confronts them with particulars as our senses do us, and (b) in respect of which they are active as, according to Kant, we are in respect of our understanding but not our intuition. A non-sensible intuition would presumably be a capacity for acting informatively, whatever that may mean. Kant emphasizes that although such an intuition is consistently supposable we cannot even speculate about what it would be like.[1]

We cannot take Kant's 'non-sensible intuition' as a precisely located possibility, because the thesis which underlies it, namely that our intuition is passive and our understanding active, is at best a drastic over-simplification. For example, when I raise my arm I actively produce changes in my sensory state; yet Kant would not count *physical activity* as an exercise of non-sensible intuition. He might plead that what really happens when I raise my arm is that I actively do something which involves no sensory changes, and that sensory changes then occur as consequences of that initial action. But this reduces the initial action to something entirely non-physical—a volition, presumably—and that way confusion lies. Or again, what about *imagination*? Kant himself says that this is an active faculty and that it confronts us with intuitions; but he would not admit that it is a kind of non-sensible intuition. Given the unclarity of his active/passive dichotomy, one simply cannot say whether or how he could avoid such an admission.

The notion of non-sensible intuition is important because of its connection with the notion of a noumenon, to which I now return.

18   The negative use of 'noumenon'

While Kant denies that we can apply to noumena 'any determinate predicate' or 'any of the concepts of the understanding', he yet holds that they are 'possible' and that we can 'think' them. How can a possibility be indescribable? And how can we 'think' something except with the concepts of the understanding? In answer, Kant introduces the 'negative' use of 'noumenon':

> The concept of a noumenon is.. a merely *limiting concept,* the function of which is to curb the pretensions of sensibility; and it is therefore only of negative employment.[2]

Presumably, curbing the pretensions of sensibility is indicating the limits on what sensibility can do—likely work for a 'limiting concept'. I take it that a 'limit' on sensibility is expressed by any true synthetic statement of the form 'All our sensory states are F' or 'None of our sensory states are F'. The restriction to synthetic truths seems reasonable: one would not want to say that our experience is 'limited' to the extent that none of our sensory states is a perception-of-something-red-

and-not-coloured, or to the extent that all our sensory states are accompanied by consciousness. On the other hand, it is reasonable to say that our experience is limited to the extent that all our auditory states are of sounds which fall within a certain range of pitch. Perhaps someone could satisfy himself that this is a genuine limit on his experience by imagining, or hearing in his mind's ear, sounds which are now too high for us; but something can be a genuine limit without our being able in this way to imagine ourselves free of it. I cannot see in my mind's eye a fourth primary colour, yet such a radical addition to my visual range is possible: it is not logically necessary that the colour-range I know is complete. Furthermore, I can say something about what it would be like for a new primary colour to be seen, for I know how I might satisfy myself that someone else could see one, what things he might say and how he might fit them in with talk about other colours.

Now, I have argued, in effect, that 'All our experience is temporal' does set a genuine limit to our experience. Yet we are unable to imagine having atemporal experience, and we cannot even say how we might know of someone else that he had atemporal experience, or apprehended an atemporal reality. In this one case, the notion of a 'limit' cannot be elucidated by an account of what would be involved in the limit's being removed; and yet it is a genuine limit for all that.

In its negative use, 'noumenon' serves as a reminder that there are facts about our experience which impose limits on what we can meaningfully say. When Kant says that an atemporal reality would be noumenal, he is saying that we can have no vocabulary, no concepts, with which to describe such a reality. When he allows that the concept of a noumenon is possible, he is saying among other things that it is not in the ordinary way analytically necessary that all data are temporal. If this interpretation is right, Kant's negative use of 'noumenon' is no longer bewildering. It does remain queer and strained, but only because the point it is making, about the place of temporality in our experience and our conceptual scheme, is itself difficult and peculiar.

Kant's point here is a good one; but the fact is that he does not make it by means of a use, even a negative use, of the concept of a noumenon. When he makes it best he *talks about* the concept of a noumenon rather than *using* it in talk about noumena.[1] What he says does not take the dangerous form: 'There might be noumena, but we have no concepts for them'. Rather, he says something like: 'The statement "There might be noumena, but we have no concepts for them" serves as a

57

reminder that our sensibility has limits which restrict what we can mean, and which therefore cannot be shown to be limits in the usual way, namely by describing their removal.' Such second-order uses of 'noumenon' are all that Kant needs. Indeed, what he wants to say can be said entirely without any such word as 'noumenon', viz. by simply describing the place which temporality has in our conceptual scheme.

A graver mistake in Kant's handling of 'noumenon', affecting the whole *Critique*, can be found in condensed form in the chapter on phenomena and noumena.[1]

I have remarked that Kant equates the noumenal with what lies outside the reach of our kind of intuition, and I have taken the atemporal as the only plausible example I could find. Now for Kant 'our kind of intuition' is passive (= sensible), and so an intuition not of our kind would be active (= intellectual). He says that 'we cannot comprehend even the possibility' of intellectual intuition,[2] but 'possibility' is there used in a strong sense. Kant does think that 'intellectual intuition' is a self-consistent phrase and—the vital point—he assumes that what lies beyond the reach of our kind of intuition is what could be known by an intellectual intuition if there were one: any being has atemporal data if, and only if, its intuition is intellectual.

Kant is presumably drawn to the phrase 'intellectual intuition' by its architectonic efficiency. An intellectual intuition would be a faculty which presented one with data but which was otherwise just like our understanding; it would, in fact, be 'an understanding which [would] know its object, not discursively through categories, but intuitively in a non-sensible intuition'.[3] Thus 'Our intuition is not intellectual' makes the same point as is made by 'Our understanding does not give us data (but only enables us to handle data reaching us from another source)'; and so two major Kantian emphases are really one.[4] To put the point teasingly, the passiveness of our intuition *is* the uninformativeness of our understanding.

This last formulation gives the game away. Clearly, the active/passive dichotomy and its still more suspect alignment with the intellectual/sensible dichotomy are here put under a theoretical load which they cannot possibly support. Even if we grant—which I do not—that something clear and true is said by 'Our intuition is passive, but there might be an intuition which was active as our understanding is', and even if we allow Kant to use 'intellectual' to mean 'active', it still does not follow that an active intuition would be 'intellectual' in the other sense of 'being a capacity for the intellectual control of data', and so it does not follow that an active intuition would be an intuitive understanding.

Worse follows. For Kant takes intellectual intuition to be free not just from the limits on human intuition but from all limits whatsoever. Sensible intuition presents us with things as they appear; intellectual intuition would present them as they are in themselves. Early in the *Critique* Kant says:

If we abstract from *our* mode of [intuition], and so take objects as they may be in themselves, then time is nothing.[1]

The caution expressed by 'may be' is later thrown to the winds:

If the senses represent to us something merely *as it appears*, this something must also in itself be a thing, and an object of a non-sensible intuition, that is, of the understanding. In other words, a [kind of] knowledge must be possible, in which there is no sensibility, and which alone has reality that is absolutely objective. Through it objects will be represented *as they are*, whereas in the empirical employment of our understanding things will be known only *as they appear*.[2]

In another passage in which this same line of thought emerges through a grammatical chaos, Kant says that in calling things phenomena we 'distinguish the mode in which we intuit them from the nature that belongs to them in themselves';[3] and that this distinction implies the notion of 'possible things, which are not objects of our senses but are thought as objects merely through the understanding', things which can be called 'intelligible entities (noumena)'.

This use of 'thought', like that in Kant's reference to 'The concept of a *noumenon*—that is, of a thing which is not to be thought as object of the senses but as a thing in itself, solely through a pure understanding',[4] points to another architectonic flourish. Noumena are intelligible; they could be *known* only through an intellectual intuition, but even we who have no such intuition can *think* them:

Appearances, so far as they are thought as objects according to the unity of the categories, are called *phaenomena*. But if I postulate things which are mere objects of understanding, and which, nevertheless, can be given as such to an intuition, although not to one that is sensible...such things would be entitled *noumena*.[5]

I cannot find, however, any clear route from 'We can only think them' to 'Only if we had an intellectual intuition could we know them'.

In any case, what is it that we are supposed to be able to think? If 'noumenon' merely points to the unamplifiable logical possibility that there should be atemporal data, then perhaps we can think noumena. But 'things as they are in themselves' is quite another matter. I can find no sense in talk about a mode of knowing, intellectual or otherwise, which presents one with things not as they appear but as they are. Such talk seems to involve a way of knowing divorced from any possibility of saying 'This is *how* I apprehend reality', e.g. of saying 'I apprehend reality as atemporal' or 'Reality appears to me as atemporal'.

Perhaps Kant's intention is less radical. He may intend knowledge of things as they are in themselves to amount only to a kind of knowledge which admits of no distinction between appearance and reality. If so, such knowledge need not exclude talk of *how* things appear or are presented, but will merely equate talk of how things *appear* with talk of how things *are*. On this interpretation of it, however, the notion of knowledge of things as they are in themselves embodies the claim that an 'absolutely objective reality'[1] might be apprehended in a way which did not admit of the possibility of error. This, if 'objective' is taken seriously, seems to be a simple mistake; and if 'objective' is not to be taken seriously then Kant is up against the difficulty which I raised for different reasons at the end of § 17: How can he deny that imagination is intuition of things, namely images, as they are in themselves?

5

INTUITIONS OF SPACE AND TIME

19 A priori concepts and a priori intuitions

In both Aesthetic and Analytic, Kant seeks to prove synthetic a priori truths about all experience. Between these two sets of results there are, he thinks, two radical differences.

Firstly, 'the concepts of space and time...must necessarily relate to objects...Only by means of such pure forms of sensibility can an object appear to us, and so be an object of empirical intuition';[1] while the concepts treated in the Analytic 'do not represent the conditions under which objects are given in intuition'[2] but only those under which objects can be brought under concepts, i.e. thought about, classified, generalized over. Here, as in the next quotation, 'object' does not mean 'objective particular' but has the very general sense of 'datum' or 'something given'. The Aesthetic, then, tells us what all our intuitions must be like, while the Analytic tells us what our intuitions must be like to be intellectually manageable.

This suggests that the Aesthetic's conditions might be met although the Analytic's were not, i.e. that there might be unconceptualizable intuitions. Kant does indeed say:

Everything might be in such confusion that, for instance, in the series of appearances nothing presented itself which might...answer to the concept of cause and effect [which, according to the Analytic, must apply to our intuitions if they are to be thinkable at all]. This concept would then be empty, null, and meaningless. But since intuition stands in no need whatsoever of the functions of thought, appearances would none the less present objects to our intuition.[3]

However, he intends this only as *prima facie* possible—as not obviously impossible—and he later argues that after all there cannot be intuitions which are not brought under concepts. In the passage just quoted, Kant is not affirming that 'intuition stands in no need whatsoever of the functions of thought'; he is putting it forward as prima facie possible, as credible to anyone who does not know the arguments for its falsity.

One could, unjustly, say that Kant has a working picture of the Aesthetic as stating what the sensibility does to intuitions as they come into existence, and of the Analytic as stating what the understanding does to them immediately thereafter. In place of this picture, shot through as it is with bad theory, I shall adopt one in which the Aesthetic states some conditions which intuitions must satisfy and the Analytic states others. The two are complementary parts of a single conceptual inquiry.

There is a second way in which Kant contrasts the conclusions of the Aesthetic with those of the Analytic. The Analytic seeks to prove that all intuitions must fall under certain concepts, such as that of cause; while the conditions which the Aesthetic lays down on all intuitions, or all outer intuitions, do not consist primarily in obedience to *concepts* at all. Kant prefers to speak of intuitions, rather than of concepts, of space and time; he even talks of space and time as being themselves intuitions. We do have concepts of space and time, he allows;[1] but he thinks that these concepts have a peculiar relationship with the corresponding intuitions: in each case the intuition somehow precedes, underlies and makes possible the concept. 'The original representation of space', Kant says, 'is an a priori intuition, not a concept.'[2]

What this comes down to as regards space is roughly the following. The Aesthetic might be taken as saying (i) that spatiality is an a priori concept: outer experience must be of things which manifest a certain kind of order and so fall under the concept of spatiality. Kant, however, takes the Aesthetic to be showing (ii) that space is an a priori intuition: outer experience must be of things which occupy Space, a particular which is given in intuition. While not rejecting (i), Kant thinks that it is, in a way I shall explain, derivative from (ii). All this applies *mutatis mutandis* to time as well.

My Strawsonian defence of the outer-sense theory has interpreted it in terms of (i), and I do not see how one could reconstruct Strawson's argument about the concept of spatiality so as to turn it into a treatment of an intuited particular called 'Space'. Apart from his desire for a synthetic theory, therefore, Kant has a further reason for denying that the Aesthetic is a Strawson-type exercise in conceptual analysis.

We must now see why Kant takes this unpromising line about the primacy of our intuitions of space and time over our concepts of spatiality and temporality. For brevity's sake I shall take over one of Kant's formulations, solecism though it is, and express the view in question in the form 'Space and time are a priori intuitions'.

Most people assume that there is only one Space and one Time: when we speak of two spaces we normally mean two parts of the single all-embracing Space; and analogously for our talk about times. Kant thinks that it is *necessary* that there is only one Space and one Time: any two spaces must be spatially related to one another and so be parts of a single Space; and any two times must be temporally related to one another and so occur in the one and only Time-series. He sees that this creates a problem. The concept of an inkwell has many instances; the concept of a natural satellite of the earth could have many; the concept of being the sole ruler of the universe cannot have more than one instance because it has singularity built in. In the first two cases it is in no way necessary, while in the third it is analytic, that the concept has at most one instance. Kant's problem is to show how it can be necessary, though not analytic, that there is only one Space and one Time; and he hopes to solve this problem through his doctrine that Space and Time are a priori intuitions, as follows.

When we say that there is only one Space and one Time we are not—according to Kant—saying of general concepts of space and time that they have only one instance each. We are not dealing with general concepts at all, because 'Space' and 'Time' are not descriptive expressions but proper names. 'There is only one Space' does not have the logical form of 'There is only one great German philosopher'; it is logically nearer to 'There is only one Immanuel Kant'. Similarly with 'There is only one Time'.

In terms of the proper name 'Space' Kant permits us to define a peculiar kind of general term 'spatial' or 'a space', this being so defined that 'x is spatial' or 'x is a space' means 'x is a part of Space'.[1] Describing x as spatial or as a space, then, is not saying that x manifests a certain kind of order; rather, it is doing something logically on a par with pointing to a particular, namely Space, and saying 'x is part of *that*'. It follows that any two 'spaces' *must* be parts of Space. Similarly, again, for times.

This account of the logic of 'space' and 'time' fails to solve Kant's problem. Kant says that the intuition of Space is prior to or more basic than any spatial concepts—which I interpret as saying that 'Space' is a proper name and that the general term 'spatial' or 'a space' must be defined in terms of it. We could grant this without granting that 'x is spatial' must mean that x is *a part of* Space, for it could mean that x is *like* Space in certain formal respects. From this definition of 'spatial' it simply does not follow that anything spatial must be a part of Space. Furthermore, this is a legitimate and natural way of deriving the adjective 'spatial' from the name 'Space'. It yields, for example, the sense which I employed in considering whether all outer experience must be of a spatial world. If Kant thinks that anything which is 'spatial' in this sense must be a part of Space, then he requires some fresh arguments: the claim that Space is an intuition—that 'Space' is a proper name—will not do the job.

Some of this applies also to the problem about the singularity of time, but a full treatment of that must wait until my next section.

Kant has some muddled supplementary reasons for presenting space and time as a priori intuitions. Firstly, his transcendental idealism about space and time could be loosely summed up by saying that *space and time are intuitions* not things in themselves. This does not make the same sort of point as the thesis that *space and time are intuitions* not concepts, but sometimes Kant seems to think that it does.[1] Secondly, Kant argues that if geometry is synthetic then space must be an intuition and not a concept, because 'from mere concepts only analytic knowledge...is to be obtained'.[2] This is just a confusion, and Kant does not even hold to it: in the Analytic he propounds some allegedly synthetic and a priori truths about certain *concepts* under which all experience must fall. Finally, Kant says: 'Pure intuition...contains only the form under which something is intuited; the pure concept only the form of the thought of an object...'.[3] This is suspiciously neat. Does Kant think that, while conditions on thinkability are concepts, conditions on intuitability must be intuitions? Surely, to speak of conditions on something is to speak of what it must be like, and that is just to speak of the concepts under which it must fall.

20 The singularity and infinity of space and time

(1) To begin with the singularity of space: we must distinguish the concept of a space from that of a complete space. S is a complete space if and only if anything which is spatially related to any part of S is itself a part of S. By this definition, a complete space must contain some given space s together with every space which is related to s; it need not contain all the spaces there are. The concept of a complete space is not one to which Kant explicitly calls attention, but he can fairly be represented as holding the view that there can be only one complete space.

A. M. Quinton argues, in his article 'Spaces and Times', that it could become more reasonable to assert than to deny that there are two complete spaces, i.e. two spaces such that no part of either relates by distance or direction to any part of the other.[4] Suppose that one night

I have a dream which is lifelike in its vividness, coherence and amplitude of detail; it involves strangers as well as myself, and seems to last about eighteen hours. The next night I have an equally verisimilar dream involving mostly the same characters and the same physical background. This continues night after night, with the dreams forming a coherently developing history interleaved with the coherent history of my waking life. When awake I can recall my previous dreams, and in any dream I can recall my waking life to date. It will eventually become unreasonable to say that these are *dreams*: they have as much right to be called experiences of reality as has my life in this world. Even conceding that what is real must be public, this conclusion stands. In so far as no one else in this world has them, the 'dreams' are admittedly private, but they contain their own public; and to divest the 'dream'-public of epistemological authority because it is only a dream-public is to beg the question. The 'dream'-public might even dismiss my reports of this world as mere dream-fiction; but they would be as wrong to do this as you would be to say that yours is the only real world I have been in. Alternatively, we can suppose that many people in this world share my 'dreams', so that one public confirms the reality of both worlds.

This shows, I think, that one could alternately inhabit two distinct worlds which had equal claims to reality. Furthermore, it could be the case that there was no reason for saying that the two worlds were spatially related to one another—or no reason except the prejudice that there can be only one complete space.

Quinton's story concerns the alternate occupancy of two complete spaces; but it is also possible that one should concurrently inhabit two spaces which have no spatial relations to one another. For example, someone might live in our world, stone deaf to all its objective noises, while also inhabiting the space of a Strawsonian auditory world.

If Kant's thesis is refuted neither by the alternate occupancy of two physical spaces, nor by the concurrent occupancy of a physical and an auditory space, what would refute it? Perhaps what is demanded is the concurrent occupancy of two complete physical spaces, i.e. the possibility that someone should bodily inhabit our space and at the same time another tactual-kinaesthetic space unrelated to ours. The question now turns on whether a person could have two bodies at once. If this is not possible then Kant's thesis, on the present interpretation of it, is true but not for the reason he gives. If a person can have two bodies at once, then it is quite unclear whether Kant is right or not: that will depend on how the two-body possibility works out in detail. In working it out we are unlikely to be helped by 'Space is an intuition, not a concept'.

(2) As regards the singularity of time: here too we need the concept of a complete time analogous to that of a complete space. Kant thinks that there can be only one complete time, i.e. that there cannot be a time which is not temporally related to *now*. This seems to be analytic, and therefore not to serve Kant's purpose. If it is analytic that everyone who is not my height is shorter or taller than me, is it not also analytic that every time other than now is either earlier or later than now? How could a time escape being simultaneous with the present except by being past or future? It seems that the concept of a complete time, like that of the sole ruler of the universe, has singularity built in.

This treatment is too glib to be final, though. Suppose it is analytic that there is only one complete time; might not some radical shift in our experience lead us to modify our temporal concepts so as to allow that there could be two distinct times which were not related to one another as earlier and later? The physics of simultaneity is irrelevant here. Granting that there *need* not be an absolute answer to the question 'Was this event simultaneous with that?', I am discussing what might follow from a negative answer to it: could we come to allow that two events might be determined as *not* simultaneous by standards which also determined that neither event preceded the other?

Well, Quinton's two-space story interferes with the metric of time but not its topology; and Quinton himself shows that his story could not be adapted to prove the possibility of two complete times.[1] I think, furthermore, that any attempt to describe experience which would lead us to say that there were two complete times would fail as completely as the attempt to describe atemporal experience: for deep logical reasons, we are as unavoidably committed to a one-dimensional, all-inclusive time-series as we are to temporality as such. Just as we cannot peel the concept of consciousness off that of a person, so we cannot strip our temporal concepts of those features which make it necessary that there is only one complete time. The reasons for this have nothing to do with time's being an intuition rather than a concept.

(3) Kant infers that space is an intuition rather than a concept, from the premiss that space is necessarily infinite.[2] The obscurity of this argument does not matter, since its sole premiss is false. Perhaps space cannot be bounded, but nevertheless it may be finite. A two-dimensional inhabitant of the surface of a sphere could learn that his space was

finite though unbounded by discovering that, although able to move where he wished, he could never break free of a certain finite region. We too could find our three-dimensional space to be finite though unbounded by discovering that however far and straight we travelled all roads led to home.

I have been told that this possibility is irrelevant to epistemology and metaphysics because although the space in question can be mathematically described it cannot be concretely imagined. The word 'curved' is sometimes invoked: only a curved space can be finite but unbounded, and a three-dimensional space cannot be pictured in the mind's eye as curved. I have dealt in § 10 with the prejudice against cosmic possibilities which cannot be portrayed in a single picture; but there is here another mistake as well, a misunderstanding about curvature. The surface of a sphere is 'curved' in the sense of having certain geometrical properties which a three-dimensional space could have too. It is also 'curved' in the untechnical sense of looking curved, feeling curved etc.; but a space which is 'curved' in this sense must be immersed in a space of higher dimensionality, in relation to which it looks and feels curved.[1] Now the plausibility of (a) 'Three-dimensional space cannot be concretely imagined as curved' depends upon (a)'s using 'curved' in this second, untechnical sense; so that if (a) is to give support to (b) 'Three-dimensional space is not curved', then (b) must use 'curved' in the untechnical sense also. But only if (b) uses 'curved' in the first, technical sense does it imply (c) 'Three-dimensional space is not finite-but-unbounded'. Therefore, on the most liberal estimate of (a)'s relevance to (b), the sense of (a) in which it may be true is one which makes it totally irrelevant to (c).

(4) Kant argues analogously from the premiss that time is necessarily infinite.[2] I have no analogous counter-argument which shows how time might be finite though unbounded. In my *Kant's Dialectic* I shall discuss infinity, including the infinity of time, more fully than I can here. That discussion will not support the view that time is an intuition rather than a concept.

ANALYTIC OF CONCEPTS

6

THE METAPHYSICAL DEDUCTION

21 Concepts and judgments

The Analytic of Concepts consists of two chapters. One is entitled
'The Clue to the Discovery of all Pure Concepts of the Understanding';
but I shall follow the universal practice, based on one passing remark of
Kant's,[1] of referring to its main line of argument as the Metaphysical
Deduction of the Categories. The second chapter bears the equally
repellent title 'Transcendental Deduction of the Categories'. In the
first chapter Kant lays down certain conditions which he thinks must
be satisfied if one is to use concepts; and in the second he argues that
only someone who uses concepts can have experience, because experience must be 'gone through in a certain way, taken up, and
connected' by the understanding.[2] In this section I shall examine
certain assumptions which lie behind the Metaphysical Deduction of
the Categories.

Someone counts as having the concept of humanity if he can correctly
use 'human' and its cognates, or 'menschlich' and its cognates, or
'humain' and its cognates etc. In saying this I treat concepts as abilities
rather than as mental states which may lead to abilities: a man's ability
to use a word properly does not merely suggest but proves that he has
the corresponding concept. I thus desert the introspectionist approach
to concepts which, as I noted in §2, Kant often adopts when he is
discussing analyticity; but then Kant himself usually deserts this too.
The Analytic of Concepts is, I think, intelligible only on the assumption
that to have a concept is to have a certain sort of linguistic skill. The
question of whether there can be a non-linguistic exercise of concepts
will be discussed in §24.

Someone who uses 'human' and its cognates correctly, i.e. in accordance with standards which are accepted by most literate speakers of
English, is said to understand these words or to know what they mean.
Someone who does not know what 'human' means may (1) have no
use for 'human' or (2) have a use for 'human' but a wrong one. The
two cases are very different: in type-(1) cases, standards of correctness
are crutches for beginners; in type-(2) cases they are correctives for
fumblers. Type-(1) cases are often stressed to the virtual exclusion of

71

type-(2), but I shall put the stress the other way: my interest is in wrong uses of words, and the normal outcome of type-(1) ignorance of the meaning of a word is not misuse but failure to use. I shall ignore wrong uses which arise not from ignorance at all but from someone's choosing to use a word in accordance with some purely personal standard although he knows what the generally accepted standards are.

Someone may show that he attaches a wrong meaning to a word by giving a thoroughly wrong definition of it, or by saying something which is obviously logically wrong and whose wrongness has to do with the meaning of the word in question—for example by saying 'Some humans are not animals' or 'He humans his lettuces every week-end' or 'To be a human is to have a brain bigger than one's stomach'. But one's understanding of a word is also shown by, and answerable to, one's use of it in ordinary synthetic sentences: in 'Humans sometimes laugh' as well as in 'Humans are animals'. Some philosophers seem to have thought that even the most eccentric set of assignments of truth-values to synthetic sentences may, however improbably, be due to misinformation rather than to a mistake about meanings. Such mis-handlings of synthetic sentences, they have thought, may *suggest* that the speaker does not know the meaning of some word he is using but can never show this for sure: the privilege of conclusive relevance is reserved for misuses of the word in which analytic sentences are deemed false, self-contradictory sentences are deemed true, nonsensical sentences are deemed meaningful, wrong definitions are offered and so on. It may be faintly plausible to associate the *explanation* of meanings with definitions, analyticities etc.; but I have suggested that we ought not to tie our theory of meaning too tightly to how meanings are explained, i.e. to cures for type-(1) ignorance of meanings. Whatever its sources, the view in question is in any case wrong. Truth-value assignments to synthetic sentences may sometimes be less directly relevant to questions about meaning than are truth-value assignments to analytic or self-contradictory ones; but if they were *never* able to force a conclusion as to whether someone understands a word, we should have to allow that someone might give 'human' its correct meaning and yet assign the wrong truth-value to every synthetic sentence in which 'human' occurs.

Different kinds of sentence can be relevant in many ways and degrees to questions about meanings, and this network of relevances cannot be embodied in a precise, general theory which could mechanically answer every question about anyone's understanding of a word. But what matters for present purposes is that such questions are answerable only on the basis of truth-value assignments to sentences of every main sort. This or that sentence may turn out to be irrelevant in a given case, but no large and clearly demarcated class of sentences can be ignored on principle.

The relevance of this to Kant is as follows. If someone understands 'human' and its cognates, then he has the concept of humanity; though the converse of this does not quite hold. If we agree, then, that someone's understanding of a word is answerable to his use of it in synthetic sentences, we are entitled to follow Kant in thinking of concepts as competences across the whole range of linguistic activity and not just across that tiny part of it which has to do with sentences which are, or are said to be, analytic or self-contradictory or meaningless. In fact, we shall see that Kant is committed to disqualifying a certain sub-class of synthetic sentences from conclusive relevance to questions about meanings; but I shall argue in §36 that even this modest thesis is false.

Before this matter is pursued further, I must say more about the relation between having concepts, making judgments and knowing meanings. To have a concept is to be able to cope with—i.e. generally to sort out true from false among—judgments of some *functional kind*. I say that a class of judgments are of a 'functional kind' if and only if they do the same sort of work, have a similarity of function: the class of judgments which treat of humans forms a functional kind, and determines the concept of humanity; while the class of complex judgments is not associated in that way with the concept of complexity or indeed with any other concept, for complex judgments do not form a functional kind—there is no task, however unspecific, which all complex judgments perform. What counts as being able to cope with judgments of a functional kind? Given the restriction to concepts as exercised in language and judgments as expressed in language, the best answer I can find is as follows. Someone can cope with judgments involving the concept of humanity, say, if and only if he understands sentences (in some language) which do the same kind of work as do English sentences containing 'human' and its cognates, and do it in the same kind of way. This brings in, as involving the concept of humanity, not only various uses of other languages but also certain uses of English which do not involve 'humanity' or any of its grammatical cognates. For example, if someone says 'If Hobbes's account of his own motivations were really correct, he would be one of the brutes and not one of *us*', the definition I have given would allow us to count this as involving the concept of humanity.

When I say 'do the same kind of work...and do it in the same kind of way' the second clause is to be understood in terms of linguistic structure. It is needed for the following reason. If a language had no short expression which could be translated as 'human' or any of its cognates, but did contain enough morphological and behavioural adjectives for the spelling out of a lengthy description roughly equivalent in meaning to 'human', we should not want to say that the concept of humanity was expressed or exercised in that language or that a user of the language had the concept of humanity. This is because the language in question, although able to handle the facts which English handles in sentences using 'human' and its cognates, would not be able to handle them in the same sort of way as English does, i.e. would not have our device for pulling *that* morphological and behavioural description together under a single short expression.

It will be noted that my account of the concept of humanity is given in terms of sentences using the English word 'human' and its cognates. This is not chauvinism, but merely reflects the fact that I have referred to the concept in question by means of an English word. Had I referred to it as 'the concept of Menschlichkeit' it would have been suitable for me to explain it in terms of sentences containing 'menschlich' and its cognates. And if I had taken as my prime example a concept which is not expressed or exercised in the English language—the concept of *Angst*, say—I should necessarily have referred to it by a non-English word and explained it in terms of non-English sentences containing that word.

Another special feature of my chosen example is that it concerns a single word, 'human'; I could as well have chosen an example which had to be based, so far as English is concerned, on a short phrase and on sentences which do the same kind of work, in the same kind of way, as sentences containing that phrase. What I could not have done, it seems, is to give any account of what is meant by 'such and such a concept' or 'such and such a functional kind of judgment' without some references to 'sentences containing such and such a word or phrase'. It should be remarked that, just as an expression of the form 'the judgment that...' may not refer unambiguously to a single judgment, so an expression of the form 'the concept of...' may not refer unambiguously to a single concept. If the sentences in which the word W occurs do two radically different kinds of work, then the expression 'the concept of W-ness' could refer to either of two concepts. The issue of how severe to be in our criterion of concept-identity might be acute in a particular case, but is not so in general: there is no profit in trying to say precisely and in general what is to count as 'doing the same kind of work'.

The reason for this has to do with our reason for wanting the 'concept' terminology at all. My rough guide to the use of 'concept' in Kant and in philosophy generally could be improved in all sorts of ways; but not in such a way as to present 'concept' as a precise technical term, for it is in fact an imprecise technical term whose utility depends upon its very imprecision. An example may help to show why it is useful in philosophy to have 'x has the concept of...' as well as 'x knows the meaning of "..."'. Hume's discussion of causality illuminates not only 'cause' and its cognates, and their dictionary-equivalents in other languages, but also such sentences as 'If the wound had been cauterized, gangrene would not have set in' and 'It is not a coincidence that left-handed parents often have left-handed children' and 'The evidence, though circumstantial, is overwhelming'. Because these do the same work as sentences containing 'cause' and its cognates, Hume's discussion of causality—not just of 'cause' but of the *concept* of cause— is relevant to them too. There is no sharp line around the sentences to which Hume's discussion of the concept of cause is relevant, and herein lies the useful imprecision of the phrase 'the concept of cause'. More generally, there is no sharp boundary to the class of sentences which 'do the same sort of work' as a given class of sentences, and in that fact lies the useful imprecision of 'concept' in all its uses.

What concepts are there? No doubt there is a concept associated with any ordinary classificatory adjective or general noun; but is there also a concept of negation, associated with 'not' and its cognates? Or of totality, associated with 'all' and its cognates? Kant answers these questions affirmatively. He uses the 'concept' terminology to codify those features of judgments which concern the sort of work they do; and he pays attention to the great variety of features of this kind which a judgment may have. The judgment that *This is a man* singles out something as human and therefore employs the concept of humanity; but it is a further fact about it that it affirms rather than denies. The judgment that *All men are mortal* is about humans, and is affirmative, and has the further feature that it says that all (rather than some or one) of a certain class have a certain property. Kant therefore includes in his inventory of concepts not only concepts like that of humanity and neurosis but also the concepts of negation and totality, singularity and conditionality, and so on.

He insists that there are important differences between these concepts and more run-of-the-mill ones: he does not regard negation and its like as optional intellectual equipment in the way in which the concept of neurosis is; and he would agree that, whereas someone who lacks the concept of neurosis can be given it by being taught how to use 'neurotic' and its cognates, there is—as I shall argue in §27—no technique for teaching the meaning of 'not' to someone who lacks the concept of negation. But this is perfectly consistent with his wanting to use 'concept' in connection with these extremely general features of judgments. Even if one cannot lack the concept of negation without lacking every concept, it remains true that a person's being able to cope with negative judgments is a fact, albeit an unsurprising one, about what he can do. Facts involving such general, basic, formal features of judgments as negativeness ought not to go without saying. In Ryle's 'Categories', on which this section has leaned heavily, the point is put thus:

In Aristotle's doctrine of the categories, the roles of 'form-words' like *all, some, the, a, any, if, and, not,* are unnoticed, and medieval followers relegated these words to limbo under the grudging appellation of 'syncategorematic'. Kant's doctrine...restores them from the limbo of logic into its workshop.[1]

22 The table of judgments

I have described the concepts of negation, totality etc. as general, basic and formal, but I claim no precision for these labels. It remains to be seen whether any sharp line can be drawn between those concepts which we should be inclined to group with those of totality and negation, and the concepts which we should group with those of humanity and neurosis. The concept of totality is obviously more basic and general than that of humanity, but Kant believes that the difference is not just one of degree. Like some philosophers today, he thinks that concepts like those of negation and totality are 'formal' while descriptive or classificatory concepts are 'material'. On this view, 'He spoke about humans' characterizes the matter of his judgment, while 'He said something universal' characterizes its form. Kant thinks that this formal/material distinction is precise and absolute; he further believes that there are twelve formal concepts out of which all other formal concepts can be defined; finally, he thinks that these twelve, just because they are the primitive formal concepts, have a complex group of privileges which entitles them to be called 'a priori concepts' or 'categories'. I shall normally use the phrase 'the categories' as a neutral label for this set of twelve concepts, not thereby conceding them any special Kantian 'categorial' status. Context will show when 'category' is being used not in this way but rather with the philosophical load which Kant puts upon it.

When Kant calls his twelve concepts 'categories', part of what he means is that to use any concepts at all one must use the twelve on his list. Since to use a concept is to make a judgment of a certain kind, it follows—subject to a qualification to be discussed in §24—that 'There are twelve concepts which must be used if any are used' is equivalent to 'There are twelve kinds of judgments which must be made if any are made'. Kant exploits this equivalence by deriving his list of supposedly indispensable concepts from a list of supposedly indispensable kinds of judgment.

The latter is introduced as a list of 'formal' features of judgments:

If we abstract from all content of a judgment, and consider only the mere form of understanding, we find that the function of thought in judgment can be brought under four heads, each of which contains three moments [= elements]. They may be conveniently represented in the following table:

> (1) *Quantity*: Singular, Particular, Universal.
> (2) *Quality*: Affirmative, Negative, Infinite.
> (3) *Relation*: Categorical, Hypothetical, Disjunctive.
> (4) *Modality*: Problematic, Assertoric, Apodeictic.[1]

Some explanations are called for.

(1) The three quantity-features are those possessed by the judgments that *My dog is stupid*, that *Some dogs are stupid* and that *All dogs are stupid*. In Kant's list the order of the three features is reversed, but this is a slip. The associated trio of concepts is given as 'unity, plurality and totality', and one remark of Kant's depends upon their being taken in that order.[2] The trio of judgment-features should therefore be given, as above, in the corresponding order.

(2) An 'infinite' judgment is one which is negative in force but affirmative in form. The general idea is as follows. In the affirmative judgment that *Henry is mortal* a thing is assigned to the restricted class of mortal beings, whereas in the negative judgment that *Henry is not mortal* the thing is not assigned to any class but is merely excluded from one and so left, as it were, wandering in the infinite range of alternative possibilities. The judgment that *Henry is non-mortal* is affirmative in

form but, unlike genuinely affirmative judgments, it merely excludes something from a certain class; and this is why Kant calls it 'infinite'. The judgment in question, by the way, is one which might be true because Henry is a mountain and mountains cannot die; it should not be confused with the judgment that *Henry is immortal*, where 'immortal' means 'alive, but not going to die'.[1]

This really won't do. The case for denying that *Henry is non-mortal* is affirmative is a case for saying that it is negative. It is uncharacteristic of Kant to say that the two sentences 'Henry is non-mortal' and 'Henry is not mortal', which do the same work in almost the same way, nevertheless express different kinds of judgment just because they differ in a minor verbal detail. I fear that part of the reason for this mistake is that Kant wants four-times-three indispensable kinds of judgment and needs infinite judgments to make up the complement.

(3) A hypothetical judgment is one which can be expressed in a sentence of the form 'If...then...'; a disjunctive judgment Kant takes to be one expressible in the form 'Either...or... (but not both)'. A categorical judgment is one which is neither hypothetical nor disjunctive.

(4) Kant's explanation of the modality-features is obscure,[2] but what he ought to say is that a judgment is problematic if it says of something that it may be the case, assertoric if it says of something that it is the case, and apodeictic if it says of something that it must be the case. The problematic must be distinguished from the possible, and the apodeictic from the necessary. The concepts associated with the modal features are supposed to be pretty much our ordinary concepts of possibility and necessity: these are involved in all judgments about the possibility or necessity of other judgments, but not in all judgments which are themselves possible or necessary—any more than the concept of complexity is involved in all complex judgments. For example, the concept of possibility is involved in the problematic judgment that *It is possible that grass is blue* but not in the possible judgment that *Grass is blue*. Similarly, the concept of necessity is involved in the apodeictic judgment that *It is necessary that* $2+2 = 4$, but not in the necessary judgment that $2+2 = 4$. In fact, there is no one concept associated with all possible judgments, or with all necessary judgments, and my explanation of 'concept' in the preceding section shows why: possible judgments do not form a functional kind; there is no kind of task which it is their duty to perform, in the way in which problematic judgments do perform the task of asserting that something is possible.

Similarly, necessary judgments do not constitute a functional kind as apodeictic judgments do. My association of functional kinds with word-occurrence also fits into place here: problematic judgments could all be expressed in sentences which do the same sort of work as English sentences containing 'possible', but nothing analogous to this could be said of possible judgments.

Kant gives something like the above account of the modality-features, but confuses the situation by saying that the antecedent of a hypothetical judgment is always problematic because it is not positively asserted as true, and by making some equally odd remarks about the parts of syllogisms. I think we can see what leads him into this mistake. The judgment that *If Lee is in command then Richmond will not be taken*, like the judgment that *It is possible that Lee is in command*, makes use of but does not positively assert the judgment that *Lee is in command*. We might even say that each expresses a sort of hesitancy or reserve with respect to this judgment. It is this vague similarity which leads Kant to say that the judgment that *Lee is in command* occurs problematic-ally in both cases; but this is too vague to be taken seriously, and anyway it nullifies everything Kant says about the associated concept of possibility.

23 The Metaphysical Deduction of the Categories

In assessing Kant's attempt to infer the indispensability of his dozen judgment-features from their formality, it is natural to start by asking just what 'formal' means.

Some writers of logic text-books still adopt the bad old assumption that between the formal and the material features of a judgment there is a distinction which, although curiously resistant to definition or clear explanation, is nevertheless absolute and important. This tradition, to which Kant's use of 'formal' also belongs, has been cogently attacked, and I shall not rehearse the objections to it here.[1] One comment, how-ever, may be worth making. Going by the examples of formality which are usually given, it seems that the words in a sentence which are relevant to the 'form' of the judgment it expresses include:

'entails'	but not	'is evidence for'
'possible'	but not	'probable'
'it is necessary that'	but not	'it is known that'
'is identical with'	but not	'is similar to'
'all'	but not	'most'.

These examples powerfully suggest that the form/content distinction is not absolute but relative—specifically, that it is relative to the judgment-features which have been intensively studied in what are called 'formal' systems of logic. Perhaps, with the growth of the systematic logical study of confirmation, probability and the so-called epistemic modalities, the first three items on the right-hand list will come to be relevant to a judgment's form rather than to its content. Anyway, there seems to be no sense of 'formal' in which we are entitled to say that the items in the left-hand column just do, while those in the right-hand column just don't, pertain to formality. Yet Kant, like many others, clearly assumes that his formal/material distinction is timelessly valid for judgments expressed in any language at all.

The falsity of that assumption bodes ill for the success of the Metaphysical Deduction of the Categories, since this is supposed to involve formality and to yield a conclusion which is valid for all humans at all times. But the Metaphysical Deduction fails in another way as well. Waiving the doubt as to whether Kant can give to 'formal' a suitably absolute sense, we can get a general picture of how he thinks a premiss about formality might support a conclusion about indispensability; and this picture, sketchy as it is, will tell us enough about Kant's argument for us to realize that the argument is certainly invalid.

Kant says that his dozen judgment-features 'specify the understanding completely, and yield an exhaustive inventory of its powers'.[1] There are of course countless intellectual operations, like thinking about humans and distinguishing hawks from handsaws, which are not on Kant's list; but he claims only that his list gives a complete 'formal' account of what the understanding can do. Consider a machine which can be adapted to drill holes, trim hedges, polish floors and so on. An exhaustive inventory of the machine's powers would have to include millions of items like 'trimming a privet hedge into the shape of a gondola', 'sanding the floor of a stockbroker's office' and so on. But one kind of account of its powers may be given 'exhaustively' yet briefly, namely a technical account of the movements of which it is capable, and of the ways in which it can be prepared for the attachment of accessories. Thus: the driving-shaft can rotate at either 1800, 2400 or 3000 r.p.m.; at any speed it can rotate in either direction; whatever the speed and direction, there is an eccentric gear which may be engaged or disengaged; a pair of attachment flanges may have to one another an angle of either 90° or 45° or 0°. A description of the machine's activities which is couched in these terms, and which omits to say what is attached to the machine or what job it is being used for, might be called a 'formal' description. In some such fashion as this— though we must not press for details—Kant thinks of his list of judg- ment-features as embodying a technical account of all the basic kinds of operation of which the understanding is capable, and as in that sense specifying the 'form' of the understanding.

The machine analogy illustrates also the argument from formality to indispensability. If it has just three speeds, two directions etc., then the machine can work at all—whether sawing wood or whipping cream— only if it goes at one of those speeds, in one of those directions, etc. Similarly, the understanding can work at all only if it operates in some way mentioned on Kant's list: no-one can make judgments without making judgments of at least some of the listed kinds.

This analogy does in fact fail because of a point which Kant seems to overlook. Every use of the machine involves one speed, one direction etc.; but it is not true that every judgment has one feature from each trio. Every categorical judgment does itself have a quantity-feature, but of a hypothetical or disjunctive judgment we can say only that its constituent judgments have quantity-features: for example, the judgment that *If all men are married then some women are single* is not itself either universal or particular or singular, though its antecedent is universal and its consequent particular. A similar point applies to proble- matic and apodeictic judgments. Nothing of importance for Kant's programme hangs on this, however, and I shall therefore pretend that it is plausible to say of each judgment that *it* has one feature from each trio.

Without knowing precisely what Kant means by his claim to have inventoried the 'formal' powers of the understanding, we can show that his argument—just because it is an argument from an inventory— shows only that all judgment-making must involve judgments with *at least* one feature from each trio; and the restriction to this limited conclusion leads in turn to the collapse of the entire argument.

The restriction is forced upon Kant in the following way. The conclusion that if the machine is ever used it must be used at one of the three stated speeds rests upon the fact that every use of the machine involves one of those speeds. To show the indispensability of *each* speed, we should have to stop talking about the conditions which *every* use of the machine must satisfy, and find some justification for saying that if the machine is ever used it must *at different times* be used at each of its three possible speeds. Such a justification could obviously not be provided by a mere inventory of the machine's possible speeds.

Similarly, since it is absurd to say that every judgment has each feature from each trio, a claim that all twelve kinds of judgment are indispensable must take some such form as 'Any extended judgment-making performance must somewhere along its length involve judgments of each of the twelve kinds' or perhaps 'Any judgment-making creature must from time to time make judgments of each of the twelve kinds'. Again, nothing of this kind can be supported by an inventory of kinds of judgment, no matter what status is claimed for the inventory's contents.

A modest conclusion may be better than none: perhaps Kant has shown at least something about the indispensability of kinds of judgment. But has he? If he retains the argument from an inventory, his conclusion may become not just modest but trivial. It is trivial in respect of a given trio of judgment-features if one of them is so defined that for a judgment to have it is simply for it to lack the other two. For example, if 'assertoric' means merely 'neither problematic nor apodeictic', then it follows that 'To judge at all one must make assertoric or problematic or apodeictic judgments' is as boring an assertion as 'To judge at all one must make judgments which are about walnut-trees or about bob-sleighs or about neither'.

If the Metaphysical Deduction is not thus to slither into triviality, the judgment-features must be so defined that it is not true by definition that every judgment has some feature from each trio. For example, an assertoric judgment must be defined as one which is neither problematic nor apodeictic but...something else instead. Kant presents his list so casually that one cannot tell whether he thinks he can construe each trio in this way; but this uncertainty does not matter, for if the trios are so construed a further difficulty arises.

Consider what is involved in saying that every judgment must have a feature from each trio, while denying that this is true by definition. The machine analogue of this is all right: that the machine should run at an unlisted speed is ruled out not by definitions but on technical grounds—it is impossible because of the way the machine is built. Kant sometimes thinks of his indispensability claim, similarly, as following from a structural description of the understanding; and thus takes 'Every judgment must have some feature from each trio' not as an application of the law of excluded middle but as a consequence of some *facts* about what the understanding—the judging faculty—is like. This approach is suggested by the phrase 'exhaustive inventory': one expects an inventory to be descriptive of that of which it is an inventory.

But what sorts of facts are facts about what the understanding is like? If they are a posteriori—like the analogous facts about the machine—then the official programme of the *Critique* collapses in ruins, and Kant knows this perfectly well. If, on the other hand, what Kant is saying about the understanding is offered as synthetic and a priori, then he is surrounded by the swarm of difficulties which beset the outer-sense theory when this was construed as an account of the mode of operation of a noumenal outer sense. Kant notes this parallel when he speaks of something as being 'as little capable of further explanation as why we have just these and no other functions of judgment, or why space and time are the only forms of our possible intuition'.[1] That he can take this so calmly does not mean that we should do likewise.

There remains the possibility that what Kant says about the understanding might be analytic but not true by definition. I think that along these lines something might be saved, analogous to the partial salvage of the outer-sense theory. Such a salvage would involve finding analytic but untrivial truths of the form 'Any extended judgment-making performance must include the making of judgments of such and such kinds' or 'Any concept-using creature must possess such and such concepts'; and it would not reify or 'noumenalize' the understanding.

Nor would it rest on the table of judgments. I shall try to show, of certain specific kinds of judgment, that they are indispensable in a certain way; but I shall not try to rescue from triviality the weak thesis that every judgment must have one feature from each trio. This thesis is a bore, whatever its status; and in any case I do not see how it can be analytic except by being true by definition. The classificatory words in the table seem to offer no prospect of complex analysis such as might be possible in respect of 'concept-employing performance' or 'use of the understanding' or the like.

It may have been unfair to take the 'inventory' metaphor literally, to press the machine analogy so hard, and to take at face value Kant's claim that his results are synthetic and a priori. But the real troubles of the Metaphysical Deduction lie deeper than that: they arise from one skeletal fact about Kant's argument, namely that he tries to derive claims about indispensability from the table of judgments. If this tedious section has lifted from our shoulders the dead weight of the argument from the table of judgments, it has been worth the labour. We shall still have to attend to Kant's list of judgment-features—but not as a list which, like the *Social Register*, purports by its mere existence to prove something about the status of its contents.

7

THE CATEGORIES CONSIDERED

24 Concepts and language

In essaying an analytic salvage of something from the Metaphysical Deduction, our first bother is that we do not know what to analyse. I have adopted Kant's equation of 'x has concepts' with 'x can make judgments', and his assumption that if x makes a judgment then x could express it in a language. These are both wrong. To 'make a judgment' in Kant's sense is to think or believe that something is the case, and in this sense judgments are often made by creatures which have no language. We say, not as a joke or a metaphor, that the scampering dog thinks that its master is holding a bone; and Kant gives no reason for eschewing this kind of talk.

On the other hand, there is little work for 'concept' to do outside the realm of language. To credit a rat with a concept of triangularity because it reacts selectively to triangles is to take a word which serves well as an imprecise technical tool in certain linguistic contexts, and to press it into a different service whose connection with its normal work is at best obscure. The formula 'A concept is a recognitional capacity',[1] though wide enough to cover the uses of 'concept' both in animal psychology and in philosophy, omits most of what is important in the philosophers' use of the word. Until we have a clearer view of how linguistic behaviour relates to selective responses to kinds of stimulus, we ought to restrict the word 'concept' to the tasks which we know it will perform. This is not a claim about what rats cannot do, but merely a counsel of caution about the use of the word 'concept'.

I therefore agree with Kant that creatures which lack a language lack concepts, though not for what seems to be his reason, namely that creatures which lack a language cannot make judgments. I wish to go further in this direction, and say that a creature cannot have concepts unless its language is of a certain special sort. If someone's linguistic behaviour consisted solely in applying words to presented bits of the world, so that he never made general statements and thus never gave reasons for what he said, what questions could we usefully raise about his *concepts*? We can find employment for the phrase 'concept of humanity' only because people can say, as well as things like 'This is not human' and 'That is a man', also things like 'Humans sometimes laugh' and 'There is a world of difference between humans and apes' and 'A human could not be made in a laboratory by a human'. A language containing nothing of these kinds would be merely a pattern of linguistic responses to sensory stimuli, and would no more put 'concept' to work than do the selective, non-linguistic responses of rats. I shall use the phrase 'concept-exercising language' as an abbreviation for 'language of the highly developed kind in connection with which "concept" can be given real work to do, i.e. whose meta-language can usefully contain the word "concept"'. To abbreviate is not, of course, to clarify.

I should remark in passing that I am deliberately giving short shrift to the view that concepts are independent entities whose association with words give the latter their meaning, and which are to be analysed by means of a kind of intuition. The picture of the philosophical analyst as using his dictionary to locate his subject-matter, and then his intuition to examine it, grotesquely misrepresents what happens when philosophers analyse concepts. The suggestion that it must be correct, because facts about word-meanings are contingent while philosophical results are necessary, is just naïve. Nor is this view of conceptual analysis supported by the fact, much stressed by Moore,[1] that we sometimes want to say something but cannot find the words for it. In such a case, it is said, we are in the presence of a concept-complex called a 'proposition', whose non-linguistic nature is shown by the fact that we have no words attached to it. What has not been shown is what this finger-snapping kind of situation has to do with serious philosophical investigations.

The Moorean methodology, in which all questions about the meanings of words are regarded as mere 'lexicographical' preliminaries to the serious business of applying intuitions to concepts, is in fact impossible. Once we have agreed on all the questions about word-uses we have agreed on all the questions there are about the analysis of concepts. If we try to isolate a disagreement about the nature of a given concept, one of two things happens. (a) The disagreement turns out to concern the uses of words, i.e. to concern—according to Moore's story—what concept is associated with a given expression rather than what the nature is of a given concept. (b) The disagreement turns out to be utterly vacuous. Thus, Moore starts with his official position:

I shall, therefore, use the word ['good'] in the sense in which I think it is ordinarily used; but at the same time I am not anxious to discuss whether I am right in thinking that it is so used. My business is solely with that object or idea, which I hold, rightly or wrongly, that the word is generally used to stand for. What I want to discover is the nature of that object or idea, and about this I am extremely anxious to arrive at an agreement.[1]

He then makes his central claim that the 'object or idea' in question is simple or, as he sometimes says, that it cannot be defined; and proceeds to draw from this a conclusion which he must call 'lexicographical':

If I am asked 'How is good to be defined?' my answer is that it cannot be defined, and that is all I have to say about it...If I am right, then nobody can foist upon us such an axiom as that 'Pleasure is the only good' or that 'The good is the desired' on the pretence that this is 'the very meaning of the word'.[2]

Let us try to rescue Moore from the 'lexicography' which dogs him, by challenging his 'Good is simple' thesis in a way which does not generate any definitions of the word 'good'. We might do this by claiming that good is not simple but complex, because it has three constituent concepts *for which there are no standard names*. This, presumably, is a disagreement purely about the nature of a concept; our dictionaries, and our attention to how words are used, are put behind us, and it is now up to our intuitions to settle the issue. But of course there is no disagreement here: we are just word-spinning. The alternative to 'lexicography' is vacuity.

I return now to the main thread of my argument. It seems that we may seek analytic conclusions of any one of three kinds: (i) 'Any creature which makes judgments at all makes judgments of such and such a kind'; (ii) 'Any language has means for expressing judgments of such and such a kind'; (iii) 'Any concept-exercising language has means for expressing judgments of such and such a kind'. Kant conflates these three, but their distinctness must be enforced.

I doubt that anything interesting of kind (ii) can be proved. Attempts to prove that this or that sort of statement must be expressible in any language have always met with failure. Admittedly, the concept of language has so far been treated but glibly and superficially, but I conjecture that a mature and suitably complex analysis of this concept, so far from yielding valuable results of kind (ii), would merely reveal that none can be had. It seems to follow that there is nothing analytic to be said of kind (i) either.

Statements of kind (iii) present a different case. The question of whether a language is a concept-exercising one does depend upon what sorts of statements can be made in it: for example, it depends partly upon whether statements of a general or reason-giving kind can be made in it. But if we seek an impressive list of results of kind (iii), we are hampered by the vagueness of the phrase 'concept-exercising language' in terms of which kind (iii) is defined. Furthermore, even if we could give precision to this phrase, there is an inhibiting worry: why should we care about what a language has to be like for this word 'concept' to be useful in describing it? Why should this one word be allowed to define a whole analytic inquiry?

The two difficulties can be taken together: clarifying and justifying here go hand in hand.

The class of possible languages divides into those whose use does, and those whose use does not, consist solely in a pattern of responses to sensory stimuli. I discuss this distinction at length in my book *Rationality*, and here sketch it only in outline.[1] A language consisting solely of statements of the form 'This is...' and 'That is...' can be seen as a technique for the linguistic handling of items which are presented to the speaker: it has been called the speaker's way of 'hitting back' at the things which sensorily bombard him. But human languages have means for making at least two sorts of statement which are not like this: general statements, and statements about the past. These do not have to be responses to, or operations upon, the environments in which they are made.

Furthermore, they express judgments which cannot be expressed except in a language. There is a natural, though weak, sense of 'express' in which it is true that many kinds of judgment can be expressed by non-linguistic behaviour; but general and past-tense judgments are not among them. It might be thought that a dog which retrieves a bone thereby expresses the judgment (i.e. shows that it thinks) that the bone was buried there last week. But the dog's digging expresses this judgment about the past only if it also expresses the general judgment that buried bones stay put. Without a language, there is no way of expressing judgments about the past without thereby expressing general judgments, or of expressing general judgments without thereby expressing judgments about the past. Are we to say, then, that the dog makes two distinct judgments which it unhappily cannot express in isolation from one another? Would it not make better sense to say that the dog makes and expresses the single judgment that *The bone is there*, and add that its past experience has caused it to make this judgment? On the other hand, if the dog had a language in which to say that the bone was buried there last week, then we should certainly agree that it was making and expressing a judgment about the past and that this was its *reason* for making a certain judgment about the present.

These uses of language which are not mere linguistic responses to stimuli, and which express judgments that cannot be expressed except in languages, overlap or coincide with the uses which are most relevant to whether a given language counts as a concept-exercising one. I think that Kant's primary interest is in judgments about general and past states of affairs, and that this is why he considers only judgments expressible in a language, and restricts himself further to languages of the developed kind which I call 'concept-exercising'.

Kant apparently believes that unless a creature can make judgments about past and general states of affairs, it cannot really make judgments at all. He would probably say that the dog does not think that the bone is there unless it has *reasons* for thinking this, and thus makes judgments about past and general states of affairs. I find this illiberal; but I do agree with Kant that a great deal turns on the difference between those who can make past and general judgments and those who cannot. I have argued in *Rationality* that this difference, more than any other, justifies the common conviction that there is an important difference of kind between human and non-human intellectual capacities; and in §§ 30–31 we shall see that it connects with the notion of self-consciousness in such a way as entirely to justify Kant's exclusive attention to the kind of intellectual capacity which includes an ability to make judgments about the past and general judgments.

I shall take it that a concept-exercising language is pretty much the same as a language in which past-tense and general statements can be made: it does not matter whether this equivalence is exact or not. Throughout the *Critique* when Kant speaks of 'judgments', of 'concepts' and of 'understanding', he is unquestionably referring to the area of intellectual competence which is roughly marked off by the phrase 'concept-exercising language'. This is what justifies a scrutiny of the notion of a concept-exercising language in a work of Kantian exegesis.

25 Some indispensable concepts

What reasons are there for saying that Kant's twelve categories must be used in any concept-exercising language? A perfunctory answer will have to do, as an exhaustive one would take half a book. It is not essential for the assessment of the *Critique* as a whole that we should decide just what concepts are indispensable or categorial, for Kant's favoured dozen serve throughout the rest of the *Critique* only as a Procrustean bed on which he hacks and wrenches his philosophical insights into a grotesque 'system'. At the ground-floor level, where he drops the running commentary and gets to work, the precise contents of the list of categories are singularly unimportant. The argument of § 26 will tend to support this twofold thesis that the list's systematic or 'architectonic' use is negligible, and that it has no other uses in the *Critique*.

Quality. The 'concept of limitation', which corresponds to the spurious class of 'infinite' judgments, is a non-starter; but it is likely that the other two categories of quality, *viz.* reality and negation, would have to occur in any concept-employing language. It seems obvious that any language must contain affirmative statements and must therefore employ Kant's 'concept of reality' if it employs concepts at all. It is arguable that any concept-exercising language must also contain negative statements: perhaps not precise analogues of the form 'It is not the case that...', but statements which reject or rule out other statements. I have argued for this in *Rationality* on the grounds—roughly—that a concept-exercising language must contain something like 'because' which in its turn requires something like 'That doesn't follow'.[1] At a non-technical level it is perhaps worth noting that any pattern of behaviour looks blind and mechanical unless it contains something of a mistake-recognizing and mistake-correcting kind. This is one reason why Spinoza's god, which neither commits nor encounters error, often strikes readers of Spinoza as merely mindless.

Quantity. A concept-exercising language is one in which reasons can be given and general statements made; and thus it must employ the concept of totality. This, together with negation, yields the concept of plurality: Kant errs in saying that no item in his dozen can be defined out of the others.

The concept of unity, which is the ability to cope with singular judgments, raises a live problem. In his *Methods of Logic*, Quine says that all the work done by statements of the form 'The F is G' could be done by the form 'It is not the case that there are no Fs, it is not the case that there are at least two Fs, and there are no Fs which are not G', and that we could therefore dispense with the former in favour of the latter. Since the latter contains no individual referring expressions such as names or definite descriptions, it seems to follow that a concept-exercising language could lack all such expressions and thus could lack the concept of unity.[2]

In his article 'Singular Terms',[1] Strawson argues that although individual referring expressions can be paraphrased out of a language which is a going concern, no language could lack such expressions *ab initio*. He argues from 'the empiricist premise...that for any universal terms to be understood, some universal terms must be learnt ostensively, by "direct confrontation"'.[2] This implies that to understand a language one must learn some meanings ostensively, and this, Strawson claims, requires that one understand such statements as that this is hot, and that is hot, and this other is not hot. Thus individual referring expressions are essential to the procedures which launch one's understanding of a language; and so, although such expressions are eliminable, they are not dispensable.

Ostensive samples can be indicated digitally as well as verbally, but this does not rebut Strawson's argument, for pointing *is* a linguistic activity.[3] It is a rule-governed procedure for calling attention to particulars, and is intimately connected with the rest of our language: its non-verbal nature is as nothing compared with the features of it which entitle it to be deemed linguistic.

Against Strawson's view, however, I suggest that one can present a child with ostensive samples without referring to them at all, if 'referring' to a thing is directing someone's attention to it in a rule-governed way. One may utter a word when the child just happens to be attending to the object to which the word applies; or one may *cause* the child to attend to the object by waving it in front of the child's face. These means are not merely permissible, they are practically unavoidable. As a matter of fact, when one tries to point something out to a very young child, the child looks at one's hand. It learns the significance of pointing, as of words like 'this', after and through its grasp of other words. One points to the door and says 'door', and the child starts to understand pointing if it already understands 'door'— and this requires its having had its attention called to doors by means which could not possibly be accounted linguistic.

Ostension, then, does not require reference. It may be that ostensive *teaching* requires reference, and that if one says 'door' while the child happens to be attending to a door one is not teaching the child but only conditioning it. I think there is virtue in so using 'teach' and 'learn' that ostensive teaching or learning does require reference, but this concedes nothing to Strawson's view. On the contrary, it is a reason for rejecting his 'empiricist premise' that for any general words to be understood some of them must have been *learned* ostensively. If 'learn' means more than 'acquire', then the premiss seems false; if it means the same as 'acquire', then the premiss does not yield the required conclusion.

Strawson seems to take as a reformulation of his 'empiricist premise' something which could be significantly different from it:

Some universal terms must be connected with our experience if any are to be understood. And these universal terms must be connected with particular bits or slices of our experience.[1]

If 'connected with' here means 'derived from', we are back where we started; but if it means 'answerable to', then this new premiss may support something like Strawson's conclusion. For now it points to issues about *use* rather than about *acquisition*. it leads us out of the nursery into the world of fully-fledged, concept-exercising linguistic behaviour, and here we have perhaps some hope of arguments for the indispensability of individual referring expressions. The only arguments I can find for such a conclusion, however, are complex and inconclusive.

In any case, there is something odd about this debate. Suppose it were shown to be necessary that a concept-exercising language should have ways of referring to individuals and saying something about them, why should we not say that the Quinean form 'It is not the case that there are no Fs...etc.' *is* such a way? Its parts have other uses as well, but that does not imply that when they are put together like this they do not 'really' express a singular judgment. We might indeed deny that the concept of unity was at work in a language in which the Quinean paraphrase was developed as an optional afterthought to the quantificational uses of its constituent parts, and in which there were no other means for referring to individuals. But it is not clear to me that Quine wants to say that there could be such a language. If he does, then I am inclined to agree with Strawson's *conclusion* that he is mistaken.

Modality. A concept-exercising language need not employ the concepts of necessity and possibility. It is sometimes thought that to know what an expression means involves knowing which sentences containing it are analytic and which self-contradictory. If this were correct, then one could understand a language only if one had the concepts of analyticity and contradictoriness and thus, perhaps, the concepts of necessity and possibility. But it is not correct. If it were true—as I have argued in §21 that it is not—that synthetic sentences are directly relevant to truth but not to meanings, then it might follow that the users of any language must have the concept of necessity if they are to be able to distinguish misinformation from misunderstanding. But I can think of no other grounds for saying that modal concepts must have a place in any concept-exercising language.

Since we can thus dismiss the modal concepts, we can snub the so-called 'concept of existence', which is the capacity to handle assertoric or non-modal judgments. Just because the modal concepts are so thoroughly dispensable, it is boring to be told that a language must contain sentences which do not involve them, in the same way as it would be boring to be told that a language must contain statements which do not involve the concept of a walnut-tree.

I have offered desultory arguments for the indispensability to any concept-exercising language of four of Kant's dozen, I have hedged about the concept of unity, and I have dismissed limitation as incoherent, necessity and possibility as dispensable, and existence as boringly indispensable. There remain the three relational categories, which need a section to themselves.

26 The relational categories

These are supposed to correspond to the judgment-features *categorical*, *hypothetical* and *disjunctive*, and Kant's names for them are 'inherence and subsistence', 'causality and dependence' and 'community'. Subject to a qualification which I shall mention in §37, he takes these to be the concepts of *substance*, *cause* and *mutual interaction* respectively, whence it follows that they do not relate to their associated judgment-features as officially they should, Whether we take 'substance' in Kant's very strong sense of 'sempiternal thing' or as 'fairly durable thing' or in some yet weaker sense, it is just not true that the only task of categorical judgments is to attribute properties to substances. Again, causal judgments are only a sub-class of hypotheticals, and the concept of cause is therefore not just the ability to handle hypotheticals. For one thing, causal judgments are as closely allied to universal as to hypothetical judgments, yet Kant does not equate the concept of cause with that of totality. I say nothing of disjunctiveness in relation to community; for the concept of community is simply constructible out of that of causality, and therefore does not need separate treatment.

Kant thinks it rather obvious that any concept-exercising language must use the other nine categories; and this is natural in one who complacently assumes that there is something ineluctably right about the structure of the Indo-European languages, and does not consider what sort of rightness it would be relevant—let alone true—to attribute to them. But no such assumption could generate the belief that any concept-exercising language must use the concepts of substance, cause and community. Even if the table of judgments were relevant—as it is not—to the categorial status of some of Kant's dozen, these three would still be left out in the cold because they do not relate as they are supposed to with their associated judgment-features.

It is therefore not surprising that later in the *Critique* Kant argues for the indispensability of the concepts of substance, cause and community with a seriousness which he at no time devotes to the other concepts on his list. He does this in a chapter called 'System of all Principles of Pure Understanding', whose relationship with the Metaphysical Deduction has confronted commentators with a puzzle for which I now offer a solution.

The 'Principles' chapter is often seen as an attempt to prove that each of the categories is a priori applicable to experience; yet Kant is committed to thinking that he has proved this before he gets as far as the 'Principles' chapter. The Transcendental Deduction will argue that we cannot have experience which is not brought under some concepts; and the Metaphysical Deduction argues that to use any concepts is to use Kant's dozen in particular; whence it should follow that there cannot be experience in connection with which Kant's dozen cannot be used. On Kant's own showing, then, what is there left for the 'Principles' chapter to prove?

A popular answer is that the Metaphysical Deduction is not meant to show that all the categories are indispensable, but only that no other concepts are indispensable. Kant's boast that the table of judgments guarantees that he has not overlooked any a priori concepts[1] suggests that the burden of the Metaphysical Deduction is just 'Any a priori concepts there may be are on the list'. This is compatible with 'Some concepts on the list are not a priori', and so leaves work for the 'Principles' chapter to do. I shall call this the 'short-list interpretation': it says that Kant intends the Metaphysical Deduction only to draw up a short list of all the possible candidates for apriority, leaving the 'Principles' chapter to decide which of the twelve candidacies is successful.

The short-list interpretation is wrong. Kant says that his list *is*—not that it *contains*—an enumeration of all the a priori concepts. The very passage in which the list's completeness is stressed bears this out, as does an earlier one in which, after giving an obscure preview of the Transcendental Deduction, Kant says that from this together with the table of judgments

there arise precisely the same number of pure concepts of the understanding which apply a priori to objects of intuition in general, as, in the preceding table, there have been found to be logical functions in all possible judgments. For these functions specify the understanding completely, and yield an exhaustive inventory of its powers. These concepts we shall, with Aristotle, call *categories*...[1]

This plainly says that all the listed concepts are indispensable, not just that any indispensable concepts there may be are on the list.

In any case, the short-list interpretation is absurd in itself. We can understand, if we do not accept, Kant's belief that the indispensability of the listed concepts follows from their vague privilege as basic and formal; but how could he think that the status of the concepts which are on the list could imply the dispensability of concepts which are *not* on it? Only by equating 'indispensable concepts' with 'concepts which define the formal powers of the understanding'; but this implies the dispensability of all unlisted concepts only by claiming the indispensability of all the listed ones, and the whole point of the short-list interpretation is to deny that Kant makes the latter claim in the Metaphysical Deduction. Since Kant's words and its own inherent inadequacy are against the short-list account, we still have a problem about what Kant is up to in the 'Principles' chapter.

The fact is that in that chapter Kant does not try to prove the apriority of each of his twelve concepts. His declared intention is to state and prove all the synthetic and a priori truths which stem from the categorial status of the twelve.[2] It would be natural to expect that Kant would at least offer a principle for each category saying that it must apply to all experience; but for nine of them he offers nothing of the sort. He evades the categories of quantity by palming off on us an entirely different concept which the label 'quantity' also fits; he ignores the concept of limitation, and discusses the concepts of reality and negation without even trying to show their a priori applicability to all experience; and for the modal categories he produces no 'principles' at all, but only 'explanations of the [modal categories] in their empirical employment',[3] giving a specious reason why this is all he can do. For the relational categories alone does Kant seriously undertake a proof of apriority. This, incidentally, is a further objection to the short-list story. The latter purports to show why there should be twelve separate indispensability-arguments in the 'Principles' chapter; now it turns out that there are only three.

Since the 'principles' associated with the relational categories are just the statements that the latter *are* categories, i.e. are applicable a priori to all experience, it is suspicious that Kant does not offer to prove analogous principles for the other nine. On the other hand, since the categorial status of all twelve concepts is supposed to be established in the Deductions, why does Kant later repeat the job for even three of them? To sort all this out must be to convict Kant of error, but we can now see that he has made one understandable mistake, not two bewildering ones. The point is that the three categories whose apriority is determinedly argued for in the 'Principles' chapter are the three which most need such argument: their indispensability has not the faintest appearance of following from the table of judgments, because they simply do not correspond to the table of judgments as Kant says they do. I do not congratulate Kant for thinking that the Metaphysical Deduction does a job which it utterly fails to do; but, given that mistake, it was reasonable for him to try to complete the job when an opportunity presented itself later in the *Critique*.

If it were just a coincidence that the 'Principles' chapter argues for the categorial status of all and only those concepts which do not relate properly to the table of judgments, it would be a remarkable coincidence indeed. It is more reasonable to say that Kant was at some level aware of what his total failures were in the Metaphysical Deduction: he was too good a philosopher not to be. But he was so much a victim of his own passion for system that he ignored the breakdown in the parallel between the table of categories and the table of judgments, and pushed doggedly on, claiming complete success for the Metaphysical Deduction and dealing evasively with the question of what is supposed to be happening in the 'Principles' chapter. Another aspect of this matter will be discussed at the end of §31.

27 The acquisition of concepts

I have spoken of discoveries which might be made about what a creature must be able to do in order to count as having concepts, or about what a pattern of behaviour must be like to count as the use of a concept-exercising language; but I have said nothing about how concepts must be acquired. My concern has been with the analysis of 'concepts', not with the genesis of concepts. This reflects Kant's own insistence that his concern is with the use of concepts and not with their '*de facto* mode of origination'.[1] He sometimes speaks of the a priori 'origin' or 'source' of the categories,[2] but these passages use 'origin' etc. oddly: they express no interest whatsoever in traditional questions about how concepts are acquired.

Philosophers have frequently discussed questions about concept-acquisition which they were not equipped to answer. Early in both *Treatise* and *Enquiry*, Hume says that to have a concept one must first be confronted with instances of it or of simpler concepts out of which it can be constructed. He presents this as an empirical hypothesis which could be killed by a counter-instance:

> Those who would assert that this position is not universally true...have only one...method of refuting it; by producing that idea which, in their opinion, is not derived from this source. It will then be incumbent on us, if we would maintain our doctrine, to produce the impression, or lively perception, which corresponds to it.[3]

Later, however, Hume uses this doctrine in an a priori way, saying that those who think they have a concept of necessary connection 'must' be wrong about this because there can be no confrontation with an instance of causal necessity.

Clearly something has gone wrong. When the detail is filled in, it can be seen that many things are very wrong:[4] this doctrine of Hume's is, of all the really fruitful contributions ever made to philosophy, the most riddled with error. The one correct feature of Hume's handling of his doctrine is the one which he drops almost immediately, namely his treatment of it as empirically falsifiable. Just because it says that *before* having a concept one must have certain experiences, the doctrine is vulnerable to the possibility that someone should have the concept without having fulfilled the doctrinal prerequisites. Hume himself taught us that there are no irrefutable statements connecting what is the case at a given time with what was the case earlier. (I do not conclude that Hume should have allowed himself to be refuted by John Doe's claim to have a concept of necessary connection. Hume's word for 'concept' is 'idea', and for him ideas are faded sensory states; and he therefore cannot say what it would be to 'produce' a counter-example to his doctrine. What he needs here is the Kantian theory of concepts as intellectual skills the proof of whose possession lies in their exercise.)

This is why prerequisites for the possession of concepts, where 'pre' has a temporal force, are not the philosopher's business. 'I don't know whether I can play the piano—I have never tried'—this is over-optimistic, but it is *logically* possible that someone should play the piano well at his first attempt. Or again, I do not believe that a man born blind could apply colour words surely and correctly from the first moment of gaining his sight; but this belief, strong as it is, gets no support from any philosophical considerations.

Within the genus concept-acquisition there is the species concept-learning, and with this philosophers may have a legitimate concern. Learning how to do something is not the only way of coming to be able to do it: Wittgenstein points out that if someone underwent a brain operation which made him able to speak Latin perfectly, we should not say that he had learned Latin on the operating table. Perhaps, then, we can establish some necessary truths about what a person must undergo before he can count as having learned a concept. Nothing is logically prerequisite to a concept's having been acquired except its being not possessed and then later possessed; but there are logical pre-requisites to a concept's having been learned, namely those which mark off learning from other sorts of acquisition.

Learning, I suggest, involves the active, rational co-operation of the learner. The acquiring of an ability may simply happen to one, but learning is something which one does, and the doing of it involves something in the nature of thinking, judging, employing concepts. The uses of 'learn' by animal psychologists are against me here, but I do not defer to them as they are utterly at variance with one another.[1] In any case, a simple stipulation is all I need: I want to talk about 'the acquiring of abilities by means which involve the use of concepts by the acquirer', and I abbreviate this to 'learning'. I think, though, that this stipulative definition squares pretty well with ordinary uses of 'learning', at least in the human context, which is all I am concerned with in the present section.

Hume and Locke provide an illustration. In Hume's account,[2] the acquirer of a concept or 'idea' is entirely passive: he has one or more visual fields, say, which leave behind a faded afterglow which is his idea of redness. This has no more required his active co-operation than does the raising of a blister on his heel by an ill-fitting shoe: note how Hume speaks of 'acquiring a custom' of using words correctly, and of customs as being 'revived' by experience. No such impression of passivity is given by Locke's telling of a comparable story.[3] Locke represents the acquiring of an idea, a process which he calls 'abstraction',

97

as an activity of the acquirer. What the latter does, roughly, is to *notice* that a number of sensory states are alike in a certain respect and to *decide* to classify further sensory states according to whether they resemble the original ones in that respect. Locke's account, like Hume's, construes ideas as quasi-sensory states, and there are other faults in it too; but it does have the merit of recognizing that a person may actively participate in his own intellectual development.

In my sense of 'learn', someone who has learned to do something must earlier have had some concepts; whence it follows that not all concepts can be learned. Furthermore, if there are any concepts whose use is required in all learning—negation and totality look eligible—they in particular cannot be learned. Abstractionist accounts of such concepts as negation and totality always have a surrealist air about them,[1] not because plausible examples of allness and notness are hard to find, but rather because someone who lacks those two concepts cannot do what the abstractionist account requires him to do—namely to notice that *all* those things share a feature which is *not* possessed by this other thing.

Are concepts like those of totality and negation therefore innate? If 'innate' meant 'possessed but not learned', the answer would be affirmative; but since it means 'possessed but not acquired', there is no reason to say that those concepts are innate. Some philosophers have overlooked the possibility of acquisition other than by learning, and have thereby tilled the ground in which the dispute over innate concepts flourishes. Locke seems to have argued that because no concepts are innate therefore all are learned;[2] while Leibniz apparently saw that not all concepts can be learned, and inferred from this that some must therefore be innate—in the sense that they are possessed at birth in a dormant form, and are somehow awakened or vitalized by experience.[3] Since Leibniz's words are inexplicit and metaphorical, any interpretation must be tentative; but I think that his point was that the procedures for concept-acquisition which Locke described can succeed only with someone who already has some concepts. This reading is reinforced by Leibniz's rejoinder to the slogan 'There is nothing in the mind which was not first in the senses'. To this he replied '...except the mind itself',[4] which may perhaps be taken to mean '...except such concepts as are prerequisite for learning anything'.

As soon as we see that an unlearned concept may nevertheless have been acquired and therefore need not be innate, we lose all temptation to posit congenital concepts, 'dormant' or not. We can thus avoid both Locke's misguided search for a way of learning the concept of totality, and Leibniz's hazardous doctrine that a baby is born with abilities which it is not yet able to exercise. A baby which has no concepts comes to have them; and its gaining of these abilities, as of the ability to control its hands, can in principle be explained causally, neuro-physiologically. This is not an evasion; for, philosophical theory apart, the only sort of explanation we should expect to find for someone's general level of intellectual capacity is a causal one, and the fact that someone has the concepts of negation and totality—unlike his possession of the concepts of neurosis and democracy—is a fact about his general intellectual level.

8

TRANSCENDENTAL DEDUCTION: THE MAIN THREAD

28 The unity of consciousness

We now turn to the jungle of the Transcendental Deduction of the Categories. Kant's justified discontent with this desperately ill-written chapter led him to rewrite it for the second edition; but the later version, though it helpfully shifts some emphases, is only marginally clearer than the earlier. Attempts have been made to canonize the whole text of the Transcendental Deduction, but the results have been derisible. Far more usefully, Vaihinger and Kemp Smith have explained the unclarity of the first version of the Deduction by the conjecture that it is a collage made up of jottings written down over the years. However this fares as a biographical hypothesis, it is at least backed by some fairly sound critical exegesis. And yet, even if the Transcendental Deduction is reshuffled in accordance with this 'patchwork theory',[1] the result, though it shows something like a linear development from primitive to sophisticated attacks on the same problems, is still dreadfully confused. The Deduction is not a patchwork but a botch. Since it contains some good things, however, it is not a negligible botch.

My aim in §§28–31 will be to lay bare certain arguments which are central to the Transcendental Deduction and from which something can be learned. While relating my remarks as closely as possible to the Kantian text, I shall leave many exegetical problems unsolved and all the exegetical debates unadjudicated.

The Transcendental Deduction can usefully be seen against the background of a possible empiricist philosopher who takes over Hume's basic epistemological doctrines and develops them into the account of objectivity-concepts which Hume himself failed to develop only because he could not see that there is clear water between the Scylla of Berkeley and the Charybdis of Locke.[2] This empiricist argues that the world might at any moment become such that the objects in it cease to obey causal laws, or even such that it will cease to contain durable objects at all. His conclusion that objectivity and causality are at any moment liable to collapse is derived from a pair of premisses. (1) There is no logical connection between the content of experience at one time and its content at another time. (2) The possibility that the world should cease to contain objects, or cease to obey causal laws, *is* the possibility that certain statements of the form 'If a sensory event of kind F occurs at t_1, then a sensory event of kind G will occur at t_2' should cease to hold true: the orderliness of our experience is not a reflection of an underlying, 'real' causality or objectivity behind the veil of perception.

Kant accepts (1); and it is nearer true than false to say that he accepts (2) also, though not quite for the reason that most empiricists would have given before his time. In so far as Hume accepted something like (2), this was because he thought that all our concepts— including those of causality and objectivity—must be *derived from* our experience; whereas Kant says only that they must be *connected to* experience, because 'they would mean nothing, were we not always able to present their meaning in appearances'.[1]

Although he accepts the empiricist's premisses, Kant dissents from the conclusion that the objectivity and causal order of the world are in constant jeopardy. His dissent rests partly on his thesis, which he proves in the 'Principles' chapter, that if we are to use any concepts we must use the concepts of object and cause. Not just *have* these concepts, but *use* or *apply* them—which can be done only if we have something objective and causally ordered to which we can apply them. If this thesis is correct, then our empiricist must concede that he has erred in representing chaotic experience as inconvenient rather than as entirely resistant to intellectual control. But he may add that this shows only that total chaos would be nastier than he had realized, not that it would be impossible. 'I grant that if causal order failed we could apply no concepts to, have no rational grasp of, our experience; but now see how much comfort you have lost and how horridly intractable your experience may, for all you know to the contrary, at any moment become.'

Kant wishes to show that this nightmare is impossible. He resists the whole sceptical trend of Hume's writings on causality, and flatly denies that our confidence in an orderly future is an act of faith or a habit of expectation engendered in us by our orderly past. He must therefore wring from our empiricist—and from Hume—a larger concession than can be forced from him just by the thesis that concepts can be applied only in a causally ordered objective realm. The Transcendental

Deduction aims to extract this larger concession by showing, roughly speaking, that there cannot be experience which is not brought under concepts at all.

There is a fashionable fable which presents sceptics and their opponents as, respectively, sapping and shoring up the confidence of the plain man in the stability and normality of his world. This has strikingly little to do with what actually happens in the pages of the great philosophers, and I would not be thought to encourage it. I have sketched the place of the Transcendental Deduction in the larger strategy of the *Critique* by treating it as part of a programme for showing that a certain alleged possibility is not in fact possible. The point of the programme, however, is not to exorcise a Humean spectre, to remove a fear about what *might* be the case; but rather to illuminate what *is* the case. If it were proved that there could not be experience which was not brought under intellectual control, this would no doubt be soothing to someone who had been neurotically worrying about the possible onset of uncontrollable experience, if such a person could be found; but it would be illuminating to anyone who cared about the relationship between the experience which we do have and the intellectual control which we do have over it—and there are many people like this.

Another way of bringing out the relationship between the Transcendental Deduction and some of Kant's predecessors, including Hume, would be this. In Hume's philosophy, the sensory and intellectual aspects of the human condition differ only in degree; and just for this reason Hume must allow that a man might have sensory states which he did not bring under any kind of intellectual control. Such a man would merely be one whose 'perceptions' were all of that degree of vividness which defines the sensory, none of them being dim enough to count as the 'ideas' which in Hume's philosophy do duty for concepts. Kant, on the other hand, distinguishes sharply between the sensory and the intellectual: he sees that facts about a man's sensory intake are *toto coelo* different from facts about what concepts a man has. This, paradoxically, makes it possible for him to argue that sensory intake and intellectual control are necessarily intertwined in a way which Hume never suspected. Kant himself sees the situation in this light:

Thoughts without content are empty, intuitions without concepts are blind... These two powers or capacities cannot exchange their functions. The understanding can intuit nothing, the senses can think nothing. Only through their union can knowledge arise. But that is no reason for confounding the contribution of either with that of the other; rather is it a strong reason for carefully separating and distinguishing the one from the other.[1]

I turn now to the central argument in the Transcendental Deduction.[2] This is scattered throughout the Deduction in A; in B it is drawn together into eleven consecutive pages.

The argument has to do with ownership of mental states. Kant says that mental states, or 'representations', can exist only as episodes in the histories of minds. He expresses this by saying that representations must be subject to the 'unity of apperception' or 'unity of conscious-ness':

The...unity of consciousness is...a condition under which every intuition must stand in order *to become an object for me*. For otherwise...the manifold would *not* be united in one consciousness.[3]

The passage goes on to say that this is analytic, because it says only that

all *my* representations...must be subject to that condition under which alone I can ascribe them to the identical self as *my* representations.

This suggests that Kant's view about the unity of consciousness is just a consequence of the statement that what is mine is mine. In fact, however, he wants to say not merely that all my representations are mine but also that every representation is someone's. If this is analytic, its being so depends upon the meaning of 'representation' or some allied term, not upon the meaning of 'mine'.

It *is* indeed analytic. The word 'representation' is here doing duty for certain more specific terms of which 'intuition' is the most important. Now, some philosophers have thought that when someone has an intuition—'apprehends a sense-datum'—there are two things involved, a man and a sense-datum, with a relation of apprehension between them; and so these philosophers have thought it sensible to wonder whether a sense-datum could exist without having that relationship to anyone. The trouble here is with the reifying premiss. Once we replace the muddled talk of the man as apprehending his sense-datum, or his pain, or his thought, by talk of the man as being in a sensory state, or suffering, or thinking, we can see that there is no question to be raised about whether there can be unapprehended sense-data. This is one reason for preferring the phrase 'sensory state': it brings out, as 'sense-datum' and 'intuition' and 'representation' do not, the logical similarity between talk about people's sense-data and talk about the properties of things. No-one would think it sensible to ask whether there could be instances of redness which did not consist in something's being red.

I do not know whether Kant would have given this reason for saying that it is analytic that all representations are someone's. One of the teasing things about the *Critique* is that, although his terminology suggests a propensity for reifying mental states, Kant stays clear of the troubles into which reifiers are usually led: he does not inquire into the niceties of the apprehension-relation between a man and his intuitions, nor discuss whether a visual sense-datum can be 'red' in the same sense as a physical surface can, nor speak of intuitions as visible or tangible or audible; and—to come back to the point—he does not think it logically possible that representations should exist except as states of minds.

There is a little more than this to Kant's thesis about the ownership of mental states. His use of the word 'unity' embodies his belief that for something to be a state of mind is for it to be unified in a certain way with other items of the same sort. This is not intended to rule out the possibility that there should be a mind which was qualitatively unvarious. Kant would in fact have rejected the extraordinary suggestion that there might be a mind of which nothing was true except its continual preoccupation with a single note of music,[1] but his reasons for that come later. In equating 'Every representation occurs in a mind' with 'Every representation is unified in a certain way with other representations', all Kant is assuming is that a mind must have a history, must last for a certain length of time. The 'unity' in which he is interested is, as we shall see, the unity which connects the earlier and the later states of a single mind.

Kant says that every representation must occur not just in some mind but specifically in the mind of a self-conscious or self-aware being. Sometimes he concedes that a representation might exist unaccompanied by self-consciousness, but insists that such a representation would 'be nothing' to its owner. Thus:

It must be possible for the 'I think' to accompany all my representations; for otherwise something would be represented in me which could not be thought at all, and that is equivalent to saying that the representation would be impossible, or at least would be nothing to me.[2]

(Despite the word 'think', Kant's concern here is with representations generally.) There is more to the same effect in a letter to Herz:

[If I had the mentality of a sub-human animal, I might have intuitions but] I should not be able to know that I have them, and they would therefore be for me, as a cognitive being, absolutely nothing. They might still...exist in me (a being unconscious of my own existence) as representations..., connected according to an empirical law of association, exercising influence upon feeling and desire, and so always disporting themselves with regularity, without my thereby acquiring the least cognition of anything, not even of these my own states.[1]

The passages just quoted suggest that Kant is armed with an account of awareness, another of self-awareness, and an argument which links the two. This would be formidable equipment indeed, but Kant does not have it; and that is hardly surprising, for there seem to be no good reasons for saying that a dog's visual field, say, is 'nothing to' the dog, or in general for saying that where there is consciousness there must be self-consciousness. Nevertheless, Kant's insistence upon self-conscious-ness is well grounded. He hopes to establish a priori truths of the form 'Whatever our experience turns out to be like, it must always have such and such features'; his aim is to show of some kinds of experience which are not obviously impossible that they are unobviously im-possible. His strategy, then, must be to start with the class of not obviously impossible kinds of experience, i.e. kinds which one can at least *prima facie* suppose oneself to have, and to thin it out. He can ignore from the outset any kind of experience which we cannot envisage ourselves as having because nothing could count as knowing that one's experience was of that kind. Now, the only states of awareness which I can regard as 'possibly mine', in the sense that I could have them and know that I had them, are ones which include an awareness of myself, an ability to have the thought that *This is how it is with me now*. There-fore, although consciousness does not imply self-consciousness, the latter must accompany any conscious states which are to fall within the ambit of Kant's inquiry, for that inquiry excludes states which one could not know oneself to be in and which therefore cannot intelligibly be made a subject for speculation.

I wish to circumscribe as clearly as possible the claim I am making. Certainly, I might suffer brain-damage and sink to a radically sub-human level at which I could no longer have a sense of myself as the owner of my mental states. Furthermore, I can talk about how in such a case I might behave, how my disability might affect others, and so on. What I cannot do is to consider what it would be like for me—on the inside, so to speak—if I were thus disabled. We do perhaps have the concept of 'what it is like for' people who suffer such a disability, of 'what it is like on the inside': this is suggested by our inclination to pity them, and our having a fear of being like them which is different from the fear of death. But we shall contradict ourselves if we try even to speculate about what it is like, for the creature concerned, to be in such a state. To do this we should have to tell what could be *his* story, and this would be to credit him with self-consciousness. We cannot say 'Perhaps something like this *would* be his story *if* he were capable of the thought "This is how it is with me now" and were therefore capable of having a story about himself.' For we cannot add self-consciousness while leaving the rest of the story intact, as though the disability consisted in X and Y and, as an isolable extra, a lack of self-consciousness. The basis for our denial that the lower animals are self-conscious *is* the basis for our assessment of their intellectual capacities: the same broad features of their behaviour are relevant in each case (see the end of §30 below). This is why, although William Golding can portray the mind of a Neanderthal man and thereby achieve something fine,[1] the purported autobiographies of horses are inevitably as unfit for adult consumption as are tales that attribute personality to shunting-engines.

So: all suppositions about possible experience must concern experience which is owned and which is accompanied by self-consciousness. It is out of these modest but not trivial asseverations that Kant spins the argumentative thread of the Transcendental Deduction.

Once again, it is necessary to insist that the consolatory aspect of Kant's conclusions does not constitute their point. We *can* see Kant as addressing himself to one who worries about what his experience might come to be like:

You cannot suppose, and thus cannot fear, that you might find yourself without a concept of yourself as the owner of your mental states. So, if I can show that experience which is accompanied by self-consciousness must have feature F, then I will have shown that finding yourself with experience which lacks feature F is not among the outcomes which you can fear.

But we can also take him to be addressing himself to a philosopher rather than to a neurotic:

When you tell a story, to yourself or to others, about the content of your mental history, you are in effect using a distinction between 'I have a story' and 'My story is as follows:...' There is nothing wrong with this distinction, but it must be properly understood. In particular, you must not assume that every aspect of your story is a simple matter of fact about the mental history which you happen to have. For there may be some feature of your experience, call it F, such that only experience which has F can be accompanied by self-consciousness; and if that is so then the fact that your experience has F lies on the 'I have a story' side of the line rather than on the 'My story is as follows:...' side of the line.

It is the latter formulation which brings out the kind of interest which the mentally stable might have in Kant's arguments.

29 Synthesis

Recall that Kant's aim is to show (a) that all experience must have certain features, and (b) that all possessors of experience must have certain capacities. The obvious parallel between (a) and what is supposed to be proved in the Aesthetic is noted by Kant in a passage which I also quote for another purpose:

The supreme principle of the possibility of all intuition in its relation to sensibility is, according to the Transcendental Aesthetic, that all the manifold of intuition should be subject to the formal conditions of space and time. The supreme principle of the same possibility, in its relation to understanding, is that all the manifold of intuition should be subject to conditions of the original synthetic unity of apperception. In so far as the manifold representations of intuition are *given* to us, they are subject to the former of these two principles; in so far as they must allow of being *combined* in one consciousness, they are subject to the latter. For without such combination nothing can be thought or known, since the given representations would not have in common the act of the apperception 'I think', and so could not be apprehended together in one self-consciousness.[1]

Most of this passage concerns (a) rather than (b), because it says that intuitions must *allow of being* combined in one consciousness. But the final sentence points to (b), for it seems to say that intuitions must *be* combined, implying presumably that their owner must be able to effect the required 'combination', whatever that may mean. (Kant usually speaks of 'synthesis' rather than 'combination'; the latter word is briefly prominent only in the second edition; but I shall use the two words interchangeably.)

The passage I have quoted makes it natural to think of combination or synthesis as something like an act of putting together; but Kant also has a different use of 'synthesis' in which a synthesis is a state of being together. The suggestion is that the outcome of a synthesis (= synthesizing act) is a synthesis (= unity or state of togetherness), as the outcome of a mustering of sheep is a mob of sheep. The analogy with the mustering of sheep has its dangers: when Kant speaks of synthesis

(= unity), he does not refer to physical proximity but rather to the togetherness, which might be called logical and is certainly not spatial, of different properties of a single object or different states of a single mind. Similarly, when he speaks of synthesis (= act of unifying), he does not mean a physical but rather a logical putting-together which, indeed, he often calls 'intellectual synthesis'.

Here is an example of intellectual synthesis. I am aware of the presence of something cold, and of something which hums; I consider the criteria for one thing's having two properties, probe my surroundings in the light of these criteria, and conclude that the cold thing is the humming thing, perhaps by identifying each with the tuning-fork which I see in my hand. Here a state of togetherness or unity has been recognized through an act of intellectual synthesis, i.e. by my arriving at a conclusion about how my sensory data relate to certain criteria. Another example: I see and handle a book, and then an hour later I see and handle a book; I wonder whether it is the same book on each occasion, and after reflection and inquiry I conclude that it is. I synthesize the two book-appearances by connecting or unifying them as appearances of a single book. The first example concerns different aspects of a thing at one time, while the second concerns aspects of a thing at different times.

These examples show that we can as well speak of 'coming to realize that x and y are united' as of 'uniting x and y'. Herding sheep into an enclosure is different from coming to realize that they are there; but the intellectual operation of assigning properties to an object *is* coming to realize, or coming to the conclusion, that they are properties of the object. It follows that the state of synthesis which is produced by an act of synthesis is not the state of affairs which consists in the cold thing's being the thing which hums, but rather that which consists in *my knowing that* the cold thing is the thing which hums: my intellectual activity did not bring it about that the tuning-fork was both cold and humming, but did bring it about that I knew that this was so. Despite this, Kant sometimes seems to say that intellectual synthesis brings about not just awareness of a unity but the unity itself. This will give us trouble later on.

In the examples above I am presented with data which are unsynthesized, i.e. which I do not know to relate to a single object, and after reflection and inquiry I synthesize them, i.e. conclude that they do relate to a single object. But I may assign several properties to something without enduring a period of agnosticism which is ended by my coming to realize that..., or coming to the conclusion that.... For example, I see and feel the pen which is now in my hand: I realize that the thing I feel is the thing I see; but I have not come to realize this, for at no stage did I have the relevant sensory data while not knowing that they related to a single object. Do I here perform an act of intellectual synthesis? Locke answered this question, or one very like it, affirmatively. He said that in such cases we are tempted to deny that we have done any concluding or interpreting only because we do this sort of thing 'so constantly, and so quick' that we cannot catch ourselves at it: the quickness of the understanding deceives the inner eye.[1] This non-empirical stab in the dark is clearly motivated by the assumption that any sort of grasp or understanding or awareness of a unity *must* have been arrived at by means of intellectual activity. There is, however, at least one kind of unity of which this assumption is false, namely the unity of mental states within one's own mind.

I cannot know that a certain mental state exists and wonder whether it is a state of my mind or of someone else's. I can wonder whose stomach is rumbling, but not whether it is my neighbour or myself who is embarrassed. Again, I may perhaps come to realize that I have a headache, but I cannot come to realize, of a given headache, that it is mine: if it is given to me at all as a possible subject of thought or discourse, it is given to me *as* mine. This is what Kant is getting at when he speaks of the unity of consciousness as 'original'. He means by this that one does not arrive at one's awareness of it by applying criteria for mental identity: I do not deem this headache to be mine by virtue of some feature of it, or some relationship between it and my other mental states. The unity of consciousness is 'original', or non-derivative, because the awareness of it is

that self-consciousness which, while generating the representation 'I think' (a representation which must be capable of accompanying all other representations...), cannot itself be accompanied by any further representation.[2]

Kant's real point here is not that the 'I think' cannot be *accompanied by* any further representation, but that it cannot be *derived from*, or asserted in virtue of, any further representation. A substitution of *abgeleitet* for *begleitet*, which has been suggested,[3] would make this explicit in the German text.

Because the unity of consciousness is 'original' in the above sense, awareness of one's ownership of mental states cannot arise from an intellectual activity, however facile and elusive, of the kind postulated by Locke. Whatever can be done quickly and easily could in principle be done slowly; but nothing could count as laboriously working out, of a given mental state, that it was one's own.

Locke's assumption is wrong for other kinds of unity as well. Even in cases where it makes sense to say that there was an act of synthesis, it is a mistake to think that there *must* have been one. The fact that I know a good deal about the things which I can now see and feel and hear may be expressed by saying that my sense-data are interpreted, understood or synthesized; but it does not follow that I must have done some interpreting, reasoned my way to an understanding, or performed an act of synthesis. To understand something, e.g. to know that the pen I feel is the pen I see, is to be able to give the right answers to certain questions, to make the right moves in solving certain physical problems and so on; and we cannot prescribe a priori the ways in which such abilities must be acquired. One can know that something is the case without previously wondering whether, and then working out, that it is the case; just as one can be able to do something without previously being unable, and then learning, to do it.

Kant sees that even a very fast act of synthesis will not do in the case of the unity of consciousness; but he does apparently flirt with Locke's assumption that any awareness of a unity must have been arrived at by some sort of reasoning or interpreting procedure—and even with the more extravagant assumption that a unity must itself be somehow created by an intellectual performance. He has in any case another reason for wanting to say that awareness of the unity of one's mind, despite its 'originality', presupposes an act of intellectual synthesis. He hopes to show that self-consciousness necessarily involves intellectual capacity of a fairly high order, and this conclusion seems to be in jeopardy if it be allowed that someone can be aware of his identity as a conscious being without having reasoned his way to this awareness. Kant therefore persists in saying that any state of unity—or at least any awareness of one—is associated with something in the nature of an act of synthesis; and he tries to reconcile this with the 'original' status of the unity of consciousness by saying that the synthesizing act involved in the latter is not empirical but 'transcendental'. There are two utterly different things which this could mean, and Kant makes free use of both without ever seeing that they are distinct. Taken in such a way that it purports to name a kind of intellectual act, Kant's phrase 'intellectual synthesis' embodies a total mistake. Taken in another way, in which it does not name an act though it is still connected with intellectual activity, 'transcendental synthesis' is a powerful philo-sophical tool which really does connect self-consciousness with intel-lectual capacity.

30 Transcendental synthesis

Taken in the sense in which it represents a mistake, the phrase, 'trans-cendental synthesis' purports to refer to an intellectual act which does not take place in the empirical time-series and therefore does not terminate a period during which the data are waiting to be synthesized. If we never catch ourselves performing the synthesizing act associated with the unity of consciousness, and are never in a position to say 'The data are before me, but are not yet synthesized', this is only to be expected if the act in question is transcendental, non-empirical, un-dated.

On this 'genetic' interpretation, as I shall call it, transcendental synthesis looks desperately unpromising. For one thing, it shares all the problems of the Aesthetic when that is taken to describe the atemporal workings of noumenal mechanisms. Furthermore, transcendental synthesis is supposed to produce either the unity of consciousness or the awareness of it, and an act of production must presumably predate the achieved product; so that transcendental synthesis must occur before certain times without occurring at any time. Worse still, since the synthesizing act is an operation upon intuitions, the latter must be available before they can be synthesized: 'The manifold to be intuited must be given prior to the synthesis of understanding, and inde-pendently of it.'[1] Yet what has driven Kant to posit a *transcendental* synthesis at all is just the fact that intuitions can be given only in the unity of consciousness and therefore only after the performance of the synthesis. It looks as though, rather than declining to date the syn-thesizing act, Kant must date it both before and after the first time at which the items to be synthesized are given.

Perhaps he would plead that 'given' is ambiguous; there are two forms which this plea might take, depending on whether the outcome of an act of synthesis is taken to be (1) a state of unity or togetherness or (2) an awareness of such a state. (1) Kant might say that before being synthesized intuitions are 'given' in the sense that they exist; afterwards they are 'given' in the stronger sense that someone has them. This will not do, though, for Kant rightly insists that intuitions cannot exist except as states of someone's mind. (2) He might say that before being synthesized intuitions are 'given' in the sense of existing as states of someone's mind; afterwards they are 'given' in the stronger sense that their owner is conscious of them. But that would commit Kant to saying that transcendental synthesis is an intellectual operation which one performs upon data which one does not know that one possesses. There seems to be no escape for Kant in a plea of ambiguity.

Obviously, it is asking for trouble to construe transcendental synthesis as a kind of act or occurrence while denying that temporal predicates apply to it. Yet Kant does beyond question sometimes adopt the genetic interpretation of 'transcendental synthesis':

I am conscious to myself a priori of a necessary synthesis [= unity] of representations—to be entitled the original synthetic unity of apperception—under which all representations that are given to me must stand, but under which they have also first to be brought by means of a synthesis [= unifying act].[1]

Thus Kemp Smith's translation. The vital word 'first', which commits Kant so explicitly to the view that transcendental synthesis is an act which predates what it produces, has no warrant in the German; but the passage clearly presents synthesis as a producer of, and therefore surely as predating, either a state of unity or an awareness of one. In any case, the predating emphasis occurs explicitly here:

To this act the general title 'synthesis' may be assigned, as indicating that we cannot represent to ourselves anything as combined in the object which we have not ourselves previously combined; and that of all representations *combination* is the only one which cannot be given through objects. Being an act of the self-activity of the subject, it cannot be executed save by the subject itself...*Analysis*, which appears to be its opposite, yet always presupposes it. For where the understanding has not previously combined [*wo der Verstand vorher nichts verbunden hat*], it cannot dissolve, since only as having been combined *by the understanding* can anything that allows of analysis be given to the faculty of representation.[2]

In many other passages Kant explicitly construes transcendental synthesis as a unifying act; the italics in the following citations are mine. He speaks of the synthesis as 'transcendental' in the sense of '*taking place* a priori';[3] he says that the understanding is 'nothing but the faculty of *combining* a priori, and of *bringing* the manifold of given representations under the unity of apperception';[4] and he refers to 'that *act* of the understanding by which the manifold of given representations (be they intuitions or concepts) is *brought* under one apperception'.[5] Those passages are all from B, but in A there are many to the same effect. A special group of these will be considered in §38; but we may now note the following:

If this manifold is to be known, the spontaneity of our thought requires that it be gone through in a certain way, taken up, and connected. This *act* I name synthesis... Synthesis is that which *gathers* the elements for knowledge, and *unites* them to [form] a certain content.[1]

If Kant had been drawn into this quagmire solely by a belief that any awareness of a unity must be reached by an intellectual process, we could leave him to sink with Locke. And if the source of the trouble were the assumption that a unity must result from a unifying procedure, and that the function of an intellectual synthesis is to produce not the awareness of a unity but the unity itself, then Kant's position would deserve even less respect still. But Kant is in fact motivated partly by a belief that self-consciousness involves intellectual capacity, and we must not dismiss this until we have seen what truth there is in it. To this end, let us turn to the better of Kant's two interpretations of 'transcendental synthesis'.

In this, the empirical/transcendental line no longer marks off what does from what does not take place in the empirical time-series: instead of an ontological distinction between two sorts of act, it is now a logical distinction between two sorts of statement—pretty much like the distinction, discussed in §8, between two sorts of idealism and between two sorts of realism.

According to this second interpretation, a transcendental synthesis is not an act at all; yet, like empirical synthesis, it underlies the awareness of states of unity. What an empirical synthesizing act has in common with the transcendental synthesis which is not an act at all is that each involves the notions of *satisfaction of criteria* and of *intellectual capacity*. The relevance of these to empirical synthesis is easy to see: arriving by an empirical synthesis at the knowledge that this book is the one I saw an hour ago involves grasping and applying criteria for the identity of physical things. But when someone is aware of a unity without having reasoned his way to this awareness, there is still a 'transcendental synthesis' in the sense that the unified items must satisfy certain criteria for unity or identity, and the person concerned must have a grasp of those criteria. 'His awareness that the book he sees is the one he saw an hour ago presupposes a transcendental synthesis'—this is not a biographical remark about how he achieved this awareness, but a philosophical remark about what it is to have this awareness. A transcendental synthesis is involved whenever someone is aware of a unity, irrespective of whether this awareness did, did not, or could not arise from an empirical synthesis. I call this the 'analytic' interpretation of 'transcendental synthesis'.

The point about criteria receives its clearest expression in the section with which Kant begins the rewritten part of the Transcendental Deduction. Here he discusses the notion of combination in all its splendid generality.[1] My examples have concerned the unity of contemporaneous properties of a thing (the pen in my hand, the tuning-fork), of stages in the history of a thing (the re-identified book), and of states of a mind. I think that Kant would have said that these are the only important species of combination or unity. What they have in common—and this defines the genus 'combination'—is that each can be described in the form 'Something is both F and G': something looks thus and feels so, something is seen by me now and was seen by me an hour ago, something experiences embarrassment and recently felt pain. Our theme is the difference between 'Something is both F and G' and 'Something is F and something is G'.

Unfortunately, Kant writes as though his concern were with the process of creating or coming to be aware of a unity; but the passage can be glossed so as to say something true about criteria for identity. It opens like this:

The manifold of representations can be given in an intuition which is purely sensible, that is, nothing but receptivity; and the form of this intuition can lie a priori in our faculty of representation, without being anything more than the mode in which the subject is affected. But the combination of a manifold in general can never come to us through the senses, and cannot, therefore, be already contained in the pure form of sensible intuition. For it is an act of spontaneity of the faculty of...understanding...All combination...is an act of the understanding...We cannot represent to ourselves anything as combined in the object which we have not ourselves previously combined, and...of all representations *combination* is the only one which cannot be given through objects.[2]

Stripping this passage of its claim that combination is an act, we can take it as saying: to be in a position to say 'Something is both F and G', one must be able to say 'Something is F and something is G, and the relevant identity-criteria entitle me to identify the thing which is F with the thing which is G'. Existentially quantified conjunctions can be true only by virtue of the satisfaction of identity-criteria ('combination...is an act of the understanding'); other concepts may or may not unpack or analyse into simpler constituents, but any concept involving combination, any identity- or unity-concept, must be analysable ('combination is the only one which cannot be given'). This evokes a picture of the passive intake of intuitions which entitle one to assert conjunctions of existentially quantified statements, and the intellectual organization of these into unities which entitle one to assert existentially quantified conjunctions; but the organization is not something which happens, but only a conceptual complexity which is *there* and which is *grasped* by the owner of the intuitions. Taken in this way, Kant's thesis applies as well to the unity of consciousness as to any other kind of unity; for it says only that membership in a single mind is obedience to criteria for mental identity, and that to be aware of mental states as one's own is to grasp these criteria and to know that the mental states in question satisfy them.

I must leave the shelter of the vague phrase 'grasp of criteria'. To grasp the criteria for a given kind of unity is to be able to handle them in an empirical synthesis: I have a grasp of the criteria for saying that the thing I feel in my hand is the thing I now see because I *could* wonder whether this identity holds and then deliberately come to the conclusion that it does. Thus transcendental synthesis, without being construed as some kind of atemporal interpretative procedure, can still be connected with intellectual activity. For, on the analytic interpretation of the phrase, 'transcendental synthesis' refers to a conceptual complexity the grasp of which consists in a capacity for ordinary, mundane, temporal, intellectual activity, i.e. for empirical synthesis.

Kant does at least sometimes adopt the analytic interpretation of 'transcendental synthesis'. Of several passages which show this,[1] I select just one:

The thought that the representations given in intuition one and all belong to me, is...equivalent to the thought that I unite them in one self-consciousness, or can at least so unite them; and although this thought is not itself the conscious-ness of [empirical] synthesis of the representations, it presupposes the possibility of that synthesis.[2]

If the word 'empirical' which I have inserted is not what Kant intended, then the passage is unintelligible; and if my interpolation is correct, then the quoted passage expresses the analytic interpretation of 'trans-cendental synthesis'.

A problem arises. It is generally allowed that a dog may *think that* the parcel in my hand is the thing that smells of meat. I do not deny the propriety of this sort of talk: indeed a primary purpose of §24 was to correct Kant's implicit denial that dogs can make judgments. But the judgment that the parcel in my hand is the thing that smells of meat does, surely, involve the sort of conceptual complexity which Kant calls 'combination'; and yet we do not wish to credit a dog with a capacity for the considered use of criteria in solving the problem of whether the parcel in my hand is...etc. It is therefore just not true that any creature which judges that P, where P involves combination, must have the kind of intellectual capacity which Kant needs for the later stages of his argument in the 'Principles' chapter.

This is a genuine gap in the central argument of the whole *Critique*. It would be both easy and fashionable to close it by denying that judgments can be made by creatures which lack a language. This is a reversion to some of the easy simplifications of Descartes; by refusing to consider epistemological questions outside the human sphere it blurs our vision of what lies within it. In particular, it reflects and reinforces the current tendency to leave unexamined, as too awesome or too special or too familiar, the judgment-expressing power of language. It treats language as a sort of magic, rather than as a sort of physical behaviour whose epistemological and logical bearings can be painfully but instructively compared with those of other kinds of physical behaviour.

The lacuna in Kant's argument can, however, be filled in another way. In §24 I have adduced reasons, which are developed at length in *Rationality*, for saying that the expression of judgments about the past does require a language, and indeed a concept-exercising one. The dog's excavations express its judgment that *The bone is there*, but without command of a fairly rich language the dog cannot express the judgment that *The bone was buried there*; and a judgment which the dog cannot express is a judgment which it does not make. This line of argument can now be taken a stage further. A creature which can make judgments about the past must not merely have a certain level of linguistic capacity, but must, specifically, be able to handle criteria in deciding whether this or that past-tense judgment is true. For a creature which makes past-tense statements can be confronted by counter-evidence and counter-assertions to them; and if it cannot cope with these according to rules or criteria, then we no longer have any reason to say that it is making past-tense statements at all. I conclude that we can accept a restricted version of the thesis which I have attributed to Kant: a capacity for empirical synthesis is required for any awareness of a unity which involves judgments about the past.

Kant can accept this restriction with equanimity. He is concerned only with what can be true of a self-conscious creature, i.e. one which can have the thought that *This is how it is with me now*. The notion of oneself is necessarily that of the possessor of a history: I can judge that this is how it is with me now only if I can also judge that that is how it was with me then. Self-consciousness can co-exist with amnesia; but there could not be a self-conscious person suffering from perpetually renewed amnesia such that he could at no time make judgments about how he was at any earlier time. Self-consciousness, then, entails a capacity to judge about the past, and so—by my argument in *Rationality*—entails the possession of a concept-exercising language.

One of the best things about the Transcendental Deduction is that it brings out that self-consciousness, far from being an unanalysable kind of glow which accompanies human and not canine mental states, involves intellectual capacity of the sort required for making past-tense judgments. As Kant says:

This thoroughgoing identity of the apperception of a manifold which is given in intuition contains a synthesis of representations, and is possible only through the consciousness of this synthesis...[The] relation [of mental states] to the identity of the subject...comes about, not simply through my accompanying each representation with consciousness, but only in so far as I *conjoin* one representation with another, and am conscious of the synthesis of them.[1]

If self-consciousness does involve the making of judgments about one's past states, and if this does require intellectual capacities of the sort Kant calls 'having concepts', then we can justify our confidence that sub-human animals are not self-conscious. Although dogs have needs and wants and aggressions, the suggestion that they might envy humans or regret being dogs seems wildly fanciful—presumably because it seems clear that a dog does not have the notion of *itself*, of *its* station in life or state of being. What makes this so clear? The only answer I know of is Kant's: in all sorts of ways—and especially by their lack of a concept-exercising language—dogs show their intellectual inability to make judgments about the past, and thus their inability to see the present as a stage in a history, and thus their lack of self-consciousness.

31 The use of criteria

By interpreting transcendental synthesis in terms of *conceptual complexity* and *capacity for empirical synthesis*, we escape from the morass of problems into which we were launched by the genetic interpretation;

but the analytic interpretation now raises a difficulty of its own. I have defended the analytic version of the doctrine of transcendental synthesis by insisting that it is to be applied solely to a kind of unity which involves the past, viz. the unity of consciousness. But how can there be an empirical synthesis—a deliberate coming to a conclusion—in respect of one's ownership of one's own mental states? Kant seems to have ruled this out by saying, rightly, that one's mental states are given to one *as* one's own: the unity of one's mind is 'original' in the sense that one's awareness of it cannot be arrived at by deliberation. How, then, can awareness of one's own identity involve a capacity for empirical synthesis? How can one have a capacity for doing something which one could not possibly do seriously?

The answer is that one can, at a given time, seriously employ criteria for mental identity in order to decide what states were one's own at *earlier* times. I do not have in mind here cases where one may say: 'That was the holiday which was ruined because one of us was feeling depressed about the international situation—now was it you or I that year?' That sort of case involves a thick social context, without which it would be impossible to refer to a given mental state while not knowing whose state it was. When I say 'That ruinous bout of depression—was it yours or mine?', I mean 'that bout of depression which we have talked about so often since', or '...which led to our going to *Parsifal* but not to *Meistersinger*', or '...which started us quarrelling about schools of psychoanalysis'. Kant therefore cannot appeal to examples of this kind. He is arguing that *any* self-conscious creature must have and exercise certain sorts of intellectual capacity; and it is no use his invoking the sort of empirical synthesis which one might try to conduct in the 'bout of depression' case or others like it. For, minimally, that kind of problem about the ownership of a mental state presupposes that one knows that there are other people as well as oneself; and Kant has no grounds for saying that a self-conscious creature must share a world with other sentient beings and know that he does so.

Nevertheless, there is another way in which one can conduct an empirical synthesis in order to decide what mental states were one's own at earlier times. Although it is only in special circumstances that I can know that someone had a certain mental state and wonder whether it was I, there is nothing special about the case where I wonder whether a past mental state was mine *by* wondering whether it was anyone's, i.e. by wondering whether it existed at all. In asking 'Did that really happen to me?', where 'that' purports to refer to a mental state, I may be asking 'Did that really happen at all?'; but my question does nevertheless involve criteria for mental identity. Furthermore, this is a kind of question which must be raisable and answerable by any self-conscious being, even one who does not know of the existence of any other sentient being.

Self-consciousness, then, involves whatever intellectual capacities may be required for the establishment—sometimes by empirical synthesis—of the truth of statements about one's own past mental states. To verify such a statement requires more than just a grasp of criteria for mental identity (Kant shows this in the 'Principles' chapter), but all that Kant needs at the present stage of his argument is that it does involve that much.

If the position I have been attributing to Kant sounds odd and implausible, this may be because one does not think of criteria for the identity of one's own mind as looming large in every question one raises about one's past mental states. The truth is that ordinarily such criteria do not, explicitly and in isolation, come into the picture at all. 'I think I noticed that discord at the time...but I'm not sure; I have heard so much about it since, and my memory may be playing tricks on me'—in trying to straighten *this* out I shall not have two separate tasks, one involving criteria for mental identity and one involving whatever else may be required for me to answer my question about my past state. Kant, however, is interested in the question of how conceptually disorganized one's experience might intelligibly be supposed to be; he has to face up to the possibility that one's experience might be so chaotic that there was no place in it for much-discussed discords, remarks made to one's companion at a concert, knowledge as to one's general level of competence at noticing discords (i.e. noticing discords which really, objectively occur); and he is saying that, however primitive and disorderly the experience is supposed to be, if it is accompanied by self-consciousness then it will have to admit of *at least* that degree of intellectual organization which is involved in one's being able to claim one's past mental states as one's own.

At the end of §30 we had to restrict Kant's claim that *To be aware of a unity one must be capable of empirical syntheses* to the special case of unities which connect one time with another and so can be known only by those who can make judgments about the past: to be aware of other kinds of unity one need not be able to perform empirical syntheses, i.e. reason one's way to a conclusion. We have now had to place the same restriction on Kant's claim, in so far as it concerns the unity of the states of one's mind, for a totally different reason: the unity of one's own present mental states not only need not, but positively cannot, be known as the outcome of an empirical synthesis.

Kant nowhere says explicitly (a) that a grasp of identity-criteria involves a capacity for using them seriously, or (b) that the only real problems about one's ownership of mental states are past-tense ones. He does, however, say something which has puzzled some commentators but which can intelligibly be seen as a half-recognized consequence of (a) and (b), namely that there cannot be first-person criteria for mental identity other than ones which concern the past ownership of mental states. To explain this, I must first make some general points about identity-criteria.

Take any general term A whose instances have histories, like rivers or mountains or pencils or people. There are two sorts of rule for the identity of an A. (i) There are rules for what constitutes an A-at-a-moment—rules which lay down, for example, when it is correct to say 'That is a mountain' rather than 'That is part of a mountain' or '...two mountains' or '...bits of three mountains'. Following Quine[1] I shall say that these are rules for what constitutes an A-*stage*. (ii) There are rules which lay down when it is correct to say of two A-stages that they are stages of the same A. These are logically distinct from rules of the former sort. Someone might know what a thing must look like to count as a single mountain-stage, but think that morphology outweighs geography in the re-identification of mountains, and so speak of climbing the same mountain in two continents; or think that a mountain stops being the same mountain when its colour changes by the falling of snow or the flowering of heather, and so speak of climbing two different mountains in the same place on consecutive days. Conversely, someone might grasp the type-(ii) rules for the identity of mountains, but not the type-(i) rules. Most people are in fact unsure about what counts as a pair of mountains rather than a single twin-peaked mountain; and someone might be abnormally hazy about this sort of thing, and yet be perfectly well able to cope with statements of the form 'This is the same mountain—or part of a mountain—or group of mountains—as I climbed last week.'

I shall speak of type-(i) as 'counting' rules, and of type-(ii) as 'identifying' rules. It is true that counting may require identification, e.g. in saying 'I have climbed twelve different mountains this year'; but my terminology is safe if one connects 'counting rules' with the special case of counting items which are all present to one at the time.

In this terminology, then, I have been saying that rules for the identity of an *A* include both counting and identifying rules, and that these are logically distinct.

It is identifying rules which are in question when philosophers discuss the relevance to personal identity of incurable amnesia, radical change of character, metempsychosis, insanity, amoebic fission of minds or bodies, and so on. It is not always seen that this is only one of the two sorts of question which jointly constitute the problem of mental identity. Locke, for example, said that two states belong to a single mind if they are or can be parts of 'the same consciousness':[1] using 'x and y are parts of the same consciousness' to say something about memory-links between distinct mind-stages, he made a real though stumbling step towards the discovery of rules for the re-identification of minds; but he also used 'x and y are parts of the same consciousness' to mean 'x and y belong to the same mind-stage', without seeing that he was thereby making 'same consciousness' do double duty.

Locke failed entirely to illuminate counting rules, but this was not merely because he conflated them with identifying rules. In H. P. Grice's article 'Personal Identity'[2] there is an impressive attempt to scour and refurbish Locke's analysis of mental identity; and one of its many merits is that Grice sees, what so many have overlooked, that there are two sorts of identity-rule. The only counting-rule for minds which he offers, however, says that two mental items belong to the same mind-stage if it is possible to know that they occur simultaneously by means of a single act of introspection or memory. I think it would now be conceded that this is unacceptably circular; but its very ingenuity suggests that there is something peculiarly elusive about counting rules for mental identity. This impression is reinforced when one rummages through the history of philosophy; attempts which have been made to state identifying rules for minds do, imperfect though they are, go some way towards reducing this difficult problem; but nothing useful has ever been said about rules or criteria governing the unity of mental states within a single mind-stage.

This history of failure is due, I suggest, to the problem's having no solution: in respect of the unity of mental states within mind-stages, Kant's doctrine of transcendental synthesis is not true. I have argued that we can be said to grasp criteria only if we can sometimes use them in solving genuine problems, and that I can have a genuine problem about whether a mental state was mine—normally by wondering whether it existed at all. But I cannot have an analogous problem about what mental states are mine now. It is true that I can wonder what interpretation to put upon my present feelings, or what estimate to make of my likely future behaviour: 'Do I really love her?', 'Am I not angry but merely jealous?' etc. And even with a relatively primitive mental state such as a uniform visual field I may grope for the *mot juste* to describe it. But problems such as these can arise only on the basis of a fairly comprehensive knowledge of what mental states are and were mine; they are not relevant to my present point, which concerns the fundamental logical structure of the concept of an individual mind. The relevant difference between the past- and present-tense cases is that I can know what it is like to be in such and such a mental state and seriously wonder whether at a given earlier time I was in a state of that kind, while for this sort of problem there is no present-tense analogue. This is the truth behind the over-bold claim that present-tense statements about sensory states are incorrigible.

Since I cannot have criteria for something unless I might use them in solving a real problem, it follows that there are no criteria whose satisfaction justifies my claim to the ownership of present mental states. There is still one kind of question which one can seriously raise about the contents of a stage of one's own mind: I can wonder, of two past sensory states, whether they were mine at the same time or at different times; and in this sense I can have a genuine problem about whether two mental items were states of my own mind-at-a-moment. But this problem essentially involves identifying criteria; and it therefore does not help us in our search for counting criteria which can be used to determine what constitutes a mind-stage, as a *preliminary* to invoking identifying criteria in order to link mind-stages together to form minds. To seek counting criteria for minds is to ask 'What makes me, now, a single conscious being (perhaps one with a history, but never mind that in the meantime)?'. This question is not answered by an account of how I establish what mental states were mine in the past, and what their chronological order was.

It does not follow that there are no rights and wrongs when we are talking about mind-stages. It is not an optional matter whether at a given time I judge that *I now have a headache*: such judgments are answerable to the facts just like any others. What is special about these judgments is only that the relationship between them and the facts which verify them cannot be expressed in rules which analyse, clarify, or tease out the relationship.

In all this I have spoken only of the use of criteria for mental identity in connection with oneself: the second- and third-person case obviously introduce considerations which take them right outside the scope of the present argument.

We can now look at the puzzling remark of Kant's to which I referred earlier. He says: 'Each representation, in so far as it is contained in a single moment, can never be anything but absolute unity';[1] and he goes on to say that the notion of a manifold, i.e. a variety which is held together within a unity, is essentially the notion of something which lasts through time and which therefore forms a unity only by being 'run through, and held together', presumably by means of identifying criteria. This gives a drastic solution to the problem of finding criteria for what constitutes a mind-stage, for it says that mind-stages are not complex and that therefore the problem does not exist.

Taken in this way, what Kant says is not true: when I say 'For the last five minutes I have been hearing a buzzing noise and suffering a headache', I do not report a rapid alternation between an auditory state and a pain. But Kant's remark about the 'absolute unity' of that which 'is contained in a single moment' does suggest that he is in some way aware that there cannot be counting criteria for minds. Having noted the one class of cases for which his doctrine of synthesis fails, Kant declares these cases to be irrelevant to the doctrine on the grounds that they do not involve that unity or conceptual complexity which the doctrine offers to analyse.

This interpretation of Kant's half-thoughts about identity-criteria is supported by his almost exclusive attention to identifying rules and by his preoccupation with temporal succession. Having said that any use of concepts must involve something of the across-time 'running through and holding together' kind mentioned above, he continues:

The word 'concept' [*Begriff*, which is cognate to *begreifen* = include, comprehend, grasp] might of itself suggest this remark. For this unitary consciousness is what combines the manifold, successively intuited...into one representation.[2]

There are other passages which similarly suggest that Kant takes his account of the unity of consciousness to be solely concerned with the uniting of mind-stages into minds, not because he overlooks counting rules but because he half-sees that there cannot be such rules for mental identity.

This brings us nearly to the end of the central argument in the Transcendental Deduction. In brief, the argument which has run through §§28–31 comes to this:– Any state of being which I can intelligibly suppose I might find myself in must include self-consciousness, and thus knowledge of my past states, and thus the intellectual ability to have and assess such knowledge. So I cannot speculate about what it would be like to lack such abilities, *or to have experience which did not enable me to exercise them.*

This last point deserves comment. When Kant argues that if I am self-conscious I must have a mental history which I can bring under concepts, he is arguing not only that I must have concepts but that my experience must 'fall under concepts'. Not until the 'Principles' chapter does Kant say anything useful about what experience must be like for past-tense judgments about it to be possible, but in the Transcendental Deduction he is preparing the way for conclusions about the limits on supposable experience.

If the Metaphysical Deduction lived up to Kant's claims for it, the limits would perhaps be set already. The Transcendental Deduction shows (a) that experience I could know myself to have must be brought under concepts, and the Metaphysical Deduction says (b) that to use concepts at all one must use Kant's favoured dozen; whence it follows that the so-called categories are indeed categories, i.e. can be known a priori to be applicable to any experience I could possibly know myself to have. But (b) is false: it is not the case that Kant's dozen are all indispensable to any exercise of concepts.

Even if we granted (b), there would be a difficulty: with most of the categories it is not at all clear what is meant by saying 'The experience of a self-conscious creature must fall under *that* concept'. For example, what sort of limit is being set to the kind of experience a self-conscious creature could have, when it is said that such experience must be capable of being brought under the concept of negation? or of totality? or of reality? or of existence? The truth is that Kant's doctrine of categories—considered as saying something not just about the intellectual abilities but also about the kind of experience one must have—has no clear content except in respect of the three relational categories, which are precisely the ones over which the Metaphysical Deduction most strikingly fails. To speak of experience which provides work for the concept of cause, or substance, or community, does seem to be to speak of a *kind* of experience. We can see what someone might be getting at if he said:

Everything might be in such confusion that, for instance, in the series of appearances nothing presented itself which might…answer to the concept of cause and effect [or of substance, or of community]. This concept would then be altogether empty, null, and meaningless.[1]

But what could be meant by an analogous remark about any of the other nine categories? This is yet another reason, additional to the one given in §26, why Kant should later argue intensively for the apriority of the relational categories but not the other nine.

Still, Kant is entitled to say that if supposable experience must be brought under concepts, this *may* imply a limit to what I can suppose my experience to be like—depending on whether it can be shown that some logically possible kinds of experience could not be brought under concepts. In the Transcendental Deduction Kant repeatedly, if obscurely, tries to get across this idea that if I am to be aware of the unity of my mental states then they must *have* that unity, i.e. must have whatever features are required for me to bring them under concepts. Thus, for example:

All possible appearances, as representations, belong to the totality of a possible self-consciousness. But as self-consciousness is a transcendental representation, numerical identity is inseparable from it, and is a priori certain. For nothing can come to our knowledge save in terms of this original apperception. Now, since this identity must necessarily enter into the synthesis of all the manifold of appearances, so far as the synthesis is to yield empirical knowledge, the appearances are subject to a priori conditions, with which the synthesis of their apprehension must be in complete accordance...Thus all appearances stand in thoroughgoing connection according to necessary laws...[2]

9

TRANSCENDENTAL DEDUCTION:
FURTHER ASPECTS

32 Objectivity and 'what solipsism means'

I want now to justify Kant's preoccupation with the first-person singular case in his treatment of mental identity, and also to introduce an important new aspect of the Transcendental Deduction. These two aims are linked by the concept of an objective state of affairs, which Kant, not quite happily, calls the concept of an object. This is the concept which marks the difference between 'I have a sensation of warmth' and 'There is something hot in my vicinity', and between 'I have a visual field as of seeing something red' and 'There is something red which I see'.

A good part of Kant's account of this concept can be found in the four paragraphs on A 104–6, but it is also scattered throughout the Transcendental Deduction in both versions: see for example the paragraph on A 128–30, and the two on B 140–2.[1] It is an account which I, like Strawson, have assumed to be fundamentally correct throughout §§11–13; but it must now be subjected to scrutiny.

Kant's analysis of the concept of an objective state of affairs rests squarely on his phenomenalism. He says that when we think we have knowledge about objects,

the object is viewed as that which prevents our modes of knowledge from being haphazard or arbitrary, and which determines them...in some definite fashion. For in so far as they are to relate to an object, they must necessarily agree with one another, that is, must possess that unity which constitutes the concept of an object.[2]

Thus, if I employ the concept of an object by saying 'I see something which is red', I do not merely report my visual field but also commit myself to something about what other intuitions I should have if I were to change my position, close my eyes, etc. That is, I bring my visual field 'under a rule' which relates it to other intuitions which I have had, do have, shall have or might have. If the rule is not obeyed, then I have either applied the concept of an object wrongly or erred in introducing it at all.

Sometimes Kant seems to deny that the obedience of my experience to appropriate rules is logically equivalent to my being confronted by objects. For example, he says: 'We have to deal only with the manifold of our representations, and...the object which corresponds to them is nothing to us [because it is] distinct from all our representations.'[1] If Kant really is here playing the noumenal, veil-of-perception game, then Kemp Smith is right to scold him for it; but perhaps he is not. The reader is referred to Kemp Smith's *Commentary*[2] and to Wolff's painstaking *Kant's Theory*[3] for an account of the place in Kant's philosophical development of passages like this and of the equally regressive hints[4] that the categories apply to noumena as well as to phenomena. What matters here is that Kant is firmly committed by the main drift of the *Critique* to a phenomenalist analysis of objectivity which does not postulate objects as noumenal items over and above the data of experience but treats them as logical constructs out of those data. This is clearly implied, for example, by his reference to 'that unity which constitutes [*ausmacht*] the concept of an object'.

Kant's treatment of objectivity marks an historic advance on the work of Berkeley and Hume. Berkeley saw that it would not do to leave objects on the other side of the veil of perception, and he expressed this insight by saying that nothing exists but minds and their 'ideas' (= intuitions).[5] But he made the disastrous mistake of saying that objects are *collections* of ideas. A collection can exist only if those conditions are satisfied which are necessary for the existence of its members; and, since an individual idea can exist only in a mind, Berkeley concluded that an object can exist only in a mind—which he took to mean that an object can exist only if perceived by a mind. In denying that objects can exist unperceived, Berkeley said something strikingly false and involved himself in a deal of philosophical trouble. Kant is absolutely clear of this error. He sometimes uses language appropriate to it, as when he says that 'objects are nothing but representations',[6] but he stays well away from the morass into which Berkeley was drawn by taking seriously and literally the claim that objects are 'collections' of mental states. Kant's considered view is that the concept of an object is a rule for intuitions; this implies that statements about objects must be translatable into statements about intuitions; but nothing follows about what the principles of translation are. For example, 'An object can exist when not perceived by any sentient being' is equivalent to *some* statement which refers to intuitions but not to objects; but this latter statement need not be 'An intuition can exist outside the mind of any sentient being'.

Hume's case is less straightforward because his only extended discussion of objectivity is so complex and so chaotic;[1] but that little-understood section does offer at least two clear points of comparison with Kant. The first is that Hume, like Berkeley, thought it useful to ask whether objects *are* 'impressions' (=intuitions). He thought that he had to choose between (i) identifying objects with impressions, (ii) accepting Locke's view that objects lie behind the veil of perception, and (iii) denying that there are objects. It was therefore natural for him to conclude that "Tis impossible upon any system to defend either our understanding or our senses' and that 'Carelessness and in-attention alone can afford us any remedy' for our perplexity over what to say about the existence of objects. What Hume needed was a clear view of the possibility that instead of an identity between objects and impressions there might be a regular, analytic relationship between them, i.e. that the concept of an object might be 'a rule for' impressions. This Kantian analysis of objectivity does indeed get much support from the thick detail of Hume's examination of that 'constancy and coherence' of experience which underlies our belief that there are objects; but Hume did not see that his own positive work on objectivity laid the foundations for a satisfactory solution of his problem. The root of the trouble was his *simpliste* account of the meanings of words as quasi-pictorial 'simple ideas' which can be quasi-mechanically fitted together to make 'complex ideas'. This doctrine militated against his seeing (a) the kind of complexity which our objectivity-concepts do have, and (b) that this kind of complexity is intellectually respectable. Hume came close to seeing (a), but did not regard this as solving his problem because he did not admit (b). Where Kant expresses (a) in such words as 'we bring our intuitions under a rule', Hume said that we acquire a 'habit' or 'custom' of talking in certain ways, and he was misled by the dyslogistic overtones of 'habit' and 'custom'.

The second relevant point is that Hume, unlike Kant, posed his problem genetically: instead of seeking an analysis of objectivity statements he sought, or purported to seek, 'the *causes* which induce us to believe' that there are objective states of affairs. This exemplifies the general penchant which philosophers have for putting a genetic rather than an analytic construction upon their problems. Very often, they are led into positive error; very often also, some useful analytic truth comes through despite the genetic formulation of the problem. This mixture of error and truth occurs in the genetic argument of Strawson's discussed in §25; and it can be found also in Hume's treatment of objectivity.

Kant scores in other ways too. For example, Berkeley and Hume wrote too often as though their problem concerned the existence of 'bodies' only, whereas actually it was about the existence of objective states of affairs of all kinds—including the sky's really being blue, and that plant's really lying in a shadow. Again, Berkeley and Hume half saw that the problem raised by 'perceptible things which are not perceived' is all of a piece with that raised by 'tangible things which are seen', 'visible things which are heard' and the like. But neither of them could isolate or explain this conceptual homogeneity, whereas it is a natural and obvious consequence of Kant's analysis of objectivity.

Kant says that the concept of an object 'can be a rule for intuitions only in so far as it represents in any given appearances...the synthetic unity in our consciousness'.[1] By this he means that a set of intuitions which hang together in such a way as to fall under the concept of an object must also hang together in such a way as to be intuitions within a single mind. As Körner puts it: 'There can be no *it* unless there is an *I*....'[2]

Granted that there can be knowledge about the world only if there are people who have it, why should so much stress be laid upon knowledge possessed by a single person? Would it not meet the case to adapt Körner's remark and say that there can be no *it* unless there is an *us*? Kant does not think so. The word 'our' in the passage I have just quoted has no warrant in the German; but even if Kant had used the plural 'our' I should still have contended that his business is with the first-person singular. For he often vacillates between singular and plural because he wants to make an essentially plural/singular point about the need for each person to think of the concept of an object in terms of his own consciousness. Hence the charming slide from plural to singular here (the italics are mine):

Since a mere modification of *our* sensibility can never be met with outside *us*, the objects, as appearances, constitute an object which is merely in *us*. Now to assert in this manner, that all these appearances, and consequently all objects with which *we* can occupy *ourselves*, are one and all in *me*, that is, are determinations of *my* identical self, is only another way of saying that there must be a complete unity of them in one and the same apperception.[3]

Kant is right to stress the first-person singular. A problem exists for me only if I have it; evidence which solves the problem exists for me only if I have it. Someone else may have evidence which bears upon my problem, but I cannot take such evidence into account until I have it too. And when someone tells me what he knows about something, he provides me with new evidence only by confronting me with new sensory data: I hear him speak, and I have evidence as to his truthfulness, i.e. as to the likelihood that the sounds he makes will tally with my experience in appropriate ways; and I therefore treat the occurrence of my auditory experience in hearing him as evidence, *my* evidence, that such and such is the case.

All this could be expressed not in terms of the 'evidence for' what I say, but in terms of the 'meaning of' what I say. Kant thinks, and I agree, that what I mean by what I say is determined solely by what difference it would or could make *to me* if I were right or wrong in saying it. Of course, I understand such a statement as 'At this moment there are at least two dogs scratching their ears in Tibet', although it is far from clear that the truth or falsity of the statement could ever be known by me. But I can attach sense to statements like that only because they are logically connected with the mainland of my language, the core of which has content for me only in so far as it bears upon my experience. My *Weltanschauung* and my conceptual scheme must ultimately rest upon my experience, including my intake of the reports of others on their experience. Kant puts this very strongly: 'A judgment is nothing but the manner in which given modes of knowledge are brought to the...unity of apperception.'[1] Substantially the same point was made by Wittgenstein when he said that 'what solipsism *means* is quite correct' and that 'the world is *my* world'.[2]

It is because of the truth of 'what solipsism means' that Kant is entitled to focus sharply on criteria for the identity of one's own mind. I can raise questions about the minds of others, and others can raise questions about my mind; I may even change my beliefs about my own past mental states in the light of what others say. But everything which I rationally say, or rationally deny, relates to evidence which I have and thus to intuitions which enter the unity of my consciousness.

33 Objectivity and the Transcendental Deduction

Kant thinks that self-consciousness is possible only to a being who has experience of an objective realm: not only does the *it* entail an *I*, but conversely the *I* entails an *it*. This conclusion is established in the 'Principles' chapter. In the Transcendental Deduction there are some anticipations of this later material, but even the best of them[3] are intelligible only in the light of the arguments which Kant deploys later on. There are also in the Transcendental Deduction certain other attempts to show that the unity of consciousness—or the awareness thereof—entails objectivity, which are not merely previews of material in the 'Principles' chapter. These are uniformly bad, but they must be expounded and exposed if we are to be liberated from that host of Kantian commentators whose respect for the *ipsissima verba* of the Transcendental Deduction has survived nearly two centuries of failure to give a tolerably clear account of what it is saying.

Part of the trouble is that Kant's use of 'object' is viciously ambiguous. As well as the sense expounded in §32, Kant sometimes gives to 'object' the sense of 'datum' or 'item which can be talked about': I have already quoted him as saying that 'the unity of consciousness is a condition under which every intuition must stand in order to become an object for me'.[1] There is no question here of objectivity in the sense I have expounded, but only of being given, of being there to be talked about. In the 'Principles' chapter Kant belatedly separates these two senses of 'object' thus:

Everything, every representation even, in so far as we are conscious of it, may be entitled object. But it is a question for deeper enquiry what the word 'object' ought to signify in respect of appearances when these are viewed not in so far as they are (as representations) objects, but only in so far as they stand for an object [i.e. are intuitions of something objective].[2]

Now, in the weak sense of 'object', it is trivial to say that all experience must in some fashion involve objects; for the data of sense are themselves objects in the weak meaning of the word. But what Kant proves in the 'Principles' chapter, and repeatedly offers to prove in the Transcendental Deduction, is that all experience must be of a realm of items which are 'objective' in the sense that they can be distinguished from oneself and one's inner states. This is not at all trivial; and from now on my concern will be solely with Kant's defence of this stronger claim; but some of the passages which I shall quote should be read with an awareness that Kant has not yet sharply separated the weak sense of 'object' from the strong.

Kant sometimes, especially in A, drifts towards the conclusion that the unity of consciousness entails objectivity by expressing its converse—that objectivity entails the unity of consciousness—in ways which invite re-conversion. For example, he says that 'this unity of possible consciousness also constitutes the form of all knowledge of objects'.[3] This is unexceptionable if it says only that the unity of consciousness constitutes certain aspects of the knowledge of objects, i.e. that any story about known objects must include a story about unified minds. But Kant infers from it that the togetherness of intuitions in a single mind 'constitutes a formal a priori knowledge of all objects...',[1] which seems to say that to be a unified mind is necessarily to possess the concept of an object. This follows from the original remark only if 'the form of all knowledge of objects' is taken to mean not just 'certain aspects of the knowledge of objects' but far more strongly 'those central, basic aspects of the knowledge of objects which make it knowledge of *objects*'. Taken in this way, the original remark is one which Kant has given us no reason to believe. Note also Kant's use of the word 'represent' when he says:

The concept of body...can be a rule for intuitions only in so far as it represents in any given appearances the necessary reproduction of their manifold, and thereby the synthetic unity in our consciousness of them.[2]

This is acceptable if it means that the concept of body 'represents' the unity of consciousness in the sense that it includes or presupposes this unity. But the word 'represent' has an ominously symmetrical sound: if A represents B, then B represents A. Only if it is taken in this symmetrical sense does the quoted statement imply that the unity of consciousness involves the concept of body; but, so taken, the quoted statement is one which Kant does not justify.

Another route whereby Kant arrives illegitimately at the conclusion that the unity of consciousness entails objectivity is best approached through his *Prolegomena*, §§18–20. Here he distinguishes between *judgments of perception* and *judgments of experience*: the former merely report the judger's sensory states, while the latter make claims about necessary connections amongst sensory states. This distinction is clearly closely allied to the distinction between judgments which do not, and judgments which do, employ the concept of an object; and we find this distinction in the Transcendental Deduction too, though not in the 'perception'/'experience' terminology. For example:

To say 'The body is heavy' is not merely to state that the two representations have always been conjoined in my perception, however often that perception be repeated; what we are asserting is that they are combined *in the object*, no matter what the state of the subject may be.[3]

Kant handles this distinction very sloppily. Just before the passage last quoted he gives as the subjective analogue of 'The body is heavy' the judgment 'If I support the body I feel an impression of weight'. But this too is an objective judgment: it employs the concept of a body and so says something about the objective realm. A similar mistake occurs in the *Prolegomena*,[1] when Kant exemplifies the distinction between judgments of experience and of perception by the pair of statements 'The sun warms the stone' and 'When the sun shines on the stone, the stone grows warm'. The best we can do by way of salvaging these examples is to say that 'The body is heavy' is more objective than 'If I support the body, I feel an impression of weight'; and that 'The sun warms the stone' is more objective, because having a greater causal commitment, than 'When the sun shines on the stone, the stone grows warm'.

Still, we can see roughly what distinction Kant wants to draw between judgments of experience and of perception, or between objective and subjective judgments. What is objectionable is the use he makes of this distinction in the section on B 140–2.[2] This was written after the *Prolegomena*, and one might have expected it to lean upon the distinction, first explicitly made in the earlier work, between judgments of experience and of perception. In fact, Kant merely denies that there are any judgments of perception, or rather he tacitly restricts the meaning of 'judgment' to that of 'judgment of experience'. Thus he refers to '...a *judgment*, that is, a relation which is *objectively valid*'.[3] This implies that every judgment involves the concept of an object, and so leads by a new route to the conclusion that all experience must fall not merely under some concepts but under objectivity concepts in particular. But this restriction on the meaning of 'judgment' is arbitrary and illegitimate: Kant gives no reason for denying what he clearly admits in the *Prolegomena*, namely that there can be judgments of perception as well as of experience. On the same page as the damaging phrase I have quoted, Kant implicitly admits this when he says that if we do not have 'a relation which is objectively valid' then 'all that I could say would be...' and he then expresses a judgment!

The limitation of 'judgment' to so-called judgments of experience is paralleled by a restriction, which appears in both versions of the Transcendental Deduction, of 'experience' to experience of an objective realm. (This, of course, explains why 'judgment of experience' means what it does for Kant.) Kant says that 'experience is knowledge by means of connected perceptions';[4] and, even more strongly: 'The a priori conditions of a possible experience in general are at the same time conditions of the possibility of objects of experience'.[5] Certainly, conditions which are necessary for experience are, a fortiori, necessary for objects of experience; but Kant seems to assert the converse of this, that there must be objects of experience if there is to be experience at all. Again, there is a curious passage in the course of which he says: 'All experience does indeed contain, in addition to the intuition of the senses through which something is given, a *concept* of an object as being thereby given...'[1] The point here may not be the meaning of 'experience', for it looks a little as though Kant thinks he is reporting an empirical truth about human experience; but if that is what is intended, then it is irrelevant to his long-term aims. (The sentence concludes '...as being thereby given, that is to say, as appearing'. This suggests yet another interpretation, namely that there cannot be appearances unless there is something, namely an object, whose appearances they are. In a variant of this, Kant elsewhere says: 'All representations have, as representations, their object',[2] apparently assuming that nothing can count as a representation unless it represents something, namely an object. This, like the argument for noumena which I noted in §8, illicitly exploits the grammar of words like 'appearance' and 'representation'.)

In so far as Kant gives to 'experience' the narrowed sense to which I have referred, my use of the word has been un-Kantian, for I have used it to mean 'intuitional sequence which one could know oneself to have'. If, to count as experience, an intuitional sequence must be experience of objects, then it is trivially true that all experience must be subsumable under the concept of an object. But Kant does not want to establish this trivial thesis; he wants to show, and later does show, that there could not be an intuitional sequence accompanied by self-consciousness which was not experience of an objective realm.

34   'Imagination' in the Transcendental Deduction

The Transcendental Deduction in A is made peculiarly difficult by Kant's use of the term 'imagination'. In the present section—which will be without philosophical content—I shall say something about this.

Kant introduces 'imagination' into his doctrine about synthesis as follows:

Since every appearance contains a manifold, and since different perceptions therefore occur in the mind separately and singly, a combination of them, such as they cannot have in sense itself, is demanded. There must therefore exist in us an active faculty for the synthesis of this manifold. To this faculty I give the title, imagination.[3]

This apparently contradicts my description of 'the synthesis of the manifold' as the concern not of imagination but of understanding. In

34. 'IMAGINATION'

fact, Kant cannot take understanding and imagination to be rivals for
the role of synthesizing faculty, for he thinks that they are collaborators.
He has a theory, to be discussed in detail later, that if a category is to be
applied to something empirical then imagination is needed to produce
'some third thing, which is homogeneous on the one hand with the
category, and on the other hand with the appearance, and which thus
makes the application of the former to the latter possible'.[1] Elsewhere
imagination is said to 'mediate' between 'the two extremes, namely
sensibility and understanding'.[2]

Yet sometimes, rather than presenting imagination as the servant of
understanding, Kant seems to identify the two outright; not just in
calling imagination the 'faculty for the synthesis of the manifold', but
also in many other passages in both editions. For example, in B Kant
says:

It is one and the same spontaneity, which in the one case, under the title of
imagination, and in the other case, under the title of understanding, brings
combination into the manifold of intuition.[3]

If Kant really means two *titles* for 'one and the same' spontaneity then
he is identifying imagination with understanding. That is probably not
his intention, but it is true that he tends in the Transcendental Deduction to give to the activities of the understanding in which it collaborates
with imagination labels which suggest activities of imagination alone.

Worse, instead of choosing one label and keeping to it, Kant shifts
restlessly from one set of technical terms to another, making no
attempt to relate them. This appears strikingly in a series of trichotomies
of which the first is:

There are three original sources...of the possibility of all experience,...
namely, *sense, imagination*, and *apperception*. Upon them are grounded (1) the
synopsis of the manifold a priori through sense; (2) the *synthesis* of this manifold
through imagination; finally (3) the *unity* of this synthesis through original
apperception.[4]

It is presumably this same trio which is presented a few pages later:

This spontaneity is the ground of a threefold synthesis which must necessarily
be found in all knowledge; namely, [1] the *apprehension* of representations as
modifications of the mind in intuition, [2] their *reproduction* in imagination, and
[3] their *recognition* in a concept.[5]

Kant explains these at some length: item (1) has to do with our having
experience which stretches over a period of time, (2) with our recalling

our past states and bringing them under concepts along with our present states, and (3) with our knowing that we are doing this correctly. Imagination, then, is closely connected—if not identical— with intellectually disciplined memory; and Kant is here expounding his view that the rational grasp of one's present experience requires the relating of it with remembered past experience.

There is a difficulty about the (2)/(3) borderline. It seems that (2) concerns something which we may do consciously and correctly; all that (3) adds is our consciousness of its correctness:

If we were not conscious that what we think is the same as what we thought a moment before, all reproduction in the series of representations would be useless...The manifold of the representation would never...form a whole, since it would lack that unity which only consciousness can impart to it.[1]

The (2)/(3) distinction is clearly a delicate one, and in Kant's hands it crumbles. Concerning (2) he says:

When I seek to...represent to myself some particular number...the various manifold representations that are involved must be apprehended by me in thought one after the other. But if I were always to drop out of thought the preceding representations (...the units in the order represented), and did not reproduce them while advancing to those that follow, a complete representation would never be obtained.[2]

And his illustration of (3) is this:

If, in counting, I forget that the units, which now hover before me, have been added to one another in succession, I should never know that a total is being produced through this successive addition of unit to unit, and so would remain ignorant of the number.[3]

The two versions of the trio which I have quoted display certain differences. In the first version the term 'synthesis' dominates only item (2), while in the second version all three items are said to concern kinds of synthesis. This, I think, arises from sheer terminological indecision on Kant's part. Another difference is that item (3), which involves consciousness of unity in both versions, is said in the first to concern 'apperception' and in the second to concern recognition 'in a concept'. A tie-up is here presupposed between apperception and the official domain of concepts, viz. the understanding. When Kant speaks of 'apperception' he refers to that kind of self-conscious grasp of past and present states which requires and is required by an ability to use concepts; and this leads him sometimes to speak of 'apperception' where one might expect a stress rather on 'understanding'. Thus, immediately after the passage last quoted, he says: 'For the concept of the number is nothing but the consciousness of this unity of synthesis'.[1] He makes another remark which—though I do not pretend to understand it—seems also to reflect this sparing use of 'understanding'. This time he introduces it as an afterthought to what is said in terms of 'imagination' on one hand and 'apperception' on the other: 'The unity of apperception in relation to the synthesis of imagination is the understanding.'[2]

Here is Kant's next version of the trio:

[1] *Sense* represents appearances empirically in *perception*, [2] *imagination* in *association* (and reproduction), [3] *apperception* in the *empirical consciousness* of the identity of the reproduced representations with the appearances whereby they were given, that is, in recognition.[3]

Here again, (3) seems to have to do with our knowing that we are doing correctly the 'reproduction' which is the concern of (2). Notice, incidentally, that 'association' seems now to be shouldering 'reproduction' aside in (2), though we are not told whether or how they differ.

A little further on we meet the trio again, only this time imagination has spread to engulf (1) as well as (2):

There must...exist in us an active faculty for the synthesis of [the] manifold. To this faculty I give the title, imagination. [1] Its action, when immediately directed upon perceptions, I entitle apprehension. Since imagination has to bring the manifold of intuition into the form of an image, it must previously have taken the impressions up into its activity, that is, have apprehended them.[4]

Kant goes on to say that we can have 'an image and a connection of the impressions' only because

[2a] There exists a subjective ground which leads the mind to reinstate a preceding perception alongside the subsequent perception to which it has passed, and so to form whole series of perceptions. This is the reproductive faculty of imagination...[5]

But (2) is not yet complete, for Kant is now splitting up what he formerly called 'reproduction' into two parts: the calling up of one's past states, and the calling of them up in an orderly or principled fashion:

[2b] If, however, representations reproduced one another in any order, just as they happened to come together, this would not lead to any determinate

connection of them, but only to accidental collocations; and so would not give rise to any knowledge. Their reproduction must, therefore, conform to a rule, in accordance with which a representation connects in the imagination with some one representation in preference to another. This...is called the *association* of representations.[1]

Our current trio is completed by Kant's reference to (3) the 'apperception which must be added to pure imagination, in order to render its function intellectual'.[2] This time, however, (3) is not reached directly through the theme of consciousness of unity, but is attached awkwardly to the end of Kant's discussion of an entirely different topic.

The patchwork theory of Vaihinger and Kemp Smith throws some light on these passages about imagination; and it may even be possible to discover precisely and in detail what thoughts lie behind the neurotically inept exposition of the Transcendental Deduction. Such a discovery would probably not be worth the trouble.

ANALYTIC OF PRINCIPLES

10

SCHEMATISM

35 Concepts and schematism

The first chapter in the Analytic of Principles is called 'The Schematism of the Pure Concepts of Understanding'. In it Kant tries, by means of a general theory about how any concept is applied to its instances, to solve an alleged problem about the application of the categories in particular. He may not have intended to offer a general theory: it may be that, starting with his problem about the categories, he just drifted into saying about every concept what he initially intended to say about the categories alone. But I shall provisionally take it that the general theory is there in its own right, and not merely as a by-product of the problem about the categories.

Kant seeks to answer the following suspect question: 'Given that I possess a concept, how can I apply it to its instances?' His answer, his general theory of concept-application, says that a concept can be applied only with the aid of its *schema*, which is a 'representation of a universal procedure of imagination in providing an image for a concept'.[1] The nasty phrase 'representation of a universal procedure' just means 'rule'. The schema of the concept of a dog is 'a rule according to which my imagination can delineate the figure of a four-footed animal in a general manner, without limitation to any single determinate figure such as experience...actually presents.'[2] In fact, Kant says this about the concept of a dog rather than about that concept's schema. I shall explain later why.

Kant's theory of schemas—whether or not it ultimately works—does at least improve on most theories which link concepts with images. Instead of associating each concept with a single image, or with a set of exactly similar images, Kant's theory associates each concept with a rule for image-production. This, as he observes, saves him from a difficulty which is fatal to other theories.[3] If the concept of a dog, for instance, is to be associated with a specific kind of image, what kind could it be? It cannot be spaniels, or dachshunds, or borzois; nor can it be, as Locke said on a related matter, all and none of these at once. Admittedly, an image or mental picture need not be entirely specific: imagined things, like fictional things and unlike real ones, can disobey the law of excluded middle. But there are limits to this sort of in-determinacy. A mental picture of a dog so sketchy as to depict every sort of dog would also, necessarily, depict foxes and jackals. Kant avoids this impasse by associating each concept with a rule; for a rule can be specific enough to generate only images of dogs, while being complex enough to allow any detailed image of any particular kind of dog.

Kant's theory says that to be able to apply a concept one must know how to *make* something, namely images; which is, on the face of it, peculiar. Recognition is clearly relevant, but where does making come in? Kant has reasons for stressing construction at the expense of recognition in mathematics:[1] a triangle, say, should be thought of not as a figure *which looks like that* but as a figure *which you get when you do this*. But he seems not to have wished to carry this emphasis over directly from mathematics to concept-application generally.

The suggestion that one might make an image by following out a rule is also peculiar. If an activity is to be covered by rules, it must be one for which there is a technique, i.e. one which resolves into sub-activities. Could there be rules for imagining a chair as there can for making a chair? Apparently not, unless one counts such rules as: 'First imagine a chair-leg, then imagine another chair-leg, then...etc.' This 'rule', its oddity aside, seems very much less resplendent than the 'representation of a universal procedure' which Kant's theory requires. Perhaps this is why he says:

This schematism of our understanding...is an art concealed in the depths of the human soul, whose real modes of activity nature is hardly likely ever to allow us to discover.[2]

The claim that there is something which we do but which we cannot catch ourselves at because it lies too deep inspires as little confidence as does Locke's assurance that we do not usually observe our conversions of raw into interpreted sense-data only because we perform them 'so constantly and so quick'.[3]

Even if Kant's claim were that to be able to apply the concept of an *F* one must have rules for making actual *F*s rather than images of *F*s, he would still be hard put to it to state an appropriate rule. He would have to admit that I can apply the concept of a chair, say, without knowing any rules about the grain of wood or the temperature of glue. All he could insist on, then, would be an entirely non-technical rule such as 'Bring it about somehow that the end-product is a chair'. But if that is a rule, then so is 'Bring it about somehow that the end-product is an image of a chair'. Clearly, such rules derive from, and so cannot be prerequisites for, the recognition of chairs.

Still, why does the schematism theory favour imagined over actual instances of a concept? Kant thinks, as I have already mentioned, that imagination plays a vital mediatory role in the application of concepts to data because it is active like the understanding, yet like sensibility it deals in intuitions. But does not physical activity also have a foot in each camp? In carpentering and walking and blinking we actively bring about changes in our sensory states. The making of chairs, then, has the same double virtue as the imagining of chairs, namely that it is an activity which results in the occurrence of intuitions. Yet schemas are said to be rules for the production, specifically, of images.

Part of the explanation is as follows. Kant's theory implies not merely something of the form 'To be able to apply a concept one must have a rule for producing...' but also something stronger, of the form 'Every time one applies a concept one must actually produce...'. If recognition requires actual production and not just knowledge of how to produce, then for overwhelming practical reasons the requirement must be for the production of images only, if images will suffice to do what needs doing.

What *is* supposed to need doing?

36 How to apply concepts

Kant wants his schematism theory, I think, to explain how we are able to recognize, classify, describe. For example: I have no doubt that this thing here in front of me is a dog; but what, for me now, links *this* with other things which I have called 'dogs', in such a way that I am entitled to call this a dog too? Kant's answer is that I can link this dog with other dogs by conjuring up a mental picture of a dog and checking it against the object which I now see. I know that my mental picture is of a dog because I have produced it in accordance with the schema of the concept of a dog. If the thing in front of me is indeed a dog, then an adequate schema of the concept of a dog will generate—as well as many images which do not help me with my present problem—at least one image which corresponds closely enough to the object now before me to justify my going ahead and calling the object a dog.

If this is intended as a perfectly general technique for concept-application, then it fails on two counts. It says that I recognize something as a dog by checking it against an image of a dog. But (a) how do I know that the image 'corresponds closely enough' with the object in front of me to justify my calling the latter a dog? And, anyway, (b) how do I know that the image is an image of a dog? Any problem which I have about classifying this object with other dogs I ought also to have about (a) classifying this object with this image, i.e. seeing that they 'correspond closely enough' to one another, and about (b) classifying this image with other dogs, i.e. seeing that it is an image of a dog. To insert an intermediate image between a concept and a putative instance of it is only to replace one concept-application by two. For the single question 'Is that object a dog?' it substitutes the pair of questions 'Does this image correspond to that object?' and 'Is this image an image of a dog?'

Wittgenstein says something like this in his *Blue Book* where he points out that, considered as explaining our ability to apply colour-concepts, colour-samples in our pockets are as good as colour-samples in our heads.[1] This incidentally suggests a further reason, or motive, for taking schemas to concern imagined rather than real instances of concepts. If real instances would serve, then one way of deciding whether *x* is a chair would be to make a chair and compare it with *x*. An intermediary chair is no worse an aid to classification than an intermediary chair-image, but its futility is more obvious.

Wittgenstein's point can be generalized to show that there could not be a technique for concept-application as such. Instructions for how to apply a concept must be of the form 'If the situation is. . ., then apply the concept', with the blank filled by a description. In the case of the intermediate-image theory, the description has to do with classifying an image and checking it against something else; but in any theory the blank must be filled by some description, and knowing whether the description fits a given situation *is* applying a concept.

Ironically, this line of argument has never been better presented than by Kant himself. In a passage just before the schematism chapter, Kant distinguishes between the *understanding*, which he calls the faculty of rules or of relating concepts to other concepts, and the *judgment*, which is the faculty of applying concepts to their instances.[2] No rule, he says, can answer the question 'To which particular things does a concept apply?'

[If we] sought to give general instructions how we are to subsume under. . . rules [i.e. concepts], that is, to distinguish whether something does or does not come under them, that could only be by means of another rule. This in turn, for the very reason that it is a rule, again demands guidance from judgment [and so raises again any *general* problem there may be about how to apply concepts]. And thus it appears that, though understanding is capable of being instructed, and of being equipped with rules, judgment is a peculiar talent which can be practised only, and cannot be taught.[1]

In brief, there can be no technique for concept-application as such, since the implementing of a technique requires the application of concepts. (Kant tries to square this with his schematism theory by arguing that the latter has to do not with the whole range of concept-application but only with 'the employment of the few pure concepts of understanding that we possess', the employment, that is, of the categories.[2] If he were right about this, the present section would be beside the point.)

This insight of Kant's is revolutionary. When Körner says that Kant is concerned not only with *non-referential rules* which relate concepts to other concepts, but also with *referential rules* which relate concepts to their instances,[3] I think that he correctly describes the intention behind the general theory of schematism; but he does not remark that the very notion of a referential rule is illegitimate. A referential rule would presumably run like this:

> You may apply the concept *C* to a thing just so long as the thing is...

ending with some description. Such a rule, however, merely relates *C* to the concepts involved in the description; that is, it says

> You may apply *C* to a thing if you are also prepared to apply...to it.

But this is presumably a *non*-referential rule.

Any rule at all must relate some concepts or general terms to others. A rule may indeed show me how to apply some one of the terms in it, if I understand the grammar of the rule and know how to apply the other terms; and such a rule might be called referential for me. The phrase 'referential for *x*' can only describe a rule's relation to a given person at a given time; a rule cannot be just referential. All this is implied by Kant's calling the understanding the 'faculty of rules' and assigning to a different faculty altogether the application of concepts to particulars: there is no place here for 'referential rules'.

Not that Kant's terminology is stable. At first: 'We can reduce all acts of the understanding to judgments, and the understanding may therefore be represented as a faculty of judgment'. Later, the understanding is called a faculty of judgment and *also*, in the very same paragraph, a faculty of rules. But now Kant calls it a faculty of rules in order to *distinguish* it from something called 'the faculty of judgment'.[1]

This apparent shift arises mainly from Kant's starting with an ordinary use of 'judgment', according to which judgments comprise not only the singular 'That is an *F*' but also the general 'rule' 'All *F*s are *G*'; and then moving over to a restricted use according to which 'rules', even if they are still themselves counted as judgments, are not the business of the faculty of judgment. Now, Kant is entitled to distinguish between rule-like judgments and others, but not to say that the understanding is concerned solely with the former. Warnock speaks of Kant's 'illegitimately separating the application of concepts from having them';[2] and this underlies Kant's idea that the understanding is restricted to the use of concepts in 'rules'. By virtue of the understanding we possess concepts, and by means of the faculty of judgment we apply them to their instances.

This is unacceptable. I might possess a concept but be unable to apply it because it had no instances or because a sensory disability prevented me from recognizing its instances. But I could not possess a concept yet be unable to apply it because of an intellectual defect, a defect in my 'judgment' which is one of 'the higher faculties of knowledge'.[3] Having a concept involves being able both to use it in 'rules' and, under favourable sensory circumstances, to apply it to its instances. You will not credit me with having the concept of a dog just because I can state many general truths about dogs, such as that they are mammals, never laugh, have legs etc. If I can do this and yet—although not sensorily disabled—apply the word 'dog' to particular birds, humans, porpoises etc., and often apply 'not a dog' to particular dogs, you must conclude that I do not understand 'mammals', 'laugh', 'legs' etc. But in that case my stock of 'general truths about dogs' is like a parrot's repertoire: it is not evidence that I understand the word 'dog' in any way at all.

Still, Kant is right—as I have argued in §24—to insist that having a concept requires the ability to use it in 'rules'. And the implication of his terminology that this ability is sufficient as well as necessary for concept-possession is, though a mistake, trivial compared with his achievement in showing the importance of the distinction between 'rules' and other sorts of judgment. His discussion of this matter is an important anticipation of Wittgenstein's fertile treatment of rules and applications.[4]

Although Kant himself shows why there cannot be a technique for concept-application as such, I have taken his general theory of schematism as an attempt to describe such a technique. Perhaps I have been wrong. What Kant is presenting may be a technique for one kind of concept-application only—a technique which does not require any concept-applications of *that* kind. His technique can be implemented if one can apply concepts in two ways: (a) in knowing, of two items which are both present, that they have a certain relation to one another, and (b) in knowing that one has performed a certain kind of action correctly. Kant would be cleared of the charge of circularity if he were offering a technique only for the kind of concept-application involved in knowing that a present item is of a certain kind, i.e. is similar to certain absent items. Calling this last the *passive-absent* use of concepts, we might say that Kant's theory of schematism shows how it is compounded out of the *active-absent* use in which one knows that the image one has produced is of a certain kind, and the *passive-present* use in which one knows that a present image relates in a certain way to some other present item.

This hypothesis has its attractions. It represents Kant (i) as trying to state rules for only one species of concept-application; (ii) as exploiting two features of imagination which he often stresses—its activeness and its concern with what is absent;[1] and (iii) as having noticed the difference between classifying *the thing before one* and classifying *what one is doing*.[2] I have no evidence, however, that Kant had these points consciously in mind; and anyway the general theory of schematism is unacceptable even on this charitable interpretation. It is true that one may classify something one does, as a means to classifying something with which one is confronted: 'Is this the right fingering for F-sharp?' —'Hand me the flute...now *that* is F-sharp, and your fingers were in that position too, so you *were* fingering correctly for F-sharp'. But not every 'passive' recognition is based on the feel of a correct performance. Here again we confront the fact that the schematizing activities which Kant describes do not usually happen: there is no reason to say that they happen too deep in the soul for us to be aware of them.

Kant might reply that they must happen 'too deep' because they must happen. This would reflect an a priori demand for an explanation of our whole ability to classify and generalize—and that demand cannot be met. If the schematism theory is taken only as invoking two kinds of concept-application in order to explain a third, the situation changes. On that interpretation, the theory is not a doomed attempt to satisfy an unsatisfiable demand; but now it must be based upon the claim that concept-applications of the third kind are *empirically* known to consist in concept-applications of the other two kinds. There are no plausible reasons for saying that two kinds of concept-application require no techniques while the third *must* have one. Analogously, I know empirically that I go through certain sub-procedures each time I clumsily determine the figure to which a syllogism belongs; but if on some occasion I classified a syllogism without being aware of these sub-procedures, I should not be entitled to insist that I *must* nevertheless have gone through them at a level too deep for empirical consciousness.

37 The 'problem' about category-application

At the start of the schematism chapter Kant raises a problem about the application of categories. He says that 'no special discussion...is required' of the application of empirical concepts, and gives the impression that the whole chapter will be devoted to solving his special problem about categories, which is as follows:– A concept must have something in common with that to which it is applied— 'the representation of the object must be *homogeneous* with the concept'.[1] But the categories have nothing empirical in them and are therefore 'quite heterogeneous from empirical intuitions'. How, then, can they be applied *to* empirical things or to our intuitions of empirical things?

The problem, it seems, concerns the relation of concepts to (intuitions of) empirical things. But later Kant says that the problem does not arise for empirical concepts because in their case 'the concepts through which the object is thought in [its] general [aspects] are not so utterly distinct and heterogeneous from those which represent it *in concreto* [that is, in all its detail]'.[2] This tells a different story, for it says that a general empirical concept is not worryingly heterogeneous from a highly specific empirical *concept*; the word 'those' must refer back to the word 'concepts'. What is it for a general concept to be homogeneous with a more specific one which falls under it? The concept of a dog is 'homogeneous with' the concept of a loyal though bad-tempered borzoi with an off-white coat and bad teeth, in the sense that the former concept is included in the latter. But then the category of substance, say, is in *that* sense 'homogeneous with' the concept of a substance which is spherical, orange-coloured, sweet-tasting, and rich in vitamin C. So what is the problem? One might say that 'dog' gives a bigger proportion of the total description of any dog than 'substance' does of the total description of any substance; and in the passage cited

Kant does take homogeneity as a matter of degree (*nicht so unter-schieden und heterogen*). But this reduces to nonsense everything else Kant says about his problem over category-application. In fact, the above passage notwithstanding, his basic concern is not with a dif-ference of degree: the problem is not 'There is a specially large gap between the categories and detailed concepts of their instances' but rather 'There is a special kind of gap between the categories and intuitions of their instances'.

What special kind of gap can this be? How can any concept, even an empirical one, be homogeneous with intuitions of its instances? If Kant took concepts to be images, he might think that empirical concepts, unlike categories, are 'homogeneous with' intuitions in the sense of resembling them; but since he does not take concepts to be images the answer must lie elsewhere. The only other sense for 'homo-geneous' which suggests itself is that in which the concept of roundness is homogeneous with an intuition of a plate if and only if the concept applies to the plate. At the start of the chapter, Kant does give precisely this meaning to 'homogeneous':

In all subsumptions of an object under a concept, the representation [= intui-tion] of the object must be *homogeneous* with the concept; in other words, the concept must contain something which is represented in the object that is to be subsumed under it. This, in fact, is what is meant by the expression, 'an object is contained under a concept'.[1]

But empirical things are contained under the categories, i.e. the categories do apply to them; and so—if we are to take seriously Kant's phrases 'in other words' and 'that is what is meant'—the categories are homogeneous with empirical intuitions. The problem about hetero-geneity has again eluded us.

Warnock offers another interpretation of Kant's talk about homo-geneity:

I think Kant's point is only that the roundness of a thing is a sensible ('intui-table') *characteristic* of it—I can *see* that a thing is round, and can be taught to use round' by having round things *pointed out* to me.[2]

Warnock compares this with such concepts as those of causality and possibility:

'This is the cause' is not like 'This is the football'; a possible President does not, at the moment of electoral triumph, lose one characteristic, possibility, and acquire a new one, actuality. What is referred to by...'cause', or 'possible', is in no case a thing that I can look at, point to, 'intuit'...[3]

The great merit of this interpretation is that it presents Kant as having a problem about the categories and about some empirical concepts but not all. I have taken the theory of schematism to be relevant to all concepts, on the strength of Kant's using the concept of a dog as an example; but Warnock can argue that the concept of a dog raises a problem which is also raised by *some* other empirical concepts and by the categories. His point is that the canine things, unlike the round things, are not marked off by a unique characteristic or set of characteristics; and in this respect 'dog' is like 'cause' and unlike 'round'.

This is an ingenious and sympathetic interpretation, but it does not point to a single prima facie problem which arises with 'cause' and 'dog' but not with 'round'. 'Causal relatedness is not a sensible characteristic of pairs of events' and 'Canineness is not a sensible characteristic of objects' do perhaps both express truths, but the truths are of quite different kinds. The truth about 'cause' is a vague one about the generality, and the distance from raw intuitions, of the concept of cause; while the truth about 'canine' is just that its meaning has a family-resemblance pattern. The difference between the two can be brought out by substituting 'dog' for 'cause' in Warnock's remark that 'What is referred to by..."cause"...is in no case a thing that I can look at, point to, "intuit"'.

Warnock and I disagree about the scope, and about the disreputability, of Kant's 'problem'. We agree, however, that Kant does not solve whatever problem he has. His solution of the hopelessly confused 'problem' about *category*-application is as follows.

A schema is a kind of counterpart to a concept, and it involves imagination. Since imagination produces intuitions, which for humans are necessarily temporal, schemas—even schemas of atemporal concepts—are all somehow temporal. The schema of the concept of substance, say, is a rule not for producing images of substances but for doing something—Kant does not make clear what—which involves imagination and therefore involves time. Each category, then, has an associated schema which carries temporality with it. This schema can 'mediate the subsumption of the appearances under the category'[1] because

[it] is so far homogeneous with the category...in that it is universal and rests upon an a priori rule [and] it is so far homogeneous with appearance, in that [it involves time and] time is contained in every empirical representation of the manifold.[2]

A schema seems to be a kind of concept. Later on, Kant says of a certain principle: 'In the principle itself we do indeed make use of the category, but in applying it to appearances we substitute for it its schema.'[1] The schema of any category, then, is just the category itself with the condition of temporality added. The schema of the category of causality-and-dependence which is associated with conditional judgments is the concept of conditionality-in-time, i.e. of something's being a sufficient condition for the subsequent occurrence of something else. The schema of the category of subsistence-and-inherence which is associated with subject-predicate judgments is the concept of a subject-in-time, i.e. a substance or thing which endures. (The schema of any empirical concept is just the concept itself; hence the identification of the concept of a dog with its schema.)

So the categories, although they have 'nothing empirical' in them, can nevertheless be brought to bear upon intuitions; for even if the naked categories cannot be applied to intuitions, at least their schemas can be so applied because they contain the empirical element of temporality.

This solves nothing. If one is wondering how the concept C can be applied to members of the class of Bs, it is no solution to say that the naked concept C does not apply to the Bs but that the specially adapted concept CB does apply to them. No difficulty about calling cats 'carnivores' could be overcome by calling them 'feline carnivores' instead. Calling something a feline carnivore is just calling it a carnivore and a cat; and saying of something that the concept of conditionality-in-time applies to it is just saying that the concept of conditionality applies to it and that it is temporal. The incoherence of Kant's problem about category-application is matched by the vacuity of its supposed solution.

Underlying all this there is a modest point which, had it not been swamped by mistakes and technicalities, might have come to something. It is just that the categories are extremely general concepts whose application to the empirical world is of no interest unless accompanied by an application of other concepts as well; and since these will always include temporal ones we might as well adjoin temporality to each of the categories from the outset. In a later chapter Kant expresses some such thought as this when he says:

The categories have this peculiar feature, that only in virtue of the general condition of sensibility [i.e. temporality] can they possess a determinate meaning and relation to any object. Now when this condition has been omitted from the pure category, it can contain nothing but the logical function for bringing the manifold under a concept. By means of this function or form of the concept, thus taken by itself, we cannot in any way know and distinguish what object comes under it, since we have abstracted from the sensible condition through which alone objects can come under it. Consequently, the categories require, in addition to the pure concept of understanding, determinations of their application to sensibility in general (schemata).[1]

In this passage, however, Kant also seems to suggest that the addition of temporality to a category is not merely necessary but sufficient for us to be able to 'know and distinguish what object comes under it'; and this is false. Furthermore, after speaking of the 'condition of sensibility [without which a category cannot] possess a *determinate* meaning and relation to any object', Kant speaks of 'the sensible condition through which alone objects can come under [a category]'. This, if I understand it, is a move from 'Without the addition of temporality, the categories say uselessly little about the empirical world' to 'Without the addition of temporality, the categories do not apply to the empirical world'. The former is true; the latter generates the 'problem' which Kant tries to solve in the schematism chapter.

It is time to correct my statement in §26 that Kant identifies two of the concepts read off from the table of judgments with our ordinary concepts of cause and substance. What he in fact says is that these are the *schemas* of concepts which are derived from the table. He is still wrong, though, for the concept of conditionality-in-time covers not merely the concept of cause but also other conditional concepts which we use in the temporal world, for example in threats; and something can be a subject-in-time without being a substance by any ordinary criterion of substantiality. His account of what we get by adding temporality to some of the other categories is even less fortunate.

11

CAUSAL NECESSITY

38 Kant and Hume on causality

Over the concept of cause, Kant is no Humean. Empiricist analyses must fail, he says, because 'the concept of a cause involves the character of necessity, which no experience can yield'.[1] Yet he describes the schema of the concept of cause thus:

> The schema of cause...is the real upon which, whenever posited, something else always follows. It consists, therefore, in the succession of the manifold, in so far as that succession is subject to a rule.[2]

This sounds like Hume's view that causal connection is a logical construction out of temporal succession and regularity. Perhaps, however, Kant takes obedience to a 'rule' to involve necessity as well as regularity. Or perhaps he thinks that the schema of cause—which is the category in its empirically usable form—need not involve the necessity which is involved in the category; for he agrees that this necessity is one 'which no experience can yield' and which is therefore, presumably, irrelevant to the details of how the concept of cause is empirically used. Kant's position is described by Körner thus:

> While Kant insists that the notion of causality is not equivalent to that of regular succession, he holds that unless it implied this notion it could not refer to anything in perception,[3]

and, we might add, he ought to hold that this implication is all we need for deciding what is causally connected with what.

Let us leave the schema. I want to know why Kant thinks there is necessity in the category—why he thinks that causal sequences are necessary as well as regular and that Hume must therefore have missed something.

One of his points against Hume is clearly valid. We do say things like 'The dam was bound to collapse', 'The water must boil soon', 'The passion-fruit cannot flourish in this climate'. Hume explains this sort of necessitarian talk as a projection onto the world of our own intellectual compulsions. Having seen many Fs followed by Gs and none not so followed, we find that when confronted by a new F we cannot help expecting a *G*; but, because 'the mind has a great propensity to spread itself on objects',[1] we say 'A *G* has to follow' instead of 'I have to expect a *G*'. This puts our reasonable expectations on a level with compulsive handwashing, as though someone who was free of these compulsions—someone who denied that the dam was bound to collapse or that the balloon had to go up—would be more rational than the rest of us. Kant protests:

The concept of cause..., which expresses the necessity of an event under a presupposed condition, would be false if it rested only on an arbitrary subjective necessity, implanted in us, of connecting certain empirical representations according to the rule of causal relation. I would not then be able to say that the effect is connected with the cause in the object, that is to say, necessarily, but only that I am so constituted that I cannot think this representation otherwise than as thus connected. This is exactly what the sceptic most desires. For if this be the situation,...[there would not] be wanting people who would refuse to admit this subjective necessity...Certainly a man cannot dispute with anyone regarding that which depends merely on the mode in which he is himself organised.[2]

I give this round to Kant. But Hume sometimes works not at discrediting but merely at analysing our necessitarian talk, showing it to be short-hand for talk about certain kinds of observable regularity. Kant still disagrees, for in his view observable regularities cannot include that 'necessity which no experience can yield'.

This seems to say that Hume uses 'cause' too generously, classifying as causal some sequences which, since they are not necessary, are not causal but merely regular. Yet Kant does not try to refute Hume by producing counter-examples; and he is certainly right not to do so, for, while counter-examples could tell against a particular empiricist analysis, they could not support Kant's claim that an empiricist analysis is the wrong thing to look for in the first place. In saying this I am not making the obvious point that to refute one execution of a programme is not conclusively to discredit the programme as such. Certainly, someone who thinks that God's existence can be proved, say, need not retract this just because particular arguments for God's existence have been shown invalid; but that is *not* my point. A programme may be to some extent discredited if specific executions of it fail: as flaws are discovered in argument after argument for God's existence, we may reasonably come to suspect that the job cannot be done. But—and this *is* my point—*empirically known* counter-examples to specific empiricist analyses have *no bearing at all* on the empiricist programme.[3] Maybe it is impossible to analyse causality solely in terms of observable features of the world; but this cannot be shown, or even suggested, by pointing out that a particular analysis treats as causal something which we know by its observable features not to be causal. For example, it has been said that Hume must take 'Whenever the 5 o'clock whistle blows at Manchester the workers in Glasgow down tools' as reporting a causal connection, which it obviously does not. But an empiricist can ask how we know there is no causal connection here, and—without making his analysis any less empiricist—amend it in the light of our answer.

If Kant does not attack Hume with crisp counter-examples, it is because he knows that they are not suitable weapons in this kind of battle.

What does Kant mean, then, when he says that there is a notion of causal necessity which must elude any empiricist analysis? One standard answer to this is as follows. In the 'Principles' chapter Kant undertakes to prove that a self-conscious being must have experience of a world which is causally ordered. Hume, on the other hand, gives the impression that our experience might at any moment turn chaotic: in his picture of the human condition, unlike Kant's, causal order looks like an optional extra. Now, it is often said that Kant asserts, against Hume, that *Causal laws are necessary* in the sense that (a) *There must be (known) causal laws* if there is to be self-consciousness. This, however, is very different from saying that *Causal laws are necessary* in the sense that (b) *Every causal law expresses some non-empirical kind of necessity.* When Kant says that 'the very concept of a cause...contains the concept of a necessity of connection with an effect',[1] he is surely making a (b)-type complaint against Hume's analysis of cause; but (a) brings against Hume a charge which is compatible with any analysis, namely that he has exaggerated the dispensability—or failed to stress the indispensability—of causal order.

Kant sometimes seems to identify these two complaints,[2] and some commentators have followed suit. Walsh separates them, but in my view not sharply enough:

Kant is emphatically not saying that some kind of inner necessity binds cause to effect...The necessity which marks the causal relation is...derived wholly from the necessity of the general principle of causality itself.[3]

But if all that is at issue is 'the necessity of the causal principle itself', i.e. the indispensability of causal order, then the phrase 'the necessity which marks the causal relation' is, at least, very misleading. As for those who entirely fail to distinguish 'Causal laws express necessity' from 'All events must fall under causal laws': perhaps they have noticed that Hume discussed the two together,[1] and have not understood why.

There is a special reason why Kant should fail to make the distinction. It concerns his doctrine of transcendental synthesis. I showed in §30 that Kant construes this sometimes as a partial analysis of the notion of a unified mind and sometimes as the theory that every mind is unified by an atemporal intellectual act. Only on the former interpretation does the doctrine embody genuine insights, but it is the latter—which is one version of the genetic interpretation—which concerns us now.

On this genetic interpretation of it, Kant's doctrine of transcendental synthesis (a) purports to say how unified minds come into being, (b) takes the understanding to be kind of synthesizing mechanism, and (c) makes a synthetic claim about how the synthesizing mechanism does in fact work. Here are the three interwoven:

An understanding…through whose representation the objects of the representation should at the same time exist would not require, for the unity of consciousness, a special act of synthesis of the manifold. For the human understanding, however, which thinks only, and does not intuit, that act is necessary.[2]

In the Transcendental Deduction, then, as in the Aesthetic, Kant exhibits three bad tendencies: to replace the analysis of a concept by claims about the genesis of its instances, to reify a faculty or capacity, and to seek an a priori guarantee for a synthetic conclusion. These can be seen as facets of a single mistake: in the Aesthetic, the mistake is that of saying that temporality is imposed on all our intuitions by inner sense; in the Transcendental Deduction, it is that of saying that certain other kinds of order are imposed on all our intuitions by the understanding. Now, in the 'Principles' chapter Kant will argue that causal order is amongst these other kinds; and so it is not surprising to find him saying that there is causal order in our experience because the understanding put it there:

The order and regularity in the appearances, which we entitle *nature*, we ourselves introduce. We could never find them in appearances, had not we ourselves, or the nature of our mind, originally set them there.[3]

The view of causal order as imposed upon experience appears also here:

That nature should direct itself according to our subjective ground of apperception, and should indeed depend upon it in respect of its conformity to law, sounds very strange and absurd. But when we consider that this nature is not a thing in itself but is merely an aggregate of appearances..., we shall not be surprised that we can discover it only...in that unity on account of which alone it can be entitled object of all possible experience, that is, nature. Nor shall we be surprised that just for this very reason this unity can be known a priori, and therefore as necessary.[1]

The second sentence of this passage is unexceptionable: it says that 'nature' = 'discoverable nature' and that what is discoverable by a mind must conform to the conditions for mental identity. The trouble is in the first sentence, where Kant says not just that the knowable world must have a certain unity but that unity is *imposed* upon the world by the mind. The imposition account of causal order finds expression in other passages too.[2]

Kant, I believe, persists in the genetic interpretation of 'transcendental synthesis' largely because it depicts causal order as stamped upon the phenomenal world by the human mind. One can feel him gloating over this picture when he describes the understanding as 'the lawgiver of nature',[3] or compares his 'new mode of thought', with that of Copernicus,[4] or condescends to Hume:

Since he could not explain...[etc., etc.] and since it never occurred to him that the understanding might itself, perhaps, through these concepts, be the author of the experience in which its objects are found...[etc., etc.].[5]

He likes the imposition account of causal order not only for its ingenuity but also for its shock-effect. I have quoted him as saying that it 'sounds very strange and absurd', and there is also this:

However exaggerated and absurd it may sound, to say that the understanding is itself the source of the laws of nature, and so of its formal unity, such an assertion is none the less correct,[6]

and this:

The question...arises, how can it be conceivable that nature should have to proceed in accordance with categories which...do not model themselves upon its pattern...The solution of this seeming enigma is as follows....[7]

The imposition account is relevant to the necessity of causes, as follows. From the mere fact that a knowable world must be causally ordered, nothing follows about whether the concept of cause involves a non-empirical kind of necessity. But if the known world is causally ordered because order is imposed on experience by the understanding, it follows that causal laws express 'necessity' in the sense that they speak not just of what does happen, but of what is transcendentally made to happen, in the known world.

Kant does not unambiguously accept this argument. Here, for example, he seems to reject it:

Pure understanding is not...in a position, through mere categories, to prescribe to appearances any a priori laws other than those which are involved...in the conformity to law of all appearances in space and time. Special laws, as concerning those appearances which are empirically determined, cannot in their specific character be *derived* from the categories, although they are one and all subject to them. To obtain any knowledge whatsoever of these special laws, we must resort to experience.[1]

What is it for individual causal laws to be 'subject to' but not 'derived from' the general lawlikeness which is 'prescribed' by the understanding? The thoroughly ambiguous passage[2] on A 92 = B 125 does not answer this, nor does Kant's remark: 'All empirical laws are only special determinations of the pure laws of understanding, under which, and according to the norm of which, they first become possible.'[3]

Kant naturally wishes to deny that 'The world obeys laws' entails the laws which the world obeys. But his picture of the understanding as 'the lawgiver of nature' credits the understanding not just with insisting that nature shall obey some laws but with prescribing which laws nature shall obey. This, I think, is why he more than once says that particular causal laws are 'special determinations'[4] of the pure laws of the understanding; and it also explains the following passage:

The laws of nature,...without exception, stand under higher principles of understanding. They simply apply the latter to special cases [in the field] of appearance. These principles alone supply the concept which contains the condition, and as it were the exponent, of a rule in general. What experience gives is the instance which stands under the rule.[5]

Again, just before a reference to 'a principle...which has its seat in the understanding', Kant says that Hume was wrong 'in inferring from the contingency of our determination *in accordance with the law* the contingency of the *law* itself';[6] and in this passage the phrase 'the law' apparently refers not to the principle that everything has a cause but to a specific law about the melting of wax.

Kant's belief that each causal law involves necessity, then, seems to be nourished by his belief that the known world's order is imposed upon it by the understanding.

Kant holds a view which will be familiar to readers of Popper:[7]

rather than observing the world passively, waiting for it to suggest causal laws to us, we take the offensive by formulating hypotheses which jump ahead of the data, and testing them. In his best passage to this effect, Kant's main thesis is that our particular observations must be underpinned by 'principles of reason', and crucially by the principle that there is a comprehensive causal order of some sort. But when he speaks of experimenting in accordance with a 'previously thought-out plan', he must have in mind the testing of specific hypotheses: while the principle that there is causal order in the word does not dictate an experimental 'plan', a specific hypothesis may do just that. This is what he says:

Reason has insight only into that which it produces after a plan of its own, and...it must not allow itself to be kept, as it were, in nature's leading-strings, [but must itself constrain] nature to give answer to questions of reason's own determining. Accidental observations, made in obedience to no previously thought-out plan, can never be made to yield a necessary law, which alone reason is concerned to discover. Reason, holding in one hand its principles, according to which alone concordant appearances can be admitted as equivalent to laws, and in the other hand the experiment which it has devised in conformity with these principles, must approach nature in order to be taught by it. It must not, however, do so in the character of a pupil who listens to everything that the teacher chooses to say, but of an appointed judge who compels the witnesses to answer questions which he has himself formulated.[1]

This view about how hypothesis relates to experiment can be made to sound like the thesis that causal order is imposed by the understanding: for example, each might be expressed in the words 'We bring laws to the world rather than drawing laws from it'. Furthermore, each runs counter to Hume who certainly did underplay the active, hypothesis-forming aspects of scientific endeavour. Kant may have tended to confuse the two views, but they are in fact distinct. The Popperian thesis concerns the making of bold conjectures and their testing by deliberate experiment; such familiar procedures are a world away from the mysterious synthesizing act postulated by the imposition doctrine.

39 Necessity and universality

I have presented four aspects of Kant's opposition to Hume:

(1) He says that 'X must result in Y' need not be an expression of the speaker's own inner compulsions. This is correct, but it does not show that the 'must' is a non-empirical one.

(2) He moves, perhaps, from 'There must be causal laws' to 'Each

causal law expresses some sort of non-empirical necessity'. To do this is to move illegitimately from a statement about the indispensability of causal laws to one about the meaning of 'causal law'.

(3) He is encouraged by the imposition interpretation of 'There must be causal laws' to think that each causal law expresses some sort of necessity. Perhaps the one does imply the other, but the imposition account is itself unacceptable.

(4) He sees further than Hume into the place of hypothesis-formation in science, and is, perhaps, inclined to connect this insight with the imposition account of causal order.

These are miserable bases for the claim that empiricist analyses of cause are bound to fail. For (2) arrives at it by an invalid move from a true premiss, and (3) by a valid move from a false premiss; while (1) and (4) are altogether irrelevant to it.

Kant's necessitarianism, however, also has a fifth source which is hinted at throughout the *Critique* and more than hinted at here:

[1] If we [were to say] that experience continually presents examples of... regularity among appearances and so affords abundant opportunity of abstracting the concept of cause, and at the same time of verifying the objective validity of such a concept, we should be overlooking the fact that the concept of cause can never arise in this manner...[2] For this concept makes strict demand that something, *A*, should be such that something else, *B*, follows from it *necessarily and in accordance with an absolutely universal rule*. [3] Appearances do indeed present cases from which a rule can be obtained according to which something usually happens, but they never prove the sequence to be *necessary*. [4] To the synthesis of cause and effect there belongs a dignity which cannot be empirically expressed, namely, that the effect not only succeeds upon the cause, but that it is posited *through* it and arises *out of* it. [5] Strict universality, also, is never a characteristic of empirical rules; they can acquire through induction only comparative universality...[1]

Sentences (1) and (2) seem to voice the old accusation—which Kant has so far failed to justify—that the necessity of causes must elude Hume's kind of analysis. The stressed phrase 'necessarily and in accordance with an absolutely universal rule' seems to mean 'not only in accordance with an absolutely universal rule (for which Hume can allow) but also necessarily (for which he cannot)'. But sentence (3) hints that there is an issue about universality after all, for it accuses Hume of fobbing us off with regularities which 'usually' hold. There is even a hint that the issue over universality *is* the issue over necessity; a regularity which 'usually' holds is treated as though it were the obvious antithesis to a regularity which 'necessarily' holds. This suggests that only a necessary universal statement can be true with no exceptions at all; and a similar suggestion is carried by the claim in sentence (5) that universality, like necessity, is unattainable by purely empirical means. In Kemp Smith's translation, (5) reads 'This strict universality of the rule is never...etc.', which positively *identifies* the necessity which is implied in (4) with the universality which is explicitly discussed in (5). But Kemp Smith's use of 'This', like his omission of 'also', has no warrant in the German.[1] Still, Kant does seem to assume in the above passage that necessity and strict universality are, as he says elsewhere, 'inseparable from one another'.[2] Obviously, a universal statement which is necessary is a fortiori true, and so has no exceptions; but Kant seems to think that, conversely, a universal statement can be true without exceptions only if it is necessary. Since 'true without exceptions' just means 'true', this amounts to saying that every non-necessary universal statement is false; which is implausible.

Its plausibility is not increased by Kant's use, above and in the passage next quoted, of the word 'strict'. We can of course use 'universally true' in a sense which is so strict, i.e. narrow, that a statement counts as universally true only if it cannot have exceptions; just as we can use 'father' so strictly, i.e. narrowly, that a man counts as a father only if he has at least three offspring. But Kant—like Berkeley before him[3]— seems to confuse this with the quite different kind of strictness which consists in a word's being used with careful attention to its proper meaning.

Now, consider the following passage:

Experience never confers on its judgments true or strict, but only assumed and comparative *universality*, through induction. We can properly only say, there-fore, that, so far as we have hitherto observed, there is no exception to this or that rule. If, then, a judgment is thought with strict universality, that is, in such manner that no exception is allowed as possible, it is not derived from experience, but is valid absolutely a priori. Empirical universality is only an arbitrary extension of a validity holding in most cases to one which holds in all...When, on the other hand, strict universality is essential to a judgment, this indicates a special source of knowledge, namely, a faculty of a priori knowledge. Necessity and strict universality are thus sure criteria of a priori knowledge, and are inseparable from one another.[4]

How does Kant get from 'a judgment [which] is *thought* with strict universality' to one which 'is *valid* absolutely a priori'? And is he really saying that we have 'a priori *knowledge*' of causal laws? These and other questions come crowding it; but I wish to explore just one thing in this protean passage, namely Kant's reference to 'a judgment [which] is thought with strict universality, that is, in such manner that no exception is allowed as possible'. If he is suggesting that it is in order for a scientist to protect his hypotheses by insisting that no exception is to be 'allowed as possible', then he is wrong. I think, however, that his point is a different and subtler one, which gives, at last, a valid reason for saying that Hume is committed to some kind of permissiveness about 'strict universality'. I shall try to explain.

Hume, like most of us, thought that a lawlike statement which proves false in even a single instance ought to be dropped: (a) because it has, or could be made to have, an unlimited number of counter-instances; and (b) because the facts it covers are also covered by some law—perhaps not yet formulated—which has no counter-instances at all. But (a) and (b) are contingent matters. Suppose they were false. Suppose, for example, that God told us that the best science the world admits of is one consisting of universal statements every one of which is falsified in a few, but only a few, instances. Should we then despair of having a genuine science at all? It would surely be more sensible to settle for weakly quantified science, i.e. one whose hypotheses all used a quantifier with the force of 'For all but a very small number of values of x, . . .'. That, at any rate, ought to be Hume's choice. Given his account of what causal laws are and why they are useful, he should say that a weakly quantified science could serve us in the same way, and nearly as well, as one consisting of genuinely universal statements. He might concede a modest loss of utility: predictions might be slightly less confident, explanations less satisfying. But he would have to allow that genuine predictions and explanations could be given in terms of a weakly quantified science. For him, all this must be a matter of degree: if God tells us that the best laws we can find will have just fifty known exceptions each, then things are moderately bad; if He tells us that the best laws we can find will have just one known exception each, then things are only one-fiftieth as bad. Strict universality is desirable, but only as the limit of something which we want in as high a degree as possible.

For Kant, on the other hand, a great gulf separates exceptionless universal statements from ones which have a single counter-instance. I think he regards the difference between one counter-instance and two (or fifty) as being of no theoretical importance: the very first counter-instance does the crucial damage. This is because it is essential to the notions of *explanation*, of something's being so *because* something else is so, of an event's *arising out of* another event, that all these must be backed by absolutely universal rules. For example, to say 'An F occurred at t_2 because a G occurred at t_1 and *nearly* every occurrence of a G is followed by the occurrence of an F' is not to give an explanation at all. The flaw in Hume's position—I think Kant thinks—is that he cannot do justice to this fact: his only reason for connecting 'explain', 'because' etc. with exceptionless rules is his contingent belief that there are such rules, and that any rule which does have one exception can be made to have many. Because he thinks that causality can be understood in purely empirical terms, Hume cannot attach philosophical importance to the difference between a rule which always holds and one which nearly always holds.

It might be misleading, but it would not be absurd, to express this point in necessitarian terms; and it concerns a feature of Hume's position which Kant, with his rigorist cast of mind, would certainly have condemned if he had noticed it. I think that he did notice it, and that the preceding two paragraphs do explain his linking of 'strict universality' with necessity, as expressed in such phrases as 'a judgment [which] is thought with strict universality, that is, in such manner that no exception is allowed as possible'.

Kant, then, has pointed to an interesting feature of Hume's position; but I think he is wrong to complain about it. The admission into one's science of statements of the form 'For all but about seven values of x, ...' need not involve a loss of intellectual respectability. I have argued elsewhere that established scientific procedures—especially in connection with unrepeatable experiments—positively require a preparedness to adopt a weakly quantified science.[1]

12

THE AXIOMS, ANTICIPATIONS, AND POSTULATES

40 The 'System of all Principles': preliminaries

The Analytic is divided like this:

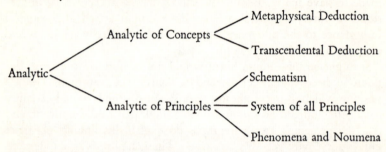

I need not offer a separate treatment of the chapter on phenomena and noumena. Nor shall I discuss the appendix to the Analytic of Principles: this is an eight-page passage entitled 'The Amphiboly of the Concepts of Reflection', followed by a twenty-three page 'Note' thereon; it criticizes Leibniz, though not on the points which make him most interesting today, and ends with a fourfold 'division of the concept of *nothing*'.[1] So there remains only the chapter whose full title is 'System of all Principles of Pure Understanding'.

In this chapter Kant undertakes to prove some a priori 'principles' involving the categories. Here, for the first time, ·we must attend to the features which distinguish the categories from one another, and not just to the categorial status which they are supposed to share.

Kant tries to impose upon the chapter a shape and unity which do not arise naturally from its contents. His naive architectonic, which is here at its worst, must be understood and disposed of if the chapter's real contents are to be grasped.

Kant's terminology is preposterous. The a priori principles about the categories of quantity are called the *Axioms of Intuition*; while the categories of quality are dealt with in the *Anticipations of Perception*, those of relation in the *Analogies of Experience*, and those of modality in the *Postulates of Empirical Thought*. The terms 'Axiom' and 'Postulate' are at least roughly equivalent to '(first) principle'; but Kant's defence of 'Analogies'[1] is absurd, and his use of 'Anticipations'[2] is based on a misapplication of the dubious distinction between the form and the matter of experience. All these daunting labels are best regarded as arbitrary, undescriptive, proper names.

One would expect Kant to present twelve principles, grouped into four trios; but in fact he does no such thing. The 'Analogies of Experience' are indeed three statements, to the effect that all experience must fall under the categories of substance, of cause, of community; and the 'Postulates of Empirical Thought' are also three in number. But under each of the headings 'Axioms of Intuition' and 'Anticipations of Perception' there is only a single a priori principle. Kant describes the single principle which he offers in each of these cases as 'the principle of' the Axioms or the Anticipations. He is apparently trying to suggest that for each trio of categories he has three statements plus an underlying 'principle'; but this picture is spoiled by his failure to produce three Anticipations, and by his admission that 'There are no axioms [of intuition] in the strict meaning of the term'.[3] It is further spoiled by the Analogies and the Postulates. These are genuine trios, as I have remarked, but Kant cannot produce convincing 'principles of' them. For the Postulates he does not even try; and his 'principle of' the Analogies is only an anaemic semi-substitute for the trio, which seems to be included only to preserve a principle-plus-trio structure.

In short, for quantity and quality all the work is done by the 'principle', while for relation and modality it is done by the trio. The reason is simple: there is a trio of statements in just those cases where there is a genuine trio of categories. The categories of quality—reality, limitation and negation—do not form a genuine trio because, as I showed in §22, limitation is spurious. As for the categories of quantity: there are three of these all right, but in the 'Principles' chapter Kant palms off something else in their place. The categories of quantity have to do with questions like 'Are all the Fs G, or only some of them, or only one of them?'; but in this chapter what comes under the heading 'quantity' bears rather on questions like 'How much is there? and 'How big is it? and 'How long did it last?' This represents a radical shift from 'quantity' as involving all/some/one to 'quantity' as involving, in Kant's phrase, 'the mathematics of appearances'.[4] In B, Kant makes a perfunctory attempt to show that this is not just a pun on 'quantity' by remarking that 'the concept of a *number*...belongs to the category of totality'.[5] This is feeble. Numerical concepts do involve totality; but so does the concept of cause, yet Kant does not introduce that under the heading of 'quantity'.

Yet another way in which the chapter goes awry is that the Postulates of Empirical Thought, which ought to be 'principles', i.e. statements, are in fact only definitions. Kant himself admits that 'the principles of modality are nothing but explanations of the concepts of possibility, actuality, and necessity, in their empirical employment',[1] and gives a lame excuse for their being no more than this. Furthermore, since a category 'in [its] empirical employment' is just a schema, these definitions or 'explanations' of the modal categories[2] ought already to have occurred in the schematism chapter; but they have not, as I shall later show.

Kant's 'Refutation of Idealism' is placed, for a silly reason, in the middle of his discussion of the Postulates. In fact, it has more in common with the second Analogy of Experience; but I shall discuss it on its own. For the rest, the Postulates can be dealt with right away.

Kant says that the concept of *possibility* in its empirical employment is the concept of consistency with 'the formal conditions of experience'; that *actuality* is the concept of 'that which is bound up with the material conditions of experience'; and that *necessity* is the concept of being entailed by the 'universal conditions of experience'. The 'formal [or universal] conditions of experience' in terms of which necessity and possibility a. explained are just those general truths about intuition and thought which Kant hopes he has proved in the Aesthetic and Analytic. Thus a proposition is 'necessary' in the present sense if it is synthetic and a priori, and it is 'possible' if it is not in conflict with anything synthetic and a priori. The account which Kant gives here of 'actuality' is clearly intended to repeat and reinforce his transcendental idealism.[3]

He apparently thinks that 'necessary' and 'possible' can be applied to the empirical world only if they are used in these special senses. But an empirical state of affairs can, after all, be properly described as *logically* possible. Connected with this point there is an oddity about the concept of necessity. Kant normally assumes that what one applies to empirical data is not a category itself but something narrower.[4] For example, causality is a special case of conditionality; substantiality is a special case of subject-hood; and the concept of possibility in its empirical employment is a special case of—is narrower or stronger than—logical possibility:

It is, indeed, a necessary logical condition that a concept of the possible must not contain any contradiction; but this is not by any means sufficient to deter-mine...the possibility of such an object as is thought through the concept.[5]

Kant seems to think also that the concept of necessity in its empirical employment is a special case of logical necessity: 'the third postulate... concerns material necessity in existence, and not merely formal and logical necessity.'[1] But the word 'merely', which suggests that logical necessity is somehow weaker than 'material necessity', is misplaced. If the two relate as weaker and stronger, wider and narrower, the relation is the other way around. Kant's ramshackle architectonic has let him down again.

Observe how different the modal concepts 'in their empirical employment' are from the modal schemas with which they ought to be identical. Kant's account of the schemas is dominated by his wish to make time central to the whole business of schematism. The schema of possibility is obscure, but the schema of actuality is plainly declared to be 'existence in some determinate time', and that of necessity to be 'existence of an object at all times';[2] none of which has much overlap with the Postulates of Empirical Thought. It may be noted, incidentally, that the schema of necessity is indistinguishable from that of substance! The latter is first described as 'permanence of the real in time',[3] and later as 'permanence (which is existence in all time)'.[4]

41 Extent

The 'principle of' the non-existent Axioms of Intuition says: 'All intuitions are extensive magnitudes'.[5] The distinction between extensive and intensive magnitude—the latter occurring in the 'principle of' the Anticipations of Perception—is difficult and interesting. Let us look at it.

The general notion of magnitude is involved in such locutions as 'how much?', 'more', 'a great deal', 'not enough' etc. Something has extensive magnitude—or, as Kant puts it, something is an extensive magnitude—if in respect of it we can ask 'How much?', meaning 'What is its extent?' We are concerned with extensive magnitude when we ask of an object how large it is, or of a process how long it lasted. We are concerned with intensive magnitude when we ask how acute a pain is, how loud a noise, or how sour a drink; the crucial idea, in these examples at least, is that of the degree of intensity of some sensation.

Some expressions could refer to both sorts of magnitude. 'My neighbour is very noisy' may complain both of the length and frequency of his noises, and of their loudness. 'Arthritis is a very painful affliction' may mean that arthritics are very often in pain, and that they sometimes suffer very acute pains. 'She is wearing the bluest ensemble you ever saw' may be a report that every item in her ensemble is blue, and that several of them are vividly, aggressively blue.

My examples of the intensive/extensive distinction have served to locate it; but my general remarks, which should have explained what distinction it is, have been circular. I have used 'extent' in explaining 'extensive', and 'intensity' in explaining 'intensive'. If we look to Kant for a general, non-circular account of extensive magnitude we learn that something has extensive magnitude if 'the representation of the parts makes possible, and therefore necessarily precedes, the representation of the whole'.[1] If we ignore the reference to what 'makes possible' and 'precedes' the representation of the whole, and take Kant to be saying just that an extensive magnitude is one which something has by virtue of having *parts*, we get an account which fits the examples I have given. My neighbour's trombone solo this morning was a temporal part of his total disturbance of me this week, and his wife's gloves and handbag are parts of her ensemble; but a trombone-blast does not have trombone-murmurs as parts, nor is the intense blueness of a handbag a whole whose parts are several more modest bluenesses.

The definition of 'extensive magnitude' as 'magnitude which something has by virtue of possessing parts' does justice not merely to my examples but to a conspicuous feature of Kant's treatment, namely his taking it that items which have extensive magnitude are all spatially or temporally extended. Things which take up space have spatial parts, and processes have temporal parts; and it is not clear that there are parts of any other kind. (Objects do not have temporal parts; but this does not conflict with what I have said, for objects do not take time either—their histories do that.) There are derivative uses of 'part' which do not directly involve extensive magnitudes. A chord played by an orchestra is complex because it has a multiplicity of features or aspects; but it would be more natural to describe this as a multiplicity of parts. But this, I think, is just a borrowing based on the fact that the various *features of the sound* correlate with the *parts of what produces it*. Similarly with the 'parts' of complex smells and tastes. These remarks do not apply to the claim that sounds and smells have parts because they occupy space—e.g. that a smell may have the same size and shape as a room. This use of 'part' may be unsatisfactory, but it is not derivative: the 'parts' in question, if we allow them at all, are spatial parts.

If I am wrong in thinking that all the primary uses of 'part' and 'whole' have to do with spatial and temporal extent, we can forget this and attend simply to Kant's equation of these two kinds of extent with what he calls 'extensive magnitude'. This equation cannot be defended on the grounds that 'extensive' connects with 'extent' and there are only these two sorts of extent; for we can properly speak of the extent of someone's ignorance or generosity. Perhaps such uses of 'extent' are derivative; but, rather than arguing that they are, I offer a more modest account of what Kant has done in calling attention to the concept of extensive magnitude. He has used the label 'extensive magnitude' to mark off definitionally two species of magnitude, namely spatial and temporal; and, even if he cannot make this demarcation interesting by correlating it with 'extent' or with 'part'/'whole', he makes it interesting by contrasting extensive with intensive magnitude (see §§ 42–3).

Sometimes Kant takes the line that 'extensive' can be defined in terms of temporal extent alone, and that the notion of spatial extent can be derived from this:

I cannot represent to myself a line, however small, without drawing it in thought, that is, generating from a point all its parts one after another...All appearances are...intuited...as complexes of previously given parts. This is not the case with magnitudes of every kind, but only with those magnitudes which are represented and apprehended by us in this *extensive* fashion.[1]

Talk about parts which are 'previously given' and which 'precede' the whole is here taken literally: something with size has extensive magnitude only because time must be expended in making or 'representing' it. Kant really means it. Much later in the *Critique* he says: 'The synthesis of the manifold parts of [any region of] space...is successive, taking place in time and containing a series.'[2] I noted in § 10 that Kant sometimes assumes that spatial configurations must be thought of in terms of what can be seen at a glance. He seems now to be denying that they can ever be thought of in that way.

This explains why he takes the notion of that which 'occupies only an instant'[3] as crucial for the explanation of intensive magnitude. A toothache's intensity has nothing to do with how long it lasts— a violent toothache may 'occupy only an instant'—and Kant seems to think that this *proves* that intensity of pain is not an extensive magnitude of any sort. It doesn't, of course. A flash of sheet-lightning has extensive magnitude, not because time is needed for the whole sheet to be spread out, or for us to 'represent' it to ourselves, but just because it is spatially extended. Spatial extension stands on its own feet: it is not a special case of temporal extension.

The definition of 'extensive' in terms of space and time gives Kant his only argument for the principle that everything empirical must have extensive magnitude: 'As the [element of] pure intuition in all appearances is either space or time, every appearance is as intuition an extensive magnitude.'[1] This slides by the Transcendental Deduction and presents the principle as a direct consequence of the Aesthetic. According to his own account of the *Critique's* structure, Kant ought to say that the principle concerns not the understanding but the sensibility, not the intellectual control of intuitions but their very existence. He ought therefore to regard the principle as one of those 'matters which do not come within the range of [the Analytic of Principles]'.[2]

Kant thinks that the principle guarantees the measurability of the experienced world. He calls it the 'transcendental principle of the mathematics of appearances [which makes] pure mathematics, in its complete precision, applicable to objects of experience'.[3] This is wrong, for a thing may have parts without being measurable. To measure a thing we must compare its magnitude with that of some standard, and this can neither be a part of the thing to be measured nor contain it as a part. Kant has shown, at most, only that we must be able to compare the magnitude of anything with the magnitudes of its own parts. It is true that no sense attaches to the notion of a period of time, or a region of space, divorced from any notion of how long or large it is; and so we may concede to Kant that if the world must be spatial and temporal then it must admit of a metric in this very weak sense. But this is far from conceding that we must be able to apply to it 'pure mathematics in its complete precision'. Kant tries to fill this gap in his argument by one of his dreadful appeals to the a priori truth of geometry.[4]

42 Intensity

What is an intensive magnitude? All I have offered so far are some examples, and a passing reference to 'the degree of intensity of some sensation'. The former lack generality, while the latter is imperfectly illuminating and, as I shall show, dubious on other grounds as well.

Kant may be attempting a positive, general account of intensive magnitude when he says that anything has intensive magnitude which is 'apprehended only as unity, and in which multiplicity can be represented only through approximation to negation'.[5] The best I can make of 'apprehended as unity' is to interpret it as 'does not have parts', which suggests a negative definition of intensive magnitude as magnitude which is not extensive. There remains the clause 'and in which multiplicity can be represented only through approximation to negation'. Kant's thought seems to be this: 'An extensive magnitude is reduced if some of a thing's parts are removed, as when a red patch in my visual field shrinks. The reduction of an intensive magnitude, as when the saturation of a red patch lessens, is not the removal of parts but....' Now we want something positive, but all Kant offers us is, in effect: '...but the magnitude's approximating more closely to negation'. This gets us nowhere. As the red patch becomes less saturated, it approximates to not being there at all; but this is equally true if the patch decreases in size. Analogously, I approximate to not having arthritic pains as my pains become ever milder, or as they diminish extensively by becoming briefer and rarer. So the idea of 'approximation to negation' does not mark off intensive from extensive magnitudes. Perhaps Kant would agree. Perhaps he is saying that with an intensive magnitude multiplicity can be represented *only* as approximation to negation, while with an extensive magnitude it can be represented not only in that way but also in another as well, namely as involving the complexity of something which has parts.

Kant makes much of the continuity of intensive magnitudes; but this does not provide a demarcation either, for a thing can shrink, as well as fade, continuously. That Kant knows this quite well is shown by his mention of infinite divisibility;[1] and he does say outright that continuity is a 'property of magnitudes'[2] of either kind.

His one other apparent attempt to describe intensive magnitude positively is his reference to 'intensive magnitude, that is, a degree'.[3] We do use 'degree'—and the Germans use *Grad*—of intensive rather than of extensive magnitudes. We speak of degrees of colour-saturation, loudness, pain-intensity etc., as in 'It was painful in the highest degree'. The word 'degree' is less at home with extensive magnitudes, apart from the accident that angles are measured in 'degrees'. We do not, for example, speak of degrees of size. But the linguistic facts are far more complicated than this, and they do not support the convenient conclusion that intensive magnitude involves degrees while extensive magnitude does not. The intensive/extensive distinction might come clearer if we had a really full picture—which I have not—of the uses of the word 'degree'.

So the best Kant can do is: intensive magnitudes are magnitudes which are not extensive. This is weak, and one would like to be able to improve upon it; but even with this unsatisfactory basis Kant is able to make excellent use of the extensive/intensive distinction, a use which I shall discuss shortly.

The principle of the Anticipations of Perception says: 'In all appearances sensation, and the *real* which corresponds to it in the object, has an *intensive magnitude*, that is, a degree.'[1] Kant speaks of 'sensation' rather than 'intuition' because he calls sensation the 'matter' of experience, and wants to exclaim over the 'surprising' fact that we have an a priori principle which permits us to 'forestall [= anticipate] experience, precisely in that which concerns what is only to be obtained through it, namely, its matter.'[2]

Setting aside the reference to 'the *real*...', the principle says that all sensations must have intensive magnitude—and indeed, Kant adds later, a sliding scale of intensive magnitudes:

Every sensation...is capable of diminution, so that it can decrease and gradually vanish. Between reality...and negation there is therefore a continuity of many possible intermediate sensations.[3]

This, however, merely says that our sensations *are* like that: it states an empirical fact, and has no place in Kant's apparatus of a priori principles. He provides no arguments for the impossibility of a world in which nothing is ever dim or in-between, in which there is only one level of pain, say, and only three degrees of saturation for each colour. Perhaps Kant would reply that even in such a world there would be 'a continuity of many *possible* intermediate sensations': such intermediate sensations need not actually occur but they must always be possible. This would make Kant's talk about 'forestalling experience' look rather feeble, but still it would suffice for the most important of his arguments involving the notion of intensive magnitude.

To understand this argument, we must first put 'real' back into the picture. Kant says that the idea of *the real in space*, i.e. of that which fills or occupies regions of space, is the idea of *that which is R*—where R is some empirical property, such as mass or impenetrability, chosen according to what one believes the basic stuff in the extended world to be like. The choice of an R may affect what kind of sensation is taken as central to the notion of being confronted by something real in space; but whatever choice is made, Kant says, confrontation-with-reality is just having-a-sensation of some favoured kind. Now, two regions of space of equal size may manifest the chosen R in different degrees: this is just to say that two things may have the same size while having different weights or degrees of hardness or rigidity etc. Some philosophers have thought that in such a case one of the two regions must be less tightly packed than the other, i.e. that the thing which is lighter or softer etc. must contain less of 'the real', and more empty space, than does the thing which is heavier or harder etc. They have taken occupancy of space as an absolute, not admitting of degrees; and so they have had to construe 'S_1 contains more reality than S_2' as equivalent to 'A greater *extent* of S_1 than of S_2 is reality-filled', and, in the special case where S_1 is the same size as S_2, equivalent to 'A greater proportion of S_1's than of S_2's extent is reality-filled'.

Kant objects that in addition to the question of whether a region of space gives rise to sensations which show that it contains something real, there is the question of how intensely such sensations are had; and differences in degrees of intensity are not necessarily due to underlying differences in the extent to which various regions of space are occupied by 'the real':

Even if the whole intuition of a certain determinate space or time is real through and through, that is, though no part of it is empty, none the less, since every reality has its degree, which can diminish to nothing (the void) through infinite gradations without in any way altering the extensive magnitude of the appearance, there must be infinite different degrees in which space and time may be filled. Intensive magnitude can in different appearances be smaller or greater, although the extensive magnitude of the intuition remains one and the same.[1]

Descartes, for one, would have benefited from sharing Kant's insight here.[2] He declared the phrase 'extended but immaterial [or incorporeal]' to be self-contradictory, and so could not explain how two congruent bodies could differ in mass, degree of hardness etc. by saying that one contains a higher proportion of vacuum, or extended non-matter, than the other. His own explanation was blatantly circular: a 'rare' body, he said, is one 'between whose parts there are many interstices filled with other bodies'; but this is no explanation unless the interstitial bodies do themselves have a low mass or degree of hardness or whatever, i.e. are themselves 'rare'. We shall see that the concept of intensive magnitude would have provided him with a vastly more satisfactory explanation.

Kant errs only in his conviction that he has to appeal to the intensive/extensive distinction as applied to sensations. Without any such appeal, he could still have pointed out that the statement 'S_1 contains more of the real than S_2' does not have to be equated with 'More of S_1 than of S_2 contains the real'. Kant's working picture here seems to be of a man who builds his *Weltanschauung* by roaming through space, receiving sensations from it, and classifying them in respect of (a) how much space they pertain to and how long they last, and (b) how intense they are. But the intensive/extensive contrast need not be restricted to this primitive level at which, presumably, the only measure of a thing's impenetrability would be the degree of pressure one felt in pushing against it. We use the extensive/intensive distinction in distinguishing a region's size from the degree of impenetrability of that which uniformly fills it, even if our techniques for measuring impenetrability are thoroughly 'extensive' and do not directly involve degrees of intensity of any sensation. For this reason, and also because Kant does not in any case *prove* anything about intensive magnitudes, he ought in the following passage to describe his argument as resting on 'a reminder of an overlooked possibility' rather than on 'a transcendental proof'. All the same, the passage is a fine one:

Almost all natural philosophers, observing...a great difference in the quantity of various kinds of matter in bodies that have the same volume, unanimously conclude that this volume, which constitutes the extensive magnitude of the appearance, must in all material bodies be empty in varying degrees...They assume that the real in space (I may not here name it impenetrability or weight, since these are empirical concepts) is everywhere uniform and varies only in extensive magnitude, that is, in amount. Now, to this presupposition, for which they could find no support in experience, and which is therefore purely metaphysical, I oppose a transcendental proof, which does not indeed explain the difference in the filling of spaces, but completely destroys the supposed necessity of the above presupposition, that the difference is only to be explained on the assumption of empty space. My proof has the merit at least of freeing the understanding, so that it is at liberty to think this difference in some other manner, should it be found that some other hypothesis is required for the explanation of the natural appearances.[1]

After citing radiant heat as an example of something real which, so far as we know, can fill the whole extent of a space in different degrees of intensity, Kant continues:

I do not at all intend to assert that [anything like] this is what actually occurs when material bodies differ in specific gravity, but only to establish...that the nature of our perceptions allows of such a mode of explanation, [and] that we are not justified in assuming the real in appearances to be uniform in degree, differing only in aggregation and extensive magnitude.[2]

This destroys the argument for the existence of empty space from the fact that there are differences in mass, impenetrability etc. Less obviously, but just as surely, it shows that the existence of empty space cannot be inferred from the fact that there is motion. Kant goes further, however, and says that there could not be empirical evidence of any kind for the existence of empty space:

The proof of an empty space or of an empty time can never be derived from experience. For, in the first place, the complete absence of reality from a sensible intuition can never be itself perceived; and, secondly, there is no appearance whatsoever and no difference in the degree of reality of any appearance from which it can be inferred.[1]

Having sensations of degree zero is not having sensory evidence that one is confronted by empty space—it is just failing to have sensations. Analogously, one could not get evidence for the existence of 'empty time'—i.e. of a period during which nothing occurs—by living through it with sensations of degree zero. So Kant is right to say: 'The complete absence of reality from a sensible intuition can never be perceived.'

Consider now the second part of his claim, namely that nothing could count as indirect evidence for the existence of empty space or empty time. In respect of time this is correct. Any measure of a period of time requires reference to what occurs during it: all that distinguishes a million years from a micro-second is a difference of content, a difference in respect of how many processes of certain standard kinds take place during them. Empty time could therefore have no metric whatsoever; it would be time to which quantitative notions just did not apply. So, putting Kant's own conclusion strongly, empty time is impossible. This is seen in the idleness of such suggestions as that every ordinary, eventful hour is interrupted by hundreds of discrete periods of empty time.

There is, however, no parallel argument for the impossibility of empty space. Because of two properties of space which are not properties of time, there are two distinct ways in which empty space could be measured. (a) Space has more than one dimension, and so a vacuum can be measured by reference to surrounding objects, i.e. ones which remain outside it. (b) The contents of a region of space can change, and so a vacuum can be measured by reference to objects which have been removed from it and not replaced by anything else. I have gleaned these two points from Leibniz, who packs the whole truth of this matter—except for the inference from immeasurability to impossibility, which he declines to draw—into one casual sentence: 'If space were only a line, and if body were immovable, it would no longer be possible to determine the length of the vacuum between two bodies.'[1]

43 Continuity

Kant's treatment of intensive magnitudes raises problems about what he calls continuity. (What he calls 'continuous' a modern mathematician would call 'dense', reserving 'continuous' for a related but stronger notion. I shall follow Kant's non-technical usage.) Although in discussing these problems about continuity I shall use some examples involving intensity, the problems arise equally in connection with extent and even with properties which are not magnitudes of any kind.

Kant takes a continuous series to be one in which no member has an immediate neighbour. The series of whole numbers is discontinuous: 53 has the immediate neighbours 52 and 54. The series of fractions is continuous: $\frac{3}{4}$ has no immediate neighbours, for there is a fraction between it and any other fraction. The key term here is 'between'. Kant is talking about continuity when he says that between any two degrees of intensity of a given sensation there is an intermediate degree.

He rightly infers from this that between any two degrees there is not just one intermediate degree but an infinite number of them.[2] This is false if we take it as saying that between any two degrees of intensity there is an infinite number of *noticeably* distinct intermediate degrees; for even if there is an infinite number of pain-levels between that of yesterday's toothache and that of today's, it would be absurd to claim that we can tell every pair of them apart.

If 'Our sensations admit of continuous degrees of intensity' is not to yield this absurd conclusion, it must be interpreted as saying something weaker than that between any two degrees there is an intermediate one which is *noticeably* distinct from both.

Before offering such an interpretation I must explain how I am using certain words. A *difference* is *discoverable* if it can be detected by any means whatsoever; but it is *noticeable* only if it can be detected by simple inspection—by having the different pains, feeling the different temperatures, looking at the different coloured surfaces, and so on. The differentia 'by simple inspection' is vague, but not fatally so. Differences which are discoverable but not noticeable include, obviously, ones whose detection requires devices like spirit-levels, thermometers and photo-finish apparatus. But technical devices are not necessary, as the following example shows. We have three coloured surfaces, A, B and C.

Of these, A and B do not differ in any way, so far as we can tell by looking at them. In some respect—degree of saturation, let us say, though we could as well take hue or size—there is a noticeable difference between A and C but not between B and C. So there is after all a difference between A and B, since they compare differently with C; and between B and C, since they compare differently with A. The diagram A—B—C presents the case: B lies between A and C in respect of saturation, and thus differs from both even though neither difference can be found by simple inspection, i.e. by looking just at A and B or just at B and C. These differences are discoverable, but only that between A and C is noticeable.

A simple extension of this terminology can be explained by examples. 'There is a *noticeable difference* between A and C in respect of their degree of saturation' = 'The degree of saturation of A is *noticeably distinct* from that of C'. 'There is a *discoverable difference* between A and B in respect of degree of saturation' = 'The degree of saturation of A is *discoverably distinct* from that of B'.

I return now to the statement: 'Our sensations admit of continuous degrees of intensity.' Clearly, if this is to be defensible, we shall have to interpret it as asserting the existence not of noticeably distinct but only of discoverably distinct intermediate degrees. This still leaves us with a choice of interpretations: (1) Between any two *noticeably* distinct degrees of intensity there is one which is discoverably distinct from both. (2) Between any two *discoverably* distinct degrees of intensity there is one which is discoverably distinct from both. I shall support (1) and attack (2).

The crucial merit of (1) is that, without entailing the existence of any infinite, it states the fact which inclines us to say that our sensations admit of continuous degrees of intensity. I take it that those who say this are reporting that the intensity-scale of their sensations seems to be full, contains no discontinuities of which they are aware; and if this were false (1) would be false, though whether the converse holds I do not know.

Now, (2) entails (1) and so, in a sense, states every fact stated by (1); but it also entails that there is an infinite number of distinct degrees of intensity. Considered as a report on experience, (2) is extravagant. Granted that '(theoretically) discoverable differences' may, and doubtless do, include many differences which we do not know how to detect, it still seems quite unwarrantable to say that there is an infinite number of them between, say, a mild pain and an acute one. It might be suggested that we could increase (2)'s plausibility without forgoing infinities: we could drop 'discoverably' from (2) altogether, thus taking it to state not what differences are *discoverable* but what differences *there are*. This suggestion, however, divorces talk of what the world is like from talk of what we might find it to be like if we took appropriate steps; or, as Kant might say, it divorces 'the actual' from 'that which is bound up with the material conditions of experience'.[1] This divorce makes serious metaphysics impossible. When someone says that differences may exist which are not even theoretically discoverable, he does not endow himself with reasons for postulating an infinity of them; he merely gives himself a licence to say what he likes.

When Kant postulates some such infinity, however, he is not forsaking his transcendental idealism, nor is he just allowing the mathematics of continuity to run away with him. To see what he *is* doing we must examine his rebuttal, in the second edition of the *Critique*, of Mendelssohn's argument for the immortality of the soul.[2]

Mendelssohn, on Kant's report of him, argued as follows. If the soul were spatially extended, it could go out of existence continuously, by a gradual reduction of size or dissipation of parts; but since it is not extended, the only mode of annihilation left to it is a discontinuous one, and this is not possible for the soul or for anything else. Therefore the soul cannot go out of existence.

Kant attacks this undistinguished argument through its premiss that only things with parts can go out of existence continuously. He points out that there is fading as well as shrinkage:

[Mendelssohn] failed...to observe that even if we admit the simple nature of the soul, namely, that it contains...no extensive quantity, we yet cannot deny to it, any more than to any other existence, intensive quantity, that is, a degree of reality in respect of all...that constitutes its existence, and that this degree of reality may diminish through all the infinitely many smaller degrees.[3]

In short, if Mendelssohn has proved the immortality of the soul he has also proved the immortality of toothaches.

Our business is with the premiss which Kant does not attack, namely that discontinuous annihilation is impossible. Mendelssohn argues that something which went out of existence discontinuously would have to exist at one instant and not at the next—'there would be no time between a moment in which it is and another in which it is not';[4] but since time is continuous there can be no next instant after any given instant. This argument infers 'Discontinuous annihilation is impossible' from 'Time is continuous'. But it is invalid, as I shall show.

Suppose that a pencil which I am holding suddenly disappears. It is unimportant that this is a miracle—the fundamental issue concerns the continuity of all change, not just of annihilation; what matters is our curiosity about whether the pencil vanished discontinuously. The miracle is repeated while being filmed at ten frames per second, and we find on the developed film that one frame shows the pencil all there while the next shows neither part nor hint of it. A Mendelssohnian says: 'So the period during which the pencil was shrinking was a very short one. Next time, run the camera faster.' We obey, and get the same result. The Mendelssohnian insists that there is *some* camera-speed, could we only achieve it, at which we should get pictures of the pencil in the act of vanishing. But he has no warrant for this: by supposing that technological advances permit camera speeds of a hundred, a thousand, a million... frames per second, we are not putting logical pressure on ourselves to suppose anything about what is seen on the developed film. There are, of course, more than merely technological limits to how fast a camera—or indeed anything else—can run, and that fact is relevant to the statement that time is continuous; but I am concerned with the entailments of that statement, not with its truth. My argument is that even if time is continuous, and even if there were no limits to how fast the camera could go, there might still be no camera-speed at which we got a picture showing the pencil in the act of vanishing. We could not empirically show that there was no such speed, but the Mendelssohnian would have no grounds for saying that there must be one.

Why does Mendelssohn think he is entitled to insist that the continuity must be there, even if we never succeed in finding it? The answer has already been quoted. Mendelssohn is arguing like this: 'There must be a continuity because "The disappearance was discontinuous" is equivalent to "There was no time between the last instant when the pencil was there and the first instant when it was not". But that makes those two instants adjacent, and if time is continuous then there is time between any instant and any other.'

This argument is based on a definition of 'discontinuous' which, if time is continuous, is simply unacceptable. Suppose we agree that time is continuous. Then, if we say that there was a last instant when something existed we must deny that there was a first instant when it did not exist. If its last instant of existing was t, then it did not exist at any time later than t; but the set of times-later-than-t has no earliest member, just as the set of fractions-greater-than-$\frac{3}{4}$ has no least member. Alternatively, we can say that there was a first instant when the thing did not exist, just so long as we deny that there was a last instant when it did exist. Mendelssohn's argument accordingly fails.

Kant is uncritical of Mendelssohn's treatment of continuity, perhaps because he accepts it. That, at any rate, would explain his thinking that between any two degrees of intensity there must be an intermediate one. If Mendelssohn's argument held for annihilation it would hold for all change; and if all change were not just apparently gradual but strictly continuous then every intensive magnitude would indeed have an infinite number of degrees. Something's degree of saturation cannot change continuously from d_1 to d_2 if between these two there is only a finite number of distinct intermediate degrees. The continuity of magnitudes, then, can be inferred from the continuity of change.

Kant does indeed make just these moves:[1] time is continuous, therefore change is continuous, therefore magnitudes are continuous— because any change from one degree to another must run through 'all smaller degrees which are contained between the first and the last',[2] with the clear implication that there is an infinite number of these:

The question...arises how a thing passes from one state...to another... Between two instants there is always a time, and between any two states in the two instants there is always a difference which has magnitude.[3]

And also:

In the [field of] appearance there is no difference of the real that is the smallest, just as in the magnitude of times there is no time that is the smallest; and the new state of reality accordingly proceeds from the first wherein this reality was not, through all the infinite [intermediate] degrees.[4]

Elsewhere Kant does better.[5] He says that the question of whether all change is continuous presupposes 'empirical principles' and thus 'lies altogether outside the limits of a transcendental philosophy'. Since he does not think that the question of whether time is continuous presupposes empirical principles he is, in effect, denying that the continuity of change can be inferred from the continuity of time.

13

THE FIRST ANALOGY

44 The Analogies of Experience: preliminaries

The Analogies of Experience assert that experience must fall under the categories of *substance, cause* and *community*. The third Analogy, concerning community, does not require extended discussion. It says: 'All substances, in so far as they can be perceived to coexist in space, are in thoroughgoing reciprocity.'[1] Kant is here making the interesting and rather Spinozist claim that we could not know that two things coexisted in the same universe unless they had causal commerce (= community) with one another. His attempt to prove this, however, is a failure which is not even incidentally valuable except for a few flickers of light which it throws on the second Analogy.

The remaining sections of my book will centre on Kant's abominably organised 'proofs' of the first and second Analogies. This thirty-page stretch of the *Critique*, for all its obscurities, ellipses and repetitions, is one of the great passages in modern philosophy.

The so-called principle of the Analogies of Experience says: 'Experience is possible only through the representation of a necessary connection of perceptions.'[2] The Analogies do indeed concern necessary connections—between the different qualities of a single substance, between cause and effect, and between things which interact with one another. The principle which covers all these at once, however, is so general as to defeat even Kant's capacity for doing philosophy at the level of the extremely abstract. Although Kant offers 'proofs' for all three Analogies, each of which entails the principle, he also tries to prove the principle itself. This 'proof' consists mainly in a sketchy restatement of the Transcendental Deduction of the Categories, against the background of a peculiar emphasis upon temporal notions. In one of its versions the principle of the Analogies says: 'All appearances are, as regards their existence, subject to a priori rules determining their relation to one another in one time';[3] and Kant also remarks that the Analogies hinge on the fact that the contents of experience must fulfil whatever conditions are necessary for 'the determination of the existence of objects in time'.[4] This last phrase can be clarified only when we move to the Analogies themselves, but it does indicate that temporal concepts are going to be central.

Time is even invoked to explain why there are just these three Analogies:[1] 'The three modes of time are *duration, succession* and *coexistence*';[2] and so the world's temporality has to do with its falling under the categories of *enduring* substance, cause and *succeeding* effect, and community of things which *coexist*! This serves only to mask the complexity of Kant's real thoughts about the first two Analogies.

45 Two senses of 'substance'

In the traditional concept of substance there are two main strands which I shall distinguish by subscripts. A *substance*$_1$ is a thing which has qualities. A *substance*$_2$ is something which can be neither originated nor annihilated by any natural process, i.e. which is, barring miracles, sempiternal. These two have often been conflated, if not identified; yet it is not obvious that they are even extensionally equivalent. To understand the first Analogy we must see how they relate to one another and to Kant's uses of the word 'substance'.

How did one word come to be used in two such different senses? Part of the answer to this, which I have adapted from an illuminating paper by Kneale,[3] seems to be as follows. It has been said, as far back as Aristotle, that while an attribute or quality can be part of the world's furniture only if there is a substance$_1$ to which it belongs, a substance$_1$ is not in the same way required to 'belong' to something else. Substances$_1$, we might say, exist *independently* of anything else. Now, if we give this a causal rather than a logical force, it says that the continued existence of a substance$_1$ does not depend causally upon the behaviour of anything else. Something which needs no outside help in order to continue existing cannot be annihilated by anything else; thus, if we hurry past the question of origination, it is sempiternal so far as natural processes go; and so it is a substance$_2$. Perhaps, then, substance$_2$ became accreted to substance$_1$ through an innocent exploitation of the ambiguity of words like 'independently'.

This suggestion is confirmed in Spinoza's writings. His doctrine that the universe is the only *indestructible thing* was expressed in his monistic thesis that the universe is the only substance; and the terminological decisions to which this led him could be summed up by saying that the universe is the only *thing which is not adjectival upon something else*. So Spinoza made 'substance' do the work both of 'substance$_1$' and of 'substance$_2$'. This is not surprising. Since he believed that causal necessity is a kind of logical necessity, Spinoza could not allow a distinction between the logical independence of substances₁ and the causal self-sufficiency of substances₂. I suggest that he was covering the old route from one sense of 'substance' to the other, but with his eyes open.

The concept of substance₂ is not just a philosophers' toy. Most of us find it natural to assume that any change is a transformation of some basic stuff which is there all the time: once it was thought to be matter, more recently it has been thought to be energy one of whose forms is matter. The hypothesis of some cosmologists that matter continually comes into existence *ex nihilo* startles the layman precisely because it seems to challenge this assumption.

I turn now to Kant. In A the first Analogy says: 'All appearances contain the permanent (substance) as the object itself, and the transitory as its mere determination, that is, as a way in which the object exists.'[1] There is more than a hint of substance₁ here, but I want to focus attention on the phrase 'the permanent (substance)'. Kant understands permanence (*Beharrlichkeit*)[2] not as relative durability but as absolute sempiternity; and so the 'substance' of which he speaks in the first Analogy is substance₂. He also says, in both editions: 'The proposition that substance is permanent is tautological.'[3] In B, however, the first Analogy says: 'In all change of appearances substance is permanent; its quantum in nature is neither increased nor diminished.'[4] This puts up for proof the same thing that, three pages later, Kant calls tautological. Like many of Kant's revisions, it is better ignored.

The a priori concepts used in this part of the *Critique* are supposed to be the schemas of categories which are read off from the table of judgments. In particular, the pre-schematism source of the concept of substance is the category associated with subject-predicate statements. This is the category of 'Inherence and Subsistence',[5] or, as Kant sometimes says, of 'substance'.[6] This apparently involves a use of 'substance' in which anything counts as a substance which can be referred to by a subject-term: thus, attributes are 'substances' in this sense, because we can say things like 'His amiability cloys'. Since Kant naturally wants his category of substance to be more limited than this, even in its pre-schematism form, he narrows it to the concept of that. which can be referred to *only* by a subject-term, i.e. the concept of 'something which can be thought only as subject, never as a predicate of something else'.[7] Thus, by disrupting the simple relationship which is supposed to hold between the categories and the table of judgments,

Kant achieves the traditional concept of substance₁—the concept of that which does not belong to or inhere in anything else as attributes do.

Kant, then, introduces substance₁ in the Metaphysical Deduction and operates with substance₂ in the first Analogy. He thinks that the latter is the schema of the former. The pre-schematism concept of substance, he says, is the unusable concept of 'simply a something which can be thought only as subject, never as a predicate of something else'; while its schema is empirically serviceable because in it 'the sensible determination of permanence' is addéd.¹ As I remarked at the end of §37, the schematism theory permits Kant to add only the sensible determination of *time*, not of permanence. Perhaps a temporal substance₁ must have duration, but why must it last for ever? Schematism, whose assigned task is to fit the categories for application to empirical data, serves rather to distort them so that in the 'Principles' chapter Kant can say what he has to say, ignoring the agenda which the Metaphysical Deduction sets before him.

We have here a quintessentially Kantian situation. Substance₂ is supposed to be derived by schematism from substance₁ which is supposed to be derived in its turn from the table of judgments; and both derivations are faulty. They are offered as a preliminary to the first Analogy, a mere locating of its key concept; but if Kant had trusted them he would have had no need for the 'proof' of the Analogy, for this is in fact a subtle inquiry into the relationship between the two concepts of substance.

46 Substances and objects

There is a confusion about 'substance' which first took root in the issues between Locke and Berkeley, and has now ramified into modern metaphysics generally.² I have already devoted an article to this, but unless I sketch it here I cannot bring the first Analogy into focus. The confusion originates in two doctrines which occur in Locke's *Essay*: (a) an account of what it is for a property to be instantiated by a particular, and (b) an account of the distinction between the subjective and the objective. In Locke's presentation of (a) there is, I think, more irony than is usually seen; but my concern is with the logical relations between the two doctrines, not with Locke's attitude to them.

(a) The 'Lockean' analysis of property-instantiation goes as follows. What concepts—or, as Locke would say, what *ideas*—are involved in the subject of the statement 'The pen in my hand is expensive'? Certainly, the concepts of being a pen and of being in my hand; but these are not all, for the statement speaks of *something which* is a pen and is in my hand. However much we enlarge our description of the thing in question, however exhaustively we list its properties, we shall come no nearer to capturing the concept of the *thing which* has the properties. There must, then, be a concept of a naked *thing which...*; and since this is an ingredient in the concept of a *thing which is F* for each value of *F*, it cannot be identical with any such concept. It is the concept of a property-bearer, or of a possible subject of predication, or—for short—of a *substance*. So there are two sorts of items: properties and substances. The function of substances is to bear properties without in their turn being borne by anything. We imply the existence of a substance every time we say that a property is instantiated.

(b) Locke was what Kant calls a transcendental realist, and not a very subtle one either. He thought that the difference between (i) seeing a tree and (ii) being in a visual state as of seeing a tree though there is no tree present, is the difference between (i) having a sensory 'idea' while in the presence of a 'real thing' which 'resembles' or 'corresponds to' the idea and (ii) having such an idea while in the presence of no such thing. In Locke's metaphysics, the whole range of our sense-experience is set over against a world of 'real things' to whose existence and nature, *we hope*, our sense-experience gives us reliable clues. In grappling with the sceptic who suggests that perhaps there is no real world after all, Locke stumbled into all the snares which Kant predicts for the transcendental realist who tries to be an empirical realist (see §8 above).

Now, Berkeley was right to reject (a) the 'Lockean' analysis of property-instantiation and (b) Locke's transcendental realism; but, unhappily, he took them to be alternative formulations of a unitary doctrine of 'material substance'. The phrase 'material substance', which hardly occurs in Locke's *Essay*, owes its association with Locke's name to this blunder of Berkeley's. Berkeley used 'matter' and its cognates for the 'real things' which figure in (b), and of course used 'substance' in connection with (a); and by uniting the two in the phrase 'material substance' he betrayed his failure to see that (a) and (b) are answers to different questions. The notorious 'Lockean doctrine of material substance' does not exist, and many passages in Berkeley wither under scrutiny because they assume that it does.[1] Sometimes, of course, Berkeley does manage to say something useful about (a) or (b) in isolation.[2]

There was some excuse for this failure of Berkeley's. He, like Locke indeed, used 'idea' in such a way that an 'idea' of something could be either a property of it or a sensory state which someone has when perceiving it. 'Qualities', he said, 'are nothing but *sensations* or *ideas*, which exist only in a mind perceiving them.'[1] It was therefore natural for him to identify the two doctrines (a) and (b), since each of them purports to offer an anchor for free-floating 'ideas'—one relating qualities to the things which have them, and the other relating sensory states to the objectively real. Berkeley's opposition to Locke could fairly enough be summed up in the form: 'Things are just collections of ideas, not something over and above them'; and this can be read as an objection equally to (a) or to (b).

Many philosophers have followed Berkeley in making this mistake, identifying not just the two doctrines but the problems they were meant to solve. For example, a famous defence of phenomenalism[2] warns us against making too much of the fact 'that we cannot, in our language, refer to the sensible properties of a thing without introducing a word or phrase which appears to stand for the thing itself as opposed to anything which may be said about it.' From this fact, we are told, 'it does not by any means follow that the thing itself is a "simple entity", or that it cannot be defined in terms of the totality of its appearances.' Something which could be said about all the properties of a thing is here said about its 'sensible properties'; these are then transmuted into 'anything which may be said about it', and then into 'the totality of its appearances'. A complete slide is thus effected from a point which is relevant to (a) property-instantiation to a point which bears upon (b) the distinction between the subjective and the objective.

Although the problems dealt with by (a) and (b) are distinct, one cannot be solved without reference to the other. For the question 'What is involved in treating something as a subject of predication?', or 'What is it for a property to be instantiated?', is so general that we cannot see how to set about answering it; but we *can* tackle the narrower question 'What is involved in treating something as an objective particular?', or 'What is it for a property to be instantiated in the objective realm?' By narrowing our inquiry to the instantiation of properties by objective particulars, or objects, we do not thereby commit Berkeley's error. For we are not now mistaking the objective/subjective borderline for the thing/property borderline; rather, we are examining how the thing/property distinction works *within* the objective realm. Our question is: 'Given that our experience is to be interpreted in terms of objective states of affairs, how are we to handle this interpretation? In particular, how are we to decide what parts of our experience relate to objects or substances₁ and what parts relate to properties of or happenings to substances₁?' Clearly, the glove on my hand is substantial₁, while the temperature of my hand is not. Almost as clearly, a battle is an incident in the histories of the combatants and is in that sense 'adjectival upon' them; it would be unnatural to regard a battle as a thing of which the combatants were aspects or properties. Other cases are less clear. Is a flash of lightning a substance₁? Some say not; but is it then a happening? If so, what does it happen *to*? Again, is the sky a substance₁? I think so, but I have heard it denied. Now, in the easy as well as the hard cases, the thing/property or thing/happening distinction rests upon criteria which could profitably be made a subject of philosophical inquiry.

It is just such an inquiry which Kant embarks on in his 'proof' of the first Analogy. This puts him in the tradition of those philosophers who, in talking about 'substance' in something like the sense of 'substance₁', have in fact concerned themselves exclusively with objective substances₁, or objects. But Kant does not owe this restriction of interest to anything like Berkeley's mistake: he does not identify the substance/property distinction with the objective/subjective one, but considers how the former is employed within the objective realm. The very wording of the first Analogy bears this out: 'All appearances contain the permanent (substance) as the object itself...' For Kant, 'appearance' covers only that which is phenomenal *and objective*:[1] the Analogy takes for granted that we have to do with objective states of affairs, and says something about how these are divided up into objects and their states or properties.

47 Alterations and existence-changes

Kant distinguishes a thing's *existence-change*, in which it goes out of or comes into existence, from its *alteration*. His word for the former is *Wechsel*, which occurs in words like *Geldwechsler* (money-changer), and has the basic sense of *ex*change or complete turnover. Kemp Smith translates it by 'change', but since this narrowing of the ordinary meaning of 'change' is hard to remember, I prefer 'existence-change'.

Here are three truisms about alteration. (1) Alterations are always of substances₁: processes and events happen but do not alter, and properties neither happen nor alter. When we say 'Its colour has altered' we ought to mean that *it* has altered in respect of its colour. Similarly, for it to be true that 'The situation has altered' it must be true that some of the things or substances₁ in the situation have altered. (2) A substance₁ must remain in existence while it is altering: nothing can undergo an existence-change and an alteration synchronously. (3) For a substance₁ to alter is for one or more of its properties to undergo an existence-change: the alteration of my face when I blush is the existence-change of my face's whiteness, which ceases to exist, and of its pinkness, which begins to exist. In a more idiomatically natural way, we might say of someone who has altered by falling ill that his illness 'dates from last Wednesday'.

Kant puts these three points as follows:

All that alters *persists*, and only its state undergoes existence-change. Since this existence-change thus concerns only the determinations [i.e. properties or states], which can cease to be or begin to be, we can say, using what may seem a somewhat paradoxical expression, that only the permanent (substance) is altered, and that the transitory suffers no alteration but only an existence-change, inasmuch as certain determinations cease to be and others begin to be.[1]

This passage, however, goes further than (1)–(3); for it says not only that alterations must be of substances₁ but that they must be of 'the permanent', i.e. of substances₂. Kant here expresses his view that the stuff of the objective world is neither originated nor annihilated, and that all happenings are alterations of this basic stuff. I remarked in §45 that most of us incline to this view, but Kant thinks he can *prove* it. His 'proof' will be my topic in the next three sections.

I shall approach Kant's thesis that every happening is an alteration of a substance₂ through the apparently weaker thesis that every happening is an alteration. This says that only properties undergo existence-changes, and that substances₁ never do. (Here, as tacitly throughout, I exclude the sort of existence-change which is really just an alteration of the substance₁'s parts, as when a book is destroyed by burning.) We like to think that this is true, but is Kant right in thinking it necessarily true? Could there not be an existence-change of a substance₁, i.e. of an objective item which had a substantival rather than an adjectival status in everyone's conceptual scheme? The obvious case to take is that of physical objects. There are empirical reasons for thinking that they cannot go out of existence except by disintegration or transformation into energy, but there seems to be no conceptual bar to supposing that a physical object might be absolutely annihilated.

To put before Kant as specific a challenge as possible, what a priori reasons could he give for saying that the following story could not come true? I produce, and submit to general inspection, a porcelain pig and a handful of coins; we find the weight and volume of the pig; watched by the bystanders, I place the coins in the pig, and put the pig inside a glass case which is then tightly sealed; finally, I put the case on a balance which I bring level by means of weights on its other arm. Then, as we watch, the porcelain pig disappears, the coins clatter to the bottom of the case, and the arm of the balance holding the case swings up; when we remove weights from the other arm, equivalent to the weight of the pig, the balance comes level again; when we unseal the glass case, the volume of air which hisses in is equal to that of the pig; and at no stage is there an explosion such as would occur if a few ounces of matter were converted into energy.

Does not this describe the existence-change of a physical object? If some other interpretation is possible, it could be ruled out by a suitable development of the story. In short, if my story does not, a similar story could, present a case in which there was no reasonable alternative to saying that a physical object was absolutely annihilated and thus underwent an existence-change.

Kant is not fundamentally challenged by this, however. He does deny that physical things can be absolutely annihilated,[1] but his argument for this uses an empirical premiss which I do not want to introduce yet. As for its other premiss, namely the thesis that all happenings must be alterations, *that* would not be regarded by Kant as falsified by the existence-change of a physical object. For Kant would say that if a pig were annihilated, as in my story, this would show only that it was not a substance$_1$ after all but just a complex of properties of the glass case, the coins, the balance, the bystanders etc. It follows that the pig's annihilation would be consistent with the thesis that all happenings are alterations, i.e. the thesis that only properties can undergo existence-changes.

Kant must admit that the porcelain pig is a 'substance$_1$' in the sense that it *has* a substantival place in our thinking and talking; but his point is that if the pig undergoes an existence-change it *ought not* to have such a place. This still looks implausible, but I shall show that Kant makes an arguable case for it.

48 Substances and properties

Kant's thinking about existence-changes centres on two questions: (a) How can we know, of something which does not exist, that it ever did exist? (b) How can we know, of something which exists, that it ever did not exist? These raise for Kant exactly the same issues. They are the two halves of the question: How can we know that something has undergone an existence-change?

In describing the annihilation of the pig, I had to mention the alterations and constancies of other things—the case, the coins, the balance, the air—which stayed in existence throughout. Things which persisted all through the experiment might have been relevant in other ways too. After the pig has vanished someone says: 'Perhaps our memories are playing us false—perhaps there never was a pig in the glass case and we have only just come to believe there was'; and we counter this by producing written, present-tense records of each stage in the experiment. Or someone says: 'Perhaps it was all a mass hallucination'; and we produce photographs, wax impressions, etc. The utility of photographs, wax impressions and written records, depends upon their having existed throughout the time of the experiment.

Kant believes that evidence for the existence-change of a substance₁—by which I mean an objective item which *is* ordinarily treated substantivally—must be based upon the alterations and constancies of other things which persist throughout the time of the existence-change. I do not know how to prove that this is right; but it strikes me as plausible in the same way as the claim that evidence of a substance₁'s having rapidly and radically altered must be based upon facts about other things which did not at the same time alter rapidly and radically. Anyway, let us see what conclusions Kant draws from this belief of his.

In the following passage, he says that if Y's existence-change can be known only through X's alteration, then Y's existence-change *is* X's alteration, and Y is therefore a property or 'determination' of X. This is uncontroversial if Y is what we should ordinarily regard as a property: clearly, someone's becoming well *is* the annihilation of his illness. But the passage contains no hint of a restriction to cases of that kind. As it stands, it clearly implies that even so thing-like an item as a porcelain pig must, if it undergoes an existence-change, be denied the title of 'substance₁' and regarded as a property or determination of other things which are evidentially relevant to the existence-change:

A coming to be or ceasing to be that is not simply a determination of the permanent but is absolute, can never be a possible perception. For this permanent is what alone makes possible the representation of the transition from one state to another, and from not-being to being. These transitions can be empirically known only as changing determinations of that which is permanent. If we assume that something absolutely begins to be, we must have a point of time in which it was not. But to what are we to attach this point, if not to that which already exists? [i.e. How can we at this time say anything about that time, except on the basis of things which existed then and still exist now?]...But if we connect the coming to be with things which previously existed, and which persist in existence up to the moment of this coming to be, *this latter must be simply a determination of what is permanent in that which precedes it.* Similarly also with ceasing to be; it presupposes the empirical representation of a time in which an appearance no longer exists. [My italics.][1]

To call a porcelain pig a property of other things looks like nonsense. It does not make sense to speak of weighing a property, or of filling it with coins. That a porcelain pig can be weighed etc. is just what makes it a typical substance₁, i.e. an objective item which is *not* adjectival on other things in the way properties are. Still, what Kant is getting at is not nonsense.

The statement that (1) my illness is a state or property of me is tied to the equally uncontroversial statement that (2) the existence-change of my illness is my becoming well or becoming unwell. Furthermore, just because this alteration *is* the existence-change of my illness, it seems right to say that (3) the alteration is not merely evidence for the existence-change.

The order of these might be reversed. If for a given X and Y we had independent grounds for saying that (3) X's alteration is not merely evidence for Y's existence-change (though not evidentially irrelevant to it either), this might lead us to say that (2) X's alteration is Y's existence-change and thus that (1) Y is a state or property of X. For example, if there were a set of statements about the alterations of the glass case, the coins etc. which gave all the evidence there could possibly be for the pig's annihilation, someone might infer from this that (3) such a set would be positively equivalent to the statement that the pig had been annihilated, rather than merely stating evidence for it. From this he might infer that (2) the sum of the alterations *was* the existence-change of the pig, and thus that (1) the pig was a state or property of the glass case, the coins etc. It is this train of thought, I submit, which leads Kant to say that every existence-change 'must be simply a determination of what is permanent' since an existence-change 'can be empirically known only as [an alteration of] that which is permanent'.

I have illustrated (1)–(3) in terms of a pig and of an illness. Consider now an example which is in a certain way intermediate between these. A magnetic field is produced by a coil through which there runs a current generated by a dynamo; and within the field there is a compass pointing south-west, a revolving coil connected to a glowing filament, and a vibrating sheet of paper on which some iron filings maintain a pattern. Then certain alterations occur: the dynamo stops, the compass needle swings to magnetic north, the filament stops glowing, the iron filings no longer form a pattern. We are inclined to say that these and like alterations are evidence that the magnetic field has ceased to exist, and to think of the field as an individual thing, an intangible substance$_1$. But we also have a contrary inclination to say that (3) such alterations are not merely evidence for the field's annihilation but (2) *are* its annihilation, and also (1) to regard the field not as a thing or substance$_1$ over and above the behaviour of the iron filings, dynamo, filament etc., but rather as a logical construction out of this and similar behaviour.

This example supports my thesis that we do in general give the same answer to (1) 'Is Y in some way adjectival upon X rather than being an independent thing in its own right?' as we give to (2) 'Is X's alteration identical with Y's existence-change?' and to (3) 'Is X's alteration more than merely evidence for Y's existence-change?' In the case of the magnetic field, we incline both towards 'Yes' and towards 'No' in answer to each question, and in this tension it becomes easier to see that the three questions are really just one.

Although it is as absurd to say 'I created a property the size of a football, and put a compass in it' as it is to say 'I weighed a property and then put coins into it', we do nevertheless speak of magnetic fields as adjectival upon, or logically constructed out of, iron filings and dynamos and the like. By this we mean that magnetic fields could be exhaustively, though clumsily, described without the use of any sub-stantival expressions referring to magnetic fields as such. Analogously, we can make sense of the claim that the porcelain pig is a property of other things: for this can be understood as saying that the history of the porcelain pig, up to and including its annihilation, could be fully recounted without the use of any substantival expression referring to the pig.

When Kant says that all happenings are alterations, however, he must mean not only that we *could*, but that in the event of its existence-change we *ought to*, deprive the pig of its substantival status and recount its history by talking about the properties and alterations of other things. I shall argue that this could be done for any pig, but in § 50 I shall deny that it ought to be done even for a pig which undergoes an existence-change.

49 Reductionism

Here is a popular reason for denying that we could treat a porcelain pig as adjectival upon other things: 'Any set of statements which do not refer directly to the pig will be logically compatible with the pig's never having existed, whereas "The pig was placed in a glass case" is not. So we cannot express the whole force of "The pig was placed in a glass case" in a language which contains no substantival expression referring to the pig. Lacking any such expression we cannot say—though we may suggest—that there was a pig in the first place.'

Something like this could be expected from those philosophers who are prone to treat phenomenalism—that least understood and oftenest 'refuted' of philosophical theories—as just a special case of the more general error of *reductionism*. With astonishing frequency we are told that, although all our evidence about Fs consists in facts about Gs, propositions about Fs cannot be reduced to propositions about Gs, are not entailed by them, cannot be deductively derived from them, and so on. These and similar assurances are given with the confident air of one who knows exactly what is meant by 'reduce', 'entails', 'deductive' and the rest; but attempts to explain these terms show how far we are from being able to draw a clinically precise line between 'all the evidence there could be for P' and 'what entails P', or between 'what could not be known' and 'what is logically impossible'.

I am not saying that the imprecision of words like 'entails' entitles us to use them as we wish, but rather that it forbids us to use them in ways which would be legitimate only if they were precise. If every question about the porcelain pig can be answered on the basis of facts about things and people other than the pig, what subtle point is made by saying that it is nevertheless 'logically possible' that these other things should be thus and so even if there were no porcelain pig? This, like the statement that the iron filings, dynamo etc. could be thus and so even if there were no magnetic field, is just idle unless we are told—as we never are—what the 'logical possibility' is being kept open for.

Idle uses of 'logical possibility', 'entails', 'deduce' etc. are sometimes backed by talk about differences of 'category' or 'type' between bodies and minds, sense-data and physical objects, facts and values, the present and the past. The notion of a difference of type or category might serve to mark off 'plain' entailments from 'fancy' ones. For example, it could distinguish (i) the grounds for saying 'A thing cannot be square without having four straight sides' from (ii) the grounds for saying

'This set of statements about sensory states cannot be true unless that statement about a physical object is true'. We might reasonably say that (ii) does, while (i) does not, involve a logical connection between one category and another. But categorial barriers are invoked not in distinguishing plain entailments from fancy ones, but rather in denying that the latter are entailments at all: statements about sensations, we are told, cannot entail statements about physical things just because the two are in different categories. Since we are not told exactly what a categorial barrier is or how such a barrier can block entailments, this merely supports one dogma with another.

In any case, differences of category or type are irrelevant to our present question; for I am not here defending—and the first Analogy does not imply—the thesis that the pig's history could be told solely in terms of sensory states. I argue only that the pig's history could be told without substantival reference to the pig—referring no doubt to visual fields and the like, but referring also to weights and coins and photographs which are presumably in the same category as the pig.

Anti-reductionism is vague to the point of non-existence. Anti-phenomenalism is not; yet it is seldom defended in ways which are worthy of critical attention. Most of the published arguments have been based on a failure to see that one can be precise about the nature of a concept's vagueness; or a failure to grasp the difference between a concept's analysis and an account of how it is acquired; or a failure to see that someone who does not wish to recommend that we change our ways of speaking may nevertheless think it worthwhile to point out that a certain change would be possible without loss of content. I hope to say more about these matters in *Kant's Dialectic*, and cannot pursue them here. I shall, however, examine the argument which Warnock brings against phenomenalism in his book *Berkeley*. Although the argument is invalid, there is more to it than the dim hopefulness of most arguments for the same conclusion. Also, the diagnosis of its error will bring out a logical point which is directly relevant to the matter of the porcelain pig.

Warnock is arguing that no set of statements about how things seem, or would seem under certain circumstances, can entail a statement about how things really are:

If the sentence 'It seems to me and to God, and it would seem to anyone else, as if there were an orange on the sideboard' *means the same as* 'There is an orange on the sideboard', then to assert the first of these and to deny the second would be *self-contradictory*. But in fact this is not the case. 'It seems to me and to God and to absolutely everyone as if there were an orange on the sideboard, but really there is no orange there'—there is no self-contradiction in this. If it seems to everyone as if they were seeing an orange on the sideboard, it might be *silly* to say 'But no orange is really there'; but there is no *contradiction* in saying so... However many people give 'their own impressions', it *makes sense* to say that they are all mistaken.[1]

This part of what Warnock says looks like routine dogma, with italics at most of the weak points. But Warnock is not just dogmatizing, for he offers an argument which I have suppressed in the above quotation. After claiming that 'there is no *contradiction*' in saying that it seems to everyone as if there were an orange but really there is not, Warnock goes on: 'Indeed, the whole point of the expression "It seems as if..." is to make this non-contradictory.' A little earlier he remarks, in a similar vein, that 'the whole force of saying "It seems as if..." is to allow for "...but not so really".'

This presumably does not mean that one's whole point in saying 'It seems as if there were an orange there' is to stop short of saying that there really is an orange there—for that objective would be better achieved by silence. Part of one's point in saying 'It seems as if there were an orange there' is to 'give one's own impressions', to record some evidence which one has for there being an orange there; and I think Warnock must be claiming something about the 'force' or 'point' of making the evidential report in that way rather than in some other.

It is difficult, though, to decide what Warnock is claiming about this. If his concern is with the logical relations between P and the simple form 'It seems as if P' then—apart from the fact that he is attacking a straw man—I cannot construe his remark about the force of 'It seems as if...'. I think he must be concerned rather with the logical relations between P and any phenomenal statements which would give one reasons for saying 'It seems as if P'. This is confirmed by his implied equation of 'seems to everyone as if *there were* an orange' with 'seems to everyone as if *they were seeing* an orange': the latter points not to the simple 'It seems as if P' but rather to the phenomenal basis upon which one might say 'It seems as if P'.

I shall take it, then, that Warnock's point concerns the force of 'It seems as if...' in such forms as 'From the [phenomenal] fact that Q, it seems as if P'. On this reading, he must be saying that in statements of that form the function of 'It seems as if...' is to prevent Q from entailing P.

But suppose that Q just does entail P? Warnock might reply: 'If Q states only phenomenal facts, and P states the existence of a physical object, then Q won't entail P.' But if Warnock says that, then his argument about 'It seems as if...' has been side-stepped and he is just dogmatizing after all.

He might say instead: 'My point is not that "It seems as if..." prevents Q from entailing P; it is just that someone who says "From the fact that Q, it seems as if P" *says that* Q does not entail P.' But this, even if it were correct, does not lead to Warnock's conclusion. Suppose it is a fact that 'From the fact that..., it seems as if...' is a way of denying that a certain phenomenal statement entails a certain physical-object statement, the question whether all such denials are true remains entirely open.

In any case, it is not true that someone who says 'From the fact that Q, it seems as if P' asserts that Q does not entail P. The following account, I suggest, is more accurate. Someone who says 'From the fact that Q, it *seems as if* P'—rather than '*I conclude that*' or '*it follows that*' or '*we are entitled to infer that*'—is stressing that he claims only a fairly weak evidential relation between Q and P. He is not positively denying that Q has to P a stronger relation such as an entailment; he is merely underlining the fact that he does not affirm that such a relation holds. If Q does in fact entail P, what he says is perhaps unsuitably worded but it need not be false.

That is all the truth I can discover in Warnock's claim that the whole force of 'It seems as if...' is to allow for '...but not so really'; and it does not support his conclusion. To take an analogous case, what Warnock says about 'It seems as if...' could as well be said about 'like a...': 'The whole force of "like a man" is to allow for "but not really a man".' Now, when we say things of the form 'In the respect that x is G, it is like an F', we are saying that x's being G constitutes a similarity between it and anything which is F. What we thus say is true even if x's being G entails its being F, though in that case some other words would be more suitable. G's being an F-entailing property is compatible with its being true that something which is G is in that respect like an F. The analogue of 'The ways in which P can seem to be true could never entail P' is 'The respects in which things can be like an F could never entail a thing's being an F', and the one is as false as the other. To be an F *is* to be F-like in enough respects: we might well be forced to the conclusion that something was an F by an accumulation of premises of the form 'It is like an F in such and such a respect'. Having reached the conclusion, we should want to reword the premises, but not to deny them.

I conclude that 'In the respect that x is G, it is like an F' may be true even if x's being G entails its being F; just as 'From the fact that Q, it seems as if P' may be true even if Q entails that P. All that has to be added in each case is that if the speaker knew that the entailment held it would be peculiar for him to make his assertion *in that way*.

This has some direct bearing on the question of the porcelain pig. If the pig's history is to be recounted without any substantival reference to the pig, it will have to include many statements which would sound very strange *in a language which did contain a phrase like 'the porcelain pig'*. If we were restricted to statements which would *ordinarily* be expressed in the form of descriptions of things other than the pig, then of course we should be unable to tell a story which entailed the pig's existence. In a normal telling of the pig's history, statements containing the phrase 'the pig' annex to themselves so much of what there is to be said that the others—i.e. the statements which it would be natural to express without substantival reference to the pig—are indeed insufficient to entail that there was a pig. But we could, abnormally, forgo any substantival reference to the pig, and tell the whole story in terms of other things. This story would include 'unnatural' statements about the distribution of air in the glass case, the positions of the coins, the visual fields of the bystanders etc.; in a language containing the phrase 'the porcelain pig' these things can be said more compactly and conveniently by saying that the pig was in the glass case, the coins were in the pig, the bystanders saw the pig, and so on.

Kant says, in effect, that we must have criteria for *our* distinctions between what is to be treated substantivally and what adjectivally.[1] I have elaborated this theme, by arguing that although we have a settled distribution of functions between nouns and adjectives, we could, with or without good reasons, redistribute these functions along different lines.

50 Substances as sempiternal

I have construed Kant's claim that every happening must be an alteration—i.e. that everything which undergoes an existence-change must be a property of other things—as implying that if something to which we had given a substantival status were annihilated, we ought retroactively to deprive it of that status and admit that we should have dealt with it in the adjectival mode all along. This is why Kant finally takes substance₂ as his only acknowledged concept of substance: anything which underwent an existence-change and so failed as a substance₂ would also lose the right to the substantival treatment which is definitive of substance₁.

This is an extravagant conclusion. In one of the passages where he stresses that *we* divide our world into substances and properties, Kant implies that the only acceptable reason for treating something substantivally is that it is sempiternal:

> If I leave out permanence (which is existence in all time), nothing remains in the concept of substance save only the logical representation of a subject—a representation which I endeavour to realise by representing to myself something which can exist only as subject and never as predicate. But not only am I ignorant of any conditions under which this logical pre-eminence may belong to anything; I can neither put such a concept to any use, nor draw the least inference from it. For no object is thereby determined for its employment, and consequently we do not know whether it signifies anything whatsoever.[1]

This is just wrong. One good reason for treating something substantivally is that it is conceptually efficient to do so. For example, the expression 'the porcelain pig which went out of existence' is preferable to equivalent expressions of the form 'the coins, glass case, balance, air, people etc. which behaved thus and so', because the former is briefer, clearer and easier to handle. We can concede something to Kant: the phrase 'the porcelain pig' would be much less useful if the pig had lasted for only a few seconds. But even if we grant that moderate durability is required for something to count as a substance₁, it is a far cry from this to saying that only the sempiternal is entitled to substantival treatment. Kant's all-or-nothing habit of thought has here carried him to an unreasonable extreme.

Still, there is one thing to be said in favour of the claim that substances₁ cannot undergo existence-changes. Some philosophers have taken the view that an existence-statement is legitimate only if it can be put in a quantified form, i.e. in the form 'There is...', 'There are...', 'There were...' etc.[2] Wanting to show that 'Lions exist' does not predicate existence of lions, as 'Lions breed' predicates fertility of them, these philosophers have said that the former statement is best understood in the form 'There are lions'. In general, they have said that statements about what exists are statements about what properties are instantiated or about what descriptions have something answering to them. If this is right—as I think it is—then the existence-change of a substance$_1$ presents a problem: how can we express in quantified form the statement that a pig existed at t_1 which did not exist at t_2? Clearly, it will not do to say 'There was a pig at t_1 and there was no pig at t_2'. Nor will it do to take some description F which fits the pig, and say 'There was a pig which was F at t_1 and which was not F at t_2'; for that could be true if the pig had merely altered between t_1 and t_2. The problem does not arise for properties: the statement that an illness which existed at t_1 did not exist at t_2 can be put in the form 'There was something which was ill at t_1 and not ill at t_2'.

To cope with the existence-changes of material things, we might equate a thing's *existing* with its *being somewhere*, and so express 'Some matter which existed at t_1 did not exist at t_2' in the form 'There was a region of space which at t_1 contained some matter which no region contained at t_2'. If we ignore the conversion of matter into energy, this formulation seems to do the job; and so the problem of how to record the existence-changes of substances$_1$ in quantified statements is perhaps solved for one vast subclass of substances$_1$, namely material things. Yet Kant still has room for manœuvre: for in equating 'x exists' with 'There is a region of space containing x' we are doing something very like treating x as adjectival upon space; just as, in recording x's existence-change in the words 'There was a region of space which contained x at t_1, and no region contained x at t_2', we are virtually treating x's existence-change as an alteration of space.

The quantified treatment of existence-statements, formalized by Frege a century later, was largely pioneered by Kant in the Dialectic[1] and may have encouraged him to think that only what is sempiternal ought to count as substantial$_1$. In any case, there is a connection between the two positions, although I have no evidence that Kant was aware of it. What I do not know is how strong the connection is: it may be possible to accept the Fregean position on existence-statements without conceding much to Kant's thesis that all happenings must be alterations.

Even if Kant's thesis were correct, it is nothing like as strong as he thinks it is. Suppose we grant that anything which undergoes an existence-change ought to be denied a substantival status: the question now arises whether the world contains anything which by this strict standard deserves substantival treatment. Kant thinks that he has given an answer:[2] he seems to assume that the existence, and indeed the omnipresence, of substances$_2$ follows from his thesis that all happenings are alterations. This is a non-sequitur. If all happenings are alterations, then throughout any happening there is something which remains in existence; but this does not entail that there is something which remains in existence throughout every happening. (The sun is always shining somewhere; but there is no place at which the sun always shines.) If Kant replies that alterations must be of substances, i.e. of substances$_2$, then of course he is just begging the question. In short, he has no grounds for saying that the world can be described entirely in terms of substances$_2$ and their properties or determinations.

In a later part of the *Critique* Kant says:

We have nothing permanent on which, as intuition, we can base the concept of a substance, save only *matter*; and even this permanence is not obtained from outer experience, but is presupposed a priori...[1]

Thus: we know a priori that something is substantial$_2$, and we discover empirically that everything other than matter is non-substantial$_2$, whence we infer that matter is substantial$_2$. It is not clear whether Kant is jumping to the conclusion that *all* matter is substantial$_2$, but it looks as though he is: the first Analogy in B says of substance that 'its quantum in nature is neither increased nor diminished',[2] and in both editions he takes the Analogy to be directly relevant to the hypothesis of the conservation of matter, understood quantitatively.[3]

Whether or not it is mediated by a lemma about the substantiality$_2$ of all matter, the conclusion that some quantitative conservation law must hold does not follow from the premiss that the world is made of substances$_2$. Might one not say 'This is precisely the same substance$_2$ as was here a moment ago, but now it is less heavy [dense, impenetrable, etc.]'? Kant does not—and his discussion of intensive magnitude suggests that he could not—give any reason for saying that the identity of a substance$_2$ must involve constancy in some quantitative respect.

This, incidentally, is one of several places where Kant can be seen as trying to show that certain key features of Newtonian mechanics must be right. Kant's relation to Newton may be a useful guide-line for historians of ideas; but it seems to me that if we are looking for the core of philosophical interest in Kant then his Newtonian preoccupations are peripheral. We have seen that out of his absorbing discussion of alterations and existence-changes Kant develops, somewhat shakily, his thesis that all happenings are alterations; from this he infers invalidly that the world is made of substances$_2$; and from this he infers, again invalidly, that some quantitative conservation law must be true. *That* is the logical pedigree of the most Newton-oriented part of the entire *Critique*.

My treatment of the first Analogy has almost no overlap with those of other commentators who have based their exposition mainly on passages which I have ignored.[1] In these Kant speaks of time as 'permanent' and 'unperceivable', and says that the permanency of time must be 'represented' by something which is both permanent and perceivable, namely substance₂. Kant seems to have attached importance to this line of argument, but unfortunately no-one has yet shown it to be intelligible. Those who have purported to understand it have merely repeated what they ought to have explained. For example, Paton:

Kant's argument amounts to this—that since time...is permanent, there must be something permanent to represent or express an unperceivable time...[2]

Prichard has a paragraph which begins with the words 'Kant's thought appears to be as follows...', and includes the following:

Therefore, to apprehend a coexistence or a succession, we must perceive something permanent. But this permanent something cannot be time, for time cannot be perceived. It must therefore be a permanent in phenomena...[3]

Other commentators do little better.[4] Some of them express dissatisfaction with the argument, but none says what argument it is.

14

THE REFUTATION OF IDEALISM

51 The realism argument

Kant has a certain line of argument which, though adumbrated in the Transcendental Deduction in A (see §33 above), appears explicitly only in B, under the heading 'Refutation of Idealism'.[1] In the Preface to B Kant rightly calls it 'the only addition, strictly so called'[2] which he has made to the content of the *Critique*.

The Refutation of Idealism is Kant's *chef d'œuvre* of compressed obscurity: no-one could claim that its one brief paragraph constitutes, as it stands, an achieved argument. If we are to take it seriously, we must speculate about what is supposed to be happening in it. Clearly, its target is anyone who denies or casts doubt on the existence of an objective realm; and the opening sentences give an impression of what the line of attack will be:

I am conscious of my own existence as determined in time. All determination of time presupposes something *permanent* in perception. This permanent cannot, however, be something in me...[3]

This seems to say: 'According to the first Analogy, a self-conscious being must have experience of something permanent. I shall now show that the latter must be objective or other-than-oneself.' Although most commentators have taken Kant at his word here,[4] there are powerful reasons for not doing so.

For one thing, the Refutation of Idealism could hold little interest if it presupposed the untruth which is the first Analogy, i.e. if it were a rider saying: '...and, furthermore, these sempiternal items must be objective'. Also, such verbal overlaps as it has with the 'proof' of the first Analogy pertain to the latter's least comprehensible part—not to the analysis of existence-change but rather to the obscure doctrine that time is permanent and unperceivable. Most important of all: if the Refutation of Idealism presupposes the first Analogy, then the 'proof' of the latter must be taken as offering, in support of the conclusion that self-consciousness requires experience of something permanent, an argument which is neutral as to whether the 'something permanent' is inner or outer. This is an impossible reading of the first Analogy, which is clearly stated in both editions as a thesis about the division of 'appearances', i.e. of the *objective* realm, into substances and properties.

In fact, the supposed connection with the first Analogy does not figure in Kant's initial statement of what is to be proved in the Refutation of Idealism:

The mere, but empirically determined, consciousness of my own existence proves the existence of objects in space outside me[1]

or in his subsequent account of what the Refutation has proved:

In the above proof it has been shown that outer experience is really immediate, and that only by means of it is inner experience—not indeed the consciousness of my own existence, but the determination of it in time—possible.[2]

Following these hints, I take the Refutation of Idealism to be a proof—or a gesture towards a proof—that self-consciousness requires experience of an objective realm, saying and assuming nothing about how such a realm should be divided into substances and properties. So construed, it does not presuppose the first Analogy, though it does set the objective scene within which the latter operates. In short, if the two are to be connected at all, Kant has them in the wrong order. Rather than arguing: 'I must have experience of substances$_2$; and these must be objective', I take him to be arguing: 'I must have experience of an objective realm; and this must contain substances$_2$'. (Cf. the last two paragraphs of §46 above.)

I have remarked that if we are not to ignore the Refutation of Idealism altogether we must bring something to it. In this spirit, I shall offer something which I call the *realism argument*. This certainly cannot be found in Kant's words, and it may not have been what he 'had in mind' in writing the Refutation of Idealism; but the hypothesis that he did have the realism argument in mind, whether it be plausible or not, is at least philosophically instructive. The two do have something to do with one another, and it can hardly be pure coincidence. The realism argument is broadly Kantian; its conclusion, namely that self-consciousness requires outer experience, is exactly that of the Refutation of Idealism; it squares with Kant's text better than any other alternative I can find; and it does not require that the proof of the first Analogy be read, absurdly, as neutral with respect to the subjective/objective or inner/outer borderline. The realism argument, furthermore, genuinely connects with Kant's *ordering argument* (discussed in §54 below), which in its turn has a large verbal overlap with the first Analogy; and this enables us to explain Kant's giving the impression—which cannot be correct—that the first Analogy lies in the background of the Refutation of Idealism. In writing the latter he was, according to my hypothesis, thinking along the lines of the realism argument; and it would be only too typical of him to get this mixed up with the ordering argument and, through it, with the first Analogy.

One other general point about the Refutation of Idealism should be noted. In it Kant refers to 'outer things', 'outer objects', 'things outside me', 'objects in space outside me' etc.; and he clearly takes these to be equivalent. Thus he links otherness with outerness, and both with objectivity, as he should have done in the Aesthetic. The Refutation of Idealism, indeed, though a wretched piece of exposition, belongs to an altogether maturer intellectual world than the early parts of the *Critique*. For example, when Kant says that 'our inner experience is possible only on the assumption of outer experience', there is no hint that he is saying something about a linkage between the mechanisms of inner and outer sense. We now have to see what, according to my exegetical hypothesis, he is saying.

The realism argument can be presented as a version of an argument which Wittgenstein uses in trying to show that there could not be a 'private language'. That is, Kant's line of thought could be the following one. How can I know now what state I was in at any earlier time? One answer is: by remembering. But then why may I trust my memory? The only possible answer to that is: because I sometimes check on it, and by and large find it reliable. So I can base an individual judgment about the past simply on a present recollection only because I can and sometimes do appeal to something other than memory. Such appeals must be to objective states of affairs: if they involved only my inner states they would raise questions of just the sort they were supposed to answer. For example, if I try to check my recollection of having been uncomfortably warm ten minutes ago by recalling that five minutes ago I recalled being uncomfortably warm five minutes before that, I replace a single problem by two others of precisely the same kind.

Here is what Kant says:

I am conscious of my own existence as determined in time. All determination of time presupposes something *permanent* in perception. But this permanent cannot be an intuition in me. For all grounds of determination of my existence which are to be met with in me are representations; and as representations themselves require a permanent distinct from them, in relation to which their change, and so my existence in the time wherein they change, may be determined.[1]

Kant's reference to the 'change' of my representations, like his stress on 'something *permanent*', is misleading: the realism argument concerns *all* past-tense statements about oneself, not only 'I was in state S which I am not in now' but also 'I was in state S which I am in still'. Change is not mentioned in Kant's statement of what is to be proved: 'The mere, but empirically determined, consciousness of my own existence proves the existence of objects in space outside me.'[1]

The 'empirically determined' consciousness of my own existence is my knowing that I have a history and knowing something of what its content has been. Later Kant words the matter a little differently, when he says that the realism argument shows 'that outer experience is really immediate, and that only by means of it is inner experience—not indeed the consciousness of my own existence, but the determination of it in time—possible.'[2] We have seen that the 'determinations' of substances are their states or properties. When Kant speaks of 'the determination in time' of my existence he means the establishment of the empirical facts about me—of what my states have been—at the various stages in my history. Later there is more to the same effect: 'The existence of outer things is required for the possibility of a determinate consciousness of the self',[3] i.e. for a consciousness of the self *as* determined in certain ways, as having this rather than that history.

Whether or not Kant really is putting forward the argument I have outlined, about the need for objective evidence as to what one's past states have been, there is a question about whether that argument is valid.

Someone might object: 'Why must we be able to check our memories? If checks were never available this would be unfortunate, but surely one *could* simply decide to trust one's memory anyway.' This objection is best answered along with another one: 'What is achieved by checking recollections against objective states of affairs? Any such check involves an inference, from present data, to the state of the world at some past time; and such an inference depends upon some general, lawlike statement. But to be entitled to trust *this* one must have evidence for its truth, and so must have beliefs about what one has observed in the past. But what entitles one to these beliefs? Unaided recollection? Then one has "checked" on one recollection by invoking others. Objective considerations, then? But these involve yet further lawlike statements, and so further beliefs about the past which require further checks, and so on ad infinitum. The whole thing is an attempt to pull oneself up by one's bootstraps.'

Both these objections have been levelled against one of Wittgenstein's arguments. In particular, Ayer has tried[1] to get from certain followers of Wittgenstein straight answers to the questions: 'Why must we have objective checks upon memory?' and 'How can we have independent checks on memory as such?' Ayer's opponents have not only failed to answer his questions but seem not to have understood why he thought it relevant to ask them. In fact the questions are relevant, and indeed fatal, to the realism argument in the form in which I have stated it and in which Wittgenstein is sometimes thought to have intended it.

There is a version of the argument which escapes these difficulties and does establish Kant's conclusion if not Wittgenstein's. Since any check on memory does itself involve a trust in memory, the reason why individual recollections must be checkable against objective states of affairs cannot be that unsupported memory is unworthy of trust. The argument must be cleansed of all references to trustworthiness, entitlement to believe, and the like. Wittgenstein says:

Justification consists in appealing to something independent.—'But surely I can appeal from one memory to another. For example, I don't know if I have remembered the time of departure of a train right and to check it I call to mind how a page of the time-table looked. Isn't it the same here?'—No: for this process has got to produce a memory which is actually *correct*. If the mental image of the time-table could not itself be *tested* for correctness, how could it confirm the correctness of the first memory? (As if someone were to buy several copies of the morning paper to assure himself that what it said was true.)[2]

This is wide open to the objections stated above. But in an earlier passage Wittgenstein proceeds differently:

In the present case I have no criterion of correctness. One would like to say: whatever is going to seem right to me is right. And that only means that here we can't talk about 'right'.[3]

This, as it stands, is too casual to be assessed; but at least it does not raise barren questions about trustworthiness; and it does in fact point towards something which, I shall argue, is true and important.

To bring out what this is, I need to refer to the theory of concept-utility presented in §14: if one has a language L in which to describe a subject-matter S, it is legitimate to add a new concept C to the stock of concepts in L in proportion as L-with-C can describe S more simply than can L-without-C. I have brought this theory to bear upon the addition of objectivity concepts to a purely phenomenal language;

I shall now apply it again, this time by considering the addition of the concept of the past to a purely present-tense phenomenal language.

Let us suppose that someone—as is at least prima facie possible—is limited to what Kant calls 'inner' experience, and has a purely present-tense language in which he describes each of his inner states as it occurs. Can he enlarge the scope of his language so as to describe not only his state at the time of his speaking but also his states at earlier times? Well, what he *now* says about his past must be based upon data which he has *now*; and since these are all 'inner', i.e. include no information about objective states of affairs, they must consist wholly in recollections of past occasions. Specifically, his present judgment about how he was at *t* must be based upon his present recollection of himself at *t*.

What is the difficulty? If his inner states include recollections, why should he not describe his past states, thus adding to his language the concept of *how I was*, the concept of *the past*? My answer is that this addition does nothing for him, since there will at any given time be a one-one relation between what he can say about his past states and what he can say about his present recollections. He can have grounds for saying 'I was thus at *t*' *if and only if* he has grounds for saying 'I recollect being thus at *t*', and so it makes no difference to the economy of his language whether he says one thing or the other. For him, the distinction between 'I was...' and 'I recollect...' is literally idle. His situation is analogous to that described in §11 of the hearer of an auditory chaos who tries to use the concept of an objective sound-sequence: this concept does no work for him because each statement he makes with it corresponds to an equally brief statement which he can make without it.

Recollections are by definition faced towards the past; and it might be thought that the man with only inner experience can easily have a concept of the past since his inner states may well include recollections. But unless we can find work for his concept of the past to do we are not entitled to assume that any of his present states can intelligibly be described as 'recollections'. My argument that he has no use for the distinction between 'I was...' and 'I recollect being...' thus turns into an argument for denying that he can even have a use for the latter.

Now, contrast this with the case of someone who has outer experience. He too must base his present judgment about his past on the data which he now has, but he is not restricted to one datum per judgment. His access to objective states of affairs enables him to bring several present data to bear on a single judgment about his past. There are at least three ways in which this may happen. (1) His recollections of various earlier times may be relevant to his judgment about what his state was at some one time: his recollection of a severe fall at t_1 may confirm his judgment that he was in pain at t_2. (2) His recollection of various aspects of his state at an earlier time may be relevant to his judgment about some one aspect of his state at that time: his recollection of seeing sunshine at t may confirm his judgment that he felt warm at t. (3) Present data other than recollections can now be relevant to a judgment about his past: that he now sees ashes confirms his judgment that he earlier saw a fire. Each of these cases involves general judgments as well—severe falls are followed by pain, sunshine is accompanied by warmth, ashes are preceded by fire—and his acceptance of any such 'law' widens still further the range of recollections which are brought to bear upon a single judgment about his past.

I do not say that because he can bring several data to bear on a single judgment about the past, he is therefore *entitled* to make such judgments: my argument does not concern the increase in trustworthiness which might be thought to accrue from piling up data. Rather, I argue that just because several of his recollections may bear on a single one of his judgments—confirming *or disconfirming* it—the person with outer experience has a complex relationship between 'I was...' and 'I recollect...'. Within the complex, ordered manifold which is his outer experience, i.e. his experience of an objective realm, he can generate a network of pros and cons; and so when he says 'I was...' he is summing up a great deal of material whose expression in terms of present data, including recollections, would be a very lengthy and complicated matter. His concept of the past, in short, is not idle.

I stress recollections because I wish to phenomenalize the story as much as possible. Most versions of the realism argument are vulnerable to the thesis that only present data can bear upon present judgments; and I am trying to show that my version is not, by building the thesis into my argument. Putting an extremely strong interpretation on the view that a present judgment can be based only on present data, my argument can be expressed in a slightly different way. Let us adopt the naively extreme premiss that the concept of what *was* the case is just the concept of what does (or, if investigations were carried far enough, would) *seem in nearly every way to have been* the case. Now, for the man who has only inner experience there is only one way in which anything can seem to have been the case, so that his so-called judgments about the past pair off neatly with his present-tense judgments about his so-called recollections. He therefore cannot construct a past out of his present data: his 'past' states collapse into his present 'recollections' of them, because no work is done by the distinction between the two. And so, in his scheme of things, the past collapses into the present.

I have argued that a concept of the past cannot operate on entirely chaotic experience, but may get a grip on experience which is so ordered as to constitute experience of an objective realm. There is an intermediate case, however. Could a creature have a working concept of the past if its experience, while falling under laws, did not allow of the distinction between 'is' and 'seems' or any of the other correlates of the inner/outer distinction? If it could, then my argument can be rescued only by weakening its conclusion. I do not know whether such a weakening is needed: the complexities of the issue have defeated me. I shall proceed as though the stronger conclusion were clearly justified. This reflects a strong suspicion that it *is* justified, and it makes for brevity.

With that caveat, then, I conclude that someone who had only inner experience could not make judgments about his past: for him to do so would be not rash but impossible. My argument is more detailed than Kant's but does have certain features in common with it. For in the Refutation of Idealism Kant is concerned with 'the empirical determination of my existence in time', which can only be understood as 'the establishment of what my sensory history has in fact been'. Also, Kant says nothing about the need for outer experience if judgments about one's past are to be *trustworthy*; what he says is that only to someone with outer experience are such judgments *possible*.

There is, however, a prima facie gap between my conclusion and Kant's. I have argued that inner experience which is not also outer could not be brought under *the concept of the past*, while Kant thinks that it could not be brought under *any concepts* and is therefore impossible. Similarly, Wittgenstein seems to conclude not that a purely 'private' language cannot have a past tense but rather that there could not be such a language.

One might try to close the gap by arguing that even a present-tense language must involve a *correct* use of general terms, i.e. one which squares with one's initial decisions as to their use and/or with one's past uses of them. This is part of Kant's point when he says:

There [could not] be an empirical synthesis of reproduction, if a certain name were sometimes given to this, sometimes to that object, or were one and the same thing named sometimes in one way, sometimes in another, independently of any rule to which appearances are in themselves subject.[1]

Wittgenstein also assumes that to use a language one must have beliefs about the past because the notion of a correct use is essentially a backwards-looking one.[1]

This assumption is too simple. There is no reason in principle why there should not be a creature which could use some large but thoroughly present-tense fragment of our language, while able neither to use nor to understand statements about the past. The pattern of linguistic behaviour which this involves could be consistently described. Although past and present are intertwined in human languages, there is no warrant for the common belief that a creature which can correctly say things like 'That is a ship' and 'This is a shoe' *must* have knowledge of its past.

Still, there is something valid in the above way of closing the gap between 'impossible' and 'not brought under the concept of the past', at least in so far as these apply to purely inner experience. We must distinguish between what one could know about some other creature and what one could know about oneself. I have argued that I could know—or reasonably believe—of some other creature that it had knowledge only of its present; but to know any such fact about it I should have to know that there was some objective realm with which both the creature and I were sensorily confronted. To know that it had a language, for example, I should have to be able to assess its linguistic performances in the light of its sensory intake; and this would require the sharing of a common world, i.e. one which was 'outer' for both of us. So *that* possibility does not prove that I could know that a creature with only inner experience had knowledge only of its present.

Well, then, could I know that I myself had purely inner experience and knowledge only of my present? I think not. It is logically impossible that I should know that I was F if F excludes self-consciousness, i.e. rules out my being able to have the thought 'This is how it is with me' (see §28 above); and self-consciousness requires knowledge of the past—'This is how it is with me now' requires 'That is how it was with me then' (see §30 above). It follows that nothing could count as my knowing that I had purely inner experience and no knowledge of the past.

In short: nothing could count as knowing that a creature both (a) had only inner experience and (b) had no knowledge of the past; for one could not know (a) of any other creature, and one could not know (b) of oneself. It may be objected that it is possible that a creature should satisfy both (a) and (b), although nothing could count as knowing that this was the case; but this use of 'possible' is idle.

I agree, then, with Kant's conclusion that purely inner experience is not to be counted as a real possibility—one which could in principle be known to be realized. As for Wittgenstein: his discussion of the possibility of a 'private language' raises exegetical problems which I cannot pursue here, but I must say something about the difference between Kant's 'inner' and Wittgenstein's 'private'.[1]

Some versions of Wittgenstein's argument for the impossibility of a private language invite the objection: 'If the argument were valid at all, it would show the impossibility of a congenital Robinson Crusoe—the sole speaker of a language with an objective subject-matter—but clearly this is not logically impossible.'[2] The standard reply is: 'The argument rules out the possibility of a language which is necessarily, not just *de facto*, private.'[3] This reply needs scrutiny.

Could there be a necessarily private hat, i.e. one which could not be worn by more than one person? The question is absurd: it is a piece of pre-Lockean essentialism, an ellipsis which we are not told how to expand. Any expression of the form 'an X which is necessarily G' requires expansion into something of the form 'an X which is F [where F is a non-modal property]—and necessarily any X which is F is G'. A hat which was never removed from any head would, *qua* hat of which that was true, be a 'necessarily private hat' in the above sense; but a hat cannot be necessarily private, or necessarily anything, except *qua* (or considered as being) a hat which has a given non-modal property. So when a philosopher asks whether there could be a necessarily private language, we must ask: 'Necessarily private—*qua* what? What non-modal feature do you have in mind which would be incompatible with a language's being understood by more than one person?' He might be asking whether there could be a language which was necessarily private *qua* language for describing the inner states of a creature which has no perceptions of anything outer. To that question the realism argument answers 'No', but I do not describe it as 'an argument for the impossibility of a necessarily private language'. That description, without actually saying what the crux of the argument is, strongly implies that the crux is *privacy*. That is, it suggests that the argument turns on the fact that a creature with only inner experience could not share a language—a fact which is totally irrelevant to the actual working of the realism argument. Some of the 'arguments for the impossibility of a necessarily private language' in the current literature turn simply on *de facto* privacy; while others, like the realism argument, have nothing to do with privacy and are concerned solely with non-modal features which do in fact entail privacy. There is a third possibility: someone might argue that a language with a certain non-modal feature is impossible, this impossibility arising *partly* from the fact that the feature entails privacy. This would be an argument for the impossibility of a language which was private in a certain way, or private for certain reasons. Even an argument like this, however— supposing there were one—would not be happily described as 'an argument for the impossibility of a necessarily private language'.

The notion of *de facto* privacy has no work to do in this general area of philosophy, but it is easy to see how someone might come to think that it has. Someone who thought that a good argument might be based on the claim (a) that memory ought to be trusted only if supported by checks which in no way presuppose trust in memory, might be led by this into thinking that his argument genuinely involved privacy because (b) the needed checks could be provided by other people but not, in the first instance at least, by objective but impersonal states of affairs. His thought might run as follows:

When I appeal to objective, impersonal clues, it is still up to me to assess them, to decide how they bear on the question about the past which I want answered. To do this I must know how the world works—how it has worked—and so the appeal to impersonal clues cannot free me from my dependence on memory. However, if I ask people instead of looking for clues, I may be given an answer to my question and not merely something out of which I must construct an answer—the latter being all I get if I 'ask' the world 'Was there fire here?' and am 'answered' with a heap of ashes.

Such a person has got off on the wrong foot by accepting (a): if (a) were correct then there could be no trustworthy source of knowledge about the past. But seeing this involves seeing that (b) is false too. That is, it involves seeing that someone who demands memory-independent checks is no better served by people than by things, and so has no reason for stressing inter-personality over objectivity. Waiving the problem of what entitles one to believe the spoken answers, the crucially damaging fact is this: the giving of an answer is a piece of behaviour, a happening in the objective realm; and like any such happening it has to be interpreted, assessed for relevance and significance. My confidence that I have been given a certain answer to my question is only as good as my confidence that the object before me is a person, that his noises are words, that the words mean what I take them to mean. All this depends upon my knowledge of how the world works— how it has worked—and so for present purposes the spoken answer is on a par with the heap of ashes. The picture of communication as the insertion of propositions into other people's minds, although always wrong, is especially harmful at our present level of epistemological grass-roots. We should replace it by the cold maxim: what people say is just a special case of what objects do.

Wittgenstein seems to flirt with the line of thought which I have been criticizing. When he says that 'it is not possible to obey a rule "privately"',[1] for example, he implies that a language which was *de facto* private could not be used according to rules. Apparently, he assumes that if I have to decide what to say then I can say what I please and can therefore have no standards for the correctness of what I say. This assumption appears strikingly in one of Malcolm's defences of this part of Wittgenstein's thought: 'On the private-language hypothesis, no one can teach me what the correct use of "same" is... But a sound that I can use *as I please* is not a *word*.'[2]

This is sad, for Wittgenstein is trying to support something for which he has an adequate argument of a quite different kind. His main concern, I believe, is to show something about the logic of the public language in which we report our inner states. Specifically, he wants to show that our public reports of our inner states are *logically* connected with the objective causes of inner states and with their objective manifestations in non-linguistic behaviour. The datum here is that what people say about their pains, for example, correlates roughly with states of their bodies and environments which we may call 'pain-causes', and with what we may call their non-linguistic 'pain-behaviour'. A simplified example: someone says 'That hurts'; he has just broken his arm, and he winces and grits his teeth. Wittgenstein's view is that pain-causes and pain-behaviour are not dispensable concomitants of pain-reports, but are necessary if we are to have a public language for reporting our pains—or, mutatis mutandis, any of our other inner states. In this sense, he thinks that facts about pain-causes and pain-behaviour enter into the meaning of what is said in our public language for reporting pains. The following objection looks plausible:

Wittgenstein seems to think that what we say in our public pain-language has meaning solely through its correlation with pain-causes and pain-behaviour; and this is rank behaviourism. In fact, (a) pain-reports correlate with (b) pain-causes and pain-behaviour only because (a) and (b) are severally correlated with items of another kind altogether—namely, *pains*. Pains correlate with (a) because we recognize pains when we have them, and with (b) because pain-causes cause pains which in their turn cause or somehow induce pain-behaviour. If we collapse these two correlations into a single one between (a) and (b) directly, we shall abolish the pains.

Wittgenstein does not wish to abolish the pains, but he opposes *this* way of getting them into the picture. He asks: might there be a failure of the alleged correlation between pains and (a) pain-reports, and a precisely compensating failure in the alleged correlation between pains and (b) pain-causes and pain-behaviour? His point is that this supposition is vacuous; and so its contradictory—namely the thesis that there are these two independent correlations—is vacuous too. Thus:

'Imagine a person whose memory could not retain *what* the word "pain" meant—so that he constantly called different things by that name—but nevertheless used the word in a way fitting in with the usual symptoms and presuppositions of pain'—in short he uses it as we all do. Here I should like to say: a wheel that can be turned though nothing else moves with it, is not part of the mechanism.[1]

This argument, which seems to me entirely successful, concerns the conditions under which there can be a public language in which inner states are reported. It has nothing to do with the possibility of a private language, or of a 'necessarily private language'—whatever that might mean. When Wittgenstein says 'in short he uses it as we all do', he places his argument squarely within the region of the question: 'What sense can I make of what others say about their inner states?' He rejects answers which do not give centrality and weight to the causal and behavioural accompaniments of our talk about inner states; but that rejection entails nothing about what sort of language I can consistently suppose myself to have, or about what conditions must obtain if I am to have any language.

If Wittgenstein could show that (i) a rule cannot be obeyed privately, it would follow that (ii) there cannot be a language which is *de facto* private, whence it would perhaps follow that (iii) someone who can bring his inner states under a language must also engage in physical behaviour, and/or be subject to physical causes, of certain sorts. The acceptance of (iii) might well predispose one to think that (iv) the causal and behavioural concomitants of our public reports of our inner states are in some way bound up with the meanings of those reports. I have tried to show, however, that Wittgenstein has an excellent argument for (iv) which does not require the cloudy move from (iii) to (iv) or the initial premiss (i) for which he has no grounds at all.

52 Kant's two refutations of empirical idealism

Kant distinguishes two kinds of empirical idealist: the 'dogmatic' one who says that there is no outer world, and the less rash 'problematic' one who regards it as not at all obvious that there is an outer world. Kant classifies Berkeley as a dogmatic idealist and Descartes as a problematic one. He is certainly right about Descartes. By the end of his second meditation, Descartes takes the nature of his inner experience to be settled beyond question, but thinks that only by a subtle theological argument can he show that he has experience of a reality distinct from himself. Kant rejects both sorts of idealism: he affirms that there is an outer world, and that this does not have to be established by an esoteric proof. He has two arguments, whose inter-relations need to be explained.

(1) Kant refutes Descartes by putting a transcendental idealist construction on his question 'Granted that my inner experience is of the usual sort, are there objects outside me?'[1] The question then answers itself, for if transcendental idealism is right then to grant that one's experience is of the sort which normal adults usually have *is* to grant that one perceives objects. In the following passage Kant expresses himself in a more Berkeleian fashion than his premisses entitle him to, saying that outer objects *are*, rather than that they are constructs out of, representations. Still, it serves to display his strategy against Descartes:

In order to arrive at the reality of outer objects I have just as little need to resort to inference as I have in regard to...the reality of my own thoughts. For in both cases alike the objects are nothing but representations, the immediate perception (consciousness) of which is at the same time a sufficient proof of their reality.[2]

Descartes of course was not a transcendental idealist. He thought he was asking whether there are real things—in some deep sense of 'real'—behind the veil of perception. Kant's view is that if Descartes' question has any meaning then, whatever Descartes may have thought, it must be one expressible in transcendental idealist terms; and, so construed, the question answers itself. (See §8 above.)

(2) Then there is the realism argument, discussed in the preceding section. The relevance of this to Descartes is obvious: someone who knows what his inner experience is like must know something of its past history and so—by the realism argument—he must inhabit an objective world and know that he does so. It is therefore impossible to

know what one's inner experience is like while wondering whether there is an objective world.

In the passage last cited, Kant virtually says that (1) is all he needs to refute idealism; but of (2) he says:

If the existence of outer things is not in any way required for the determination of one's own existence in time, the assumption of their existence is a quite gratuitous assumption, of which no proof can ever be given.[1]

In short, he says that (1) is sufficient, and that (2) is necessary, for the refutation of empirical idealism. Since (1) does not entail (2), this must be wrong.

It might be thought that Kant changed his mind between the two editions of the *Critique*, since (1) is most fully expounded in a passage occurring only in A, while (2) is only in B. But it would be wrong to infer that Kant became dissatisfied with his first anti-idealist argument and therefore replaced it by another, i.e. that he called (2) necessary because he *no longer* thought (1) sufficient for the refutation of idealism. Since (1) is valid, Kant has no reason to jettison it; and most of it can in fact be found in a passage occurring in both editions.

Further evidence of Kant's desire to hold both that (1) is sufficient and that (2) is necessary is given by the fact that in B he tries to reconcile these two claims.[2] What he says is that (1) is sufficient to refute dogmatic idealism, but that (2) is necessary for the refutation of the less vulnerable problematic idealism. This seems to conflict with the passage I have quoted in which Kant deploys (1) against the problematic idealist; but, as I have remarked, that passage is too Berkeleian to be true to Kant. If Kant were to say not that 'outer objects are representations' but only that outer objects are constructs out of representations, or that the content of statements about outer objects is expressible purely in statements about representations, then perhaps problematic idealism is not after all refuted by (1) the argument from transcendental idealism. For Kant's phenomenalism, when thus properly expressed, leaves it open for him to say that every statement about the objective realm, however well attested, is open to refutation by the *future* course of experience. (Phenomenalism is not motivated solely by a passion for certainty. Someone who regards objectivity statements as permanently corrigible[3] may nevertheless think that phenomenalism gives a *correct* analysis of them; he will not reject the sceptic's claim 'We can never know for sure', but only the reasons the sceptic gives for it.) Good reasons have been given for rejecting this corrigibilist thesis;[4] but Kant, for whom substances must be sempiternal and causal laws strictly universal, is just the man to keep tables and chairs permanently on probation. This could lead him to think that, against someone who says 'It *may* all be a rather durable mirage', he needs bigger guns than (1) his transcendental idealism; and that these are provided by (2) the realism argument, which does imply something about the future, specifically about what our experience *will* be like for as long as we have known inner states of any kind. If this is Kant's position, though, it is unsatisfactory; for he admits that the realism argument does not guarantee the truth of any particular objectivity statement,[1] and so it cannot have much force against this form of problematic idealism.

Perhaps Kant has something different in mind. He may think that (2) the realism argument is effective not against Descartes' claim that he *ought to*, but rather against his claim that he *does*, suspend judgment on the question of whether there is an objective realm. For the realism argument, if it shows anything, shows that a self-conscious being must inhabit an objective realm and know that he does so:

In order to determine to which given intuitions objects outside me actually correspond, and which therefore belong to outer *sense*..., we must in each single case appeal to the rules according to which experience in general...is distinguished from imagination—the proposition that there is such a thing as outer experience being always presupposed.[2]

But this interpretation seems not to fit Kant's objection to problematic idealism. His complaint is not that Descartes says he doubts something which in fact he must 'presuppose', but rather that he finds 'doubtful and indemonstrable' something which can be 'proved'.

The distinction between problematic and dogmatic idealism is, I suggest, a red herring. When we set it aside we can see that there is, after all, a case to be made for saying that (1) is in some way sufficient, and that (2) is in some way necessary, for the refutation of idealism. For (1) is sufficient, when combined with certain sensory facts, to refute idealism; but if one wants to refute it without invoking empirical data then (2) is necessary. Consider this version of (1):

The transcendental idealist is...an empirical realist, and allows to matter, as appearance, a reality which does not permit of being inferred, but is immediately perceived. Transcendental realism, on the other hand,...regards the objects of outer sense as something distinct from the senses themselves...On such a view as this, however clearly we may be conscious of our representation of these things, it is still far from certain that, if the representation exists, there exists also the object corresponding to it.[3]

This passage contrasts the ways in which transcendental idealism and transcendental realism respectively handle the given sensory facts: it is by appealing to these that (1) settles Descartes' doubts. Argument (2), on the other hand, makes no appeal to sensory facts, for it argues that if one can tell any story at all about one's sensory states one must have experience of an objective realm. Could there be an idealist whose question 'Do I perceive an objective world?' was not answered by (1) because he, unlike Descartes, did not himself have the requisite sensory states? There could not; and this is shown by (2) the realism argument but not by (1) the argument from transcendental idealism.

15

THE SECOND ANALOGY

53   The object/process argument

The second Analogy says: 'All alterations take place in conformity with the law of the connection of cause and effect.'[1] Kant's 'proof' of this is sometimes said to be a sequence of six arguments with no acknowledged breaks between them;[2] while Weldon calls it a single argument with an introduction and a postscript.[3] I think that the 'proof' is too much of a jumble for either of these descriptions to be apt. Here, even more than usual, respect for Kant's genius requires an irreverent approach to his text.

A dominant theme in the 'proof' of the second Analogy is the relationship between causality and objectivity. Kant has two arguments about this. One of them argues that since self-conscious creatures must have outer experience, they must have experience of a realm which is causally ordered:

> If we enquire what new character *relation to an object* confers upon our representations, what dignity they thereby acquire, we find that it results only in subjecting the representations to a rule, and so in necessitating us to connect them in some one specific manner.[4]

This point was illustrated in §12, where sensory chaos was turned into experience of objective sound-sequences by means of a primitive causal law associating non-master with master sounds; and again in §13, where the sound-sequences were allowed to move and alter, but at a rate limited by yet further causal laws so that the auditory world should not revert to a non-objective chaos. These examples point to Kant's central insight that objectivity is a certain kind of order.

An objective realm must indeed obey causal laws, but the obedience need not be perfect. The physical world would not be shown to be a figment of my imagination just by the occurrence in it of occasional flurries of disorder, occasional happenings which—so far as I could tell—fell under no causal law. Kant, therefore, is still short of his conclusion that *all* alterations conform to 'the law of the connection of cause and effect'.

One would hardly expect him to concede this. His view that causal laws must be true with absolutely no exceptions (§ 39) leaves open the possibility that some alterations might not be wholly causally determined: without allowing that the true science may sometimes give the wrong answer, Kant might allow that it could sometimes give no answer, to questions about what will happen next. Against this we must set his deeply rigorist cast of mind: he seems to have been incapable of taking in the idea that some important aspect of our conceptual scheme might depend upon something's being the case in a *fairly high degree*; and so we might expect him to treat an argument for the world's moderate obedience to causal laws as though it were an argument for total determinism. Be that as it may, Kant does in fact proceed as though he *did* see a gap between objectivity and perfect causal order; for he produces a second argument about the object/cause relationship, one which seems intended to succeed where the first argument fails.

This second argument is prefaced by a paragraph[1] in which Kant considers one aspect of the distinction between 'appearance' (objective) and 'the representations of apprehension' (subjective). His concern is with the logic of the concept of a *survey*, which is my word for a *series of perceptions of different parts or aspects of an unchanging object*. Kant notes that when we inspect a house, room by room, we have a succession of different visual states, yet 'no-one will grant' that 'the manifold of the house is also in itself successive' even though the house is a logical construct out of our perceptions of it. He concludes, in effect, that the mode of construction must be such as to reconcile the successiveness of the survey with the unchangingness of the house.

What is the mode of construction, then? What are our criteria for the distinction between surveying an *object* and perceiving an *objective process*? Kant often veils this distinction by speaking of 'the concept of an object' when he means 'the concept of an objective state of affairs', but now he turns the distinction to account in an attempt to prove that all objective processes must conform to causal laws.

Consider (a) watching a ship sail out of a harbour, and (b) looking over a house, room by room. In each case my sensory state changes, but in (a) the changes in me are associated with changes in the perceived objects, while in (b) they are attributed to the way in which I perceived something which did not change. According to Kant, the distinction turns on whether the order in which my sensory states occur can be re-arranged: saying that what I apprehend is an objective process 'is only another way of saying that I cannot arrange the apprehension otherwise than in this very succession'. When I view the house, I can start and finish where I please, but when I watch the ship's departure the order in which my visual states occur is not up to me. In the following passage, Kant says this and also takes it a step further:

In the perception of an event there is always a rule that makes the order in which the perceptions (in the apprehension of this appearance) follow upon one another a *necessary* order...The objective succession will therefore consist in that order of the manifold of appearance according to which, *in conformity with a rule*, the apprehension of that which happens follows upon the apprehension of that which precedes. Thus only can I be justified in asserting, not merely of my apprehension, but of appearance itself, that a succession is to be met with in it. This is only another way of saying that I cannot arrange the apprehension otherwise than in this very succession. In conformity with such a rule there must lie in that which precedes an event the condition of a rule according to which this event invariably and necessarily follows.[1]

Thus, the perception of an objective process involves a necessary order of representations and so a necessary order of the episodes which make up the process itself. Whence it follows, Kant thinks, that every objective process is totally governed by causal laws.

The last step is certainly a non-sequitur. 'X and Y could not have occurred in the order Y–X' entails 'Given that X and Y happened non-synchronously, they had to happen in the order X–Y', but it does not entail 'Given that X happened, Y had to follow'. The rule which forbids a professor to precede the Vice-Chancellor in a procession does not forbid him to opt out of the procession altogether.

In any case the premiss of the argument, namely Kant's analysis of the concept of an objective process, is wrong. First we must clear up an ambiguity in it. If I have had a certain sequence of intuitions, I cannot now have *them* in a different order—in making this point in his 'proof' of the third Analogy, Kant wrongly takes it to be relevant to the concept of an objective process.[2] The fact that I cannot re-have past intuitions in a different order because they are all over and done with, so far from connecting objective succession with necessary order, has nothing to do with either. It is irrelevant to objectivity because it holds for every past sequence of intuitions, even those involved in a survey; and it is irrelevant to order because it holds for the re-having of past intuitions in no matter what order.

Perhaps we can take Kant's remark 'I cannot arrange the apprehension otherwise than in this very succession' to mean that my sensory states when I saw the ship leave the harbour *could not have* occurred in any other order. But does not this apply equally to a survey? Given that I walked and looked where I did, my visual states as I surveyed the house *could not have* occurred in any other order.

Kant might reply that in the survey I could have re-arranged my visual states, that their order would have been different if I had behaved differently; whereas when I saw the ship leave the harbour no action of mine could have altered the order in which my visual states occurred. This may do for the sailing-ship, but for some objective processes it is wrong. Here is a counter-example. (a) I saw a long-boat being rowed out of the harbour; which, if Kant's analysis is right, entails not just that my visual states *did* occur in a certain order but that (b) I *could not have* had them in any other order. But since the coxswain of the boat was under orders from me, I *could have* secured for myself the spectacle of the boat being back-paddled, stern foremost, into the harbour. So, (a) is true and (b) false, and Kant's analysis of (a) is therefore wrong.

No doubt the distinction between perceiving a process and surveying an object does have something to do with whether and how the percipient could have brought it about that his sensory states occurred in a different order—how much stage-managing would have been required, and of what kinds. So Kant might safely say: 'When I survey an object, the order of my perceptions depends in a certain way on how I act at the time; whereas when I perceive a process the order of my perceptions does not depend in *that* way—though it may depend in other ways—on how I act at the time.' This, though, is at best a preliminary sketch for an analysis of the object/process distinction, and there is no reason to think that if the detail were filled in it would constitute a proof of the second Analogy.

Since the distinction between perceiving a process and surveying an object requires that the percipient shall have a body, or at least a 'point of view' which he can control, Kant's analysis—in which bodies are not even mentioned—was bound to fail. His neglect of the fact that humans have bodies connects with his failure to see that when I survey an object an objective process is involved, namely my own movements.

54 The ordering argument

Weldon says that the second Analogy is concerned with 'a problem as to the manner in which we come to know about the physical as distinct from the psychological order of events'.[1] He gives an example: if I am 300 yards from a choir which I hear both directly and through a radio at my elbow, 'I shall hear the actual choir as an echo of the wireless', but my knowledge of physics assures me that every sound from the radio is emitted slightly later than the corresponding sound from the choir.

Weldon presumably has in mind a passage where Kant says:

Let us suppose that there is nothing antecedent to an event, upon which it must follow according to rule. All succession of perception would then be only in the apprehension, that is, would be merely subjective, and would never enable us to determine objectively which perceptions are those that really precede and which are those that follow.[1]

This, on the face of it, is concerned with the criteria for deciding whether X objectively followed Y or Y objectively followed X. Yet one sentence later Kant goes on:

I could not then assert that two states follow upon one another in the appearance [i.e. in the objective realm], but only that one apprehension follows upon the other.

Now this refers to the object/process distinction: rather than the question 'Which came first?' its concern is with the question 'Was there an objective succession at all?' I suggest that the previous passage would be better read as another, somewhat careless, formulation of the problem about objects and processes. It is unlikely to be addressed to Weldon's problem, which concerns the very rare case in which someone can know that he perceives an objective process while not knowing in what order its episodes occur. Significantly, Weldon's radio example is anachronistic, and I cannot replace it by one which Kant might have had in mind and thought crucial to one's conceptual grasp of any possible objective realm.

Kant does have a problem about temporal order, which generates what I call his 'ordering argument'. One of its features (a) marks it off sharply from the object/process argument and also from Weldon's problem; and another (b) marks it off from the realism argument as well.

(a) The object/process argument deals with one aspect of the way in which subjective data—'I have had such and such intuitions, in such and such an order'—are brought under objectivity concepts. The ordering argument, on the other hand, deals with an aspect of the way in which the subjective data themselves are established; specifically, with how one knows in what order certain events—including the occurrence of intuitions—have happened. This separates it from Weldon's problem as well, but not from the realism argument.

(b) The realism and ordering arguments both turn on the conditions under which something can be recalled in memory. The former says that if someone is to have any recollections at all he must have some experience of an objective realm; but the latter says that recollections *of a certain kind* are possible only if *each* of them is backed by objective considerations. The ordering argument is weaker than the realism argument in that it invokes objectivity in connection with only a sub-class of recollections, but stronger in that it demands objective backing for each recollection of that kind and not merely as a general background. The realism argument is analogous to the rule: 'No children may come unless several adults come', and the ordering argument to the rule: 'No child under five may come unless accompanied by an adult'.

The ordering argument occurs in fragments, just below the surface of Kant's text. Although it was clearly not part of his consciously held and explicitly formulated doctrine, I want to show what its textual basis is, for several parts of the text become more intelligible if they are seen to be coloured by a subliminal awareness of the ordering argument. These are passages where a treatment of the general relationship between objectivity and causality, or a deployment of the object/process argument, is unsatisfactory in a way which can be understood if we see that Kant is half-consciously trying to pack in something of the ordering argument as well. For example, while discussing the perception of an objective process Kant says:

In this case, therefore, we must derive the *subjective succession* of apprehension from the *objective succession* of appearances. Otherwise the order of apprehension is entirely undetermined, and does not distinguish one appearance from another. Since the subjective succession by itself is altogether arbitrary, it does not prove anything as to the manner in which the manifold is connected in the object[ive realm].[1]

The remark in the last sentence that the subjective succession 'does not prove anything as to the manner in which the [objective] manifold is connected' is appropriate to the object/process argument; but why does Kant call the subjective succession 'altogether arbitrary'? In the preceding sentence, too, as well as saying that the subjective succession does not determine what if any objective succession there is, Kant calls it 'entirely undetermined'. This, like his use of 'arbitrary', seems to point to a difficulty about what the subjective succession actually *is*. And in the first sentence Kant says outright that to know in what order one's inner states do or did occur one must have knowledge of an objective realm. The whole passage hints at a problem not about the relation between one's subjective and objective stories, but about the establishment of one's subjective story and, in particular, its temporal ordering. It is this more radical problem which provides fuel for the ordering argument.

Here again, hints of the ordering argument are mixed up with other things:

I perceive that appearances follow one another, that is, that there is a state of things at one time the opposite of which was in the preceding time. Thus I am really connecting two perceptions in time. Now connection is not the work of mere sense and intuition, but is here the product of a synthetic faculty of imagination, which determines inner sense in respect of the time-relation. But imagination can connect these two states in two ways, so that either the one or the other precedes in time. For time cannot be perceived in itself, and what precedes and what follows cannot, therefore, by relation to it, be empirically determined in the object. [I am conscious only that my imagination sets the one state before and the other after, not that the one state precedes the other in the object. In other words, the *objective relation* of appearances that follow upon one another is not to be determined through mere perception.] In order that this relation be known as determined, the relation between the two states must be so thought that it is thereby determined as necessary which of them must be placed before, and which of them after, and that they cannot be placed in the reverse relation.[1]

The sentences I have bracketed pertain to the object/process argument; but if the whole passage is a treatment of the objective order in which events occur then what can we make of the clause: 'which determines *inner* sense in respect of the time relation'? And what would the relevance be of the unperceivability of time? Both these aspects of the passage can be explained on the assumption that it does, at least in part, concern the ordering argument.

Kant's claim that 'time cannot be perceived in itself', which figured so obscurely in the 'proof' of the first Analogy, is the key to the explanation. By this Kant means that the position in time—or, for short, the date—of an event which I experience is not a perceptible feature of it. I experience it at a particular time, but I do not *perceive that* it has the feature of occurring at that time. The consequence of this which is crucial for the ordering argument is that because an event's date is not perceptible it is not recollectable either. I heard a loud bang at noon yesterday: I can recall its loudness by recalling *it*, but if I can be said to recall when it occurred this can only be because I recall other things as well as the bang—for example, the look of the clock or sound of the radio or state of my appetite at the time.

Paton, whose interpretation I am mainly following here, says that if time could be perceived then an event's date would be perceptible in a way 'akin to empirical perception', and would therefore be recollectable as one of its empirical features among others:

The death of Julius Caesar would, I suppose, be actually given to perception with the mark upon it of a particular moment on the Ides of March, BC 44, and all subsequent efforts to recall his death in imagination would necessarily recall that particular mark as an inseparable part of the whole event recalled.[1]

There is no need to say that, in recalling the death, Cassius would 'necessarily' recall its date; it is enough to say that he *could* do so. The point about the unperceivability of time is not that an event's date can be forgotten but rather than it cannot ever be recalled in the way in which one can sometimes recall what an event was like in respect of its perceptible features.

The reason for this is just that an event's date is a logical construct out of its temporal relations with other events. One can no more recall an event's date by recalling what *it* was like than one can recall what forebears and progeny a man had by recalling what *he* was like. It follows that we cannot establish the temporal order of past events by recalling their dates and ordering them upon that basis; rather, we must establish their order, and then date them.

This applies to the dating of subjective as well as objective events in the past. In the following passage Kant handles the unperceivability of time in the way I have outlined; and here, as in the long passage last quoted, what he says of 'appearances' is clearly valid for subjective events also:

Since absolute time is not an object of perception, this determination of [temporal] position cannot be derived from the relation of appearances to [absolute time]. On the contrary, the appearances must determine for one another their position in time, and make their time-order a necessary order.[2]

The last clause of this will be explained shortly.

Now, if Kant's concern in the long quoted passage is with the ordering or dating of past events, subjective or objective, then 'imagination' must there mean something like 'memory unaided by objective considerations'. For example, he says: 'Imagination can connect these two states in two ways, so that either the one or the other precedes in time.' I take this to mean that unaided recollection may inform me that X occurred and that Y occurred, but that nothing in my 'imaginative' recall of the two happenings can dictate which happened first.

That point concerns the *order* of past events. As well as denying that past events can be dated, and then ordered on that basis, Kant is denying that we can, forgoing the dates, just recall what the order was. In the following passage too:

All empirical knowledge involves the synthesis of the manifold by the imagination. This synthesis is always successive, that is, the representations in it are always sequent upon one another. In the imagination this sequence is not in any way determined in its order, as to what must precede and what must follow, and the series of sequent representations can indifferently be taken either in backward or in forward order.[1]

The picture here is one of 'imagination' conjuring up past episodes one by one, with the question inevitably arising: 'What is the relation between the order in which the events are conjured up and the order in which they actually occurred?' The answer, of course, is that there need be no regular relationship: this morning I recalled a childhood holiday, while last night I recalled yesterday's lunch. But this example seems to miss Kant's point; and to see what he *is* getting at we shall have to give up his unduly narrow picture of sequences of imaginative conjurings. What I take him to be saying is that if we are to recall that X preceded Y, we must be able to appeal to objective considerations, not just as a prerequisite for having any working concept of the past, but in support of that particular recollection. To take a simple example: if I am to recollect digging in the garden *before* having a bath, I must be able to appeal to objective considerations over and above those which are necessarily involved in my recollecting digging in the garden and recollecting having a bath. That is, I must be able to appeal to facts about the behaviour of clocks, or the fact that I always have a bath after gardening, or the fact that the mud which I recall washing off in the bath could have come only from my digging in the garden. Nothing could count as recalling that X preceded Y that did not involve objective considerations bearing directly on that specific temporal ordering. In short, the order in which events occur is no more a perceptible or recollectable feature of them than are their dates.

Something like this, I think, is what Kant has in mind when he says that 'we must derive the subjective succession of apprehension from the objective succession of appearances';[1] that if we cannot appeal to objective considerations 'the order of apprehension is entirely undetermined and...altogether arbitrary'; that 'imagination...determines inner sense in respect of the time-relation [but can connect] two states in two ways, so that either the one or the other precedes in time'; that '[if] the relation between two states [is to be determined it] must be so thought that it is thereby determined as necessary which of them must be placed before, and which of them after'; and that 'in the imagination this sequence is not in any way determined in its order, as to what must precede and what must follow, and the series of sequent representations can indifferently be taken either in backward or in forward order.'

This thesis of Kant's does not hold without exceptions; for here are three ways in which the order of a pair of events can be *simply recalled*, i.e. recalled without recourse to objective or causal considerations bearing specifically upon that ordering. (1) If Y occurred so soon after X that one can recall a specious present containing both, then one can simply recall that X preceded Y. If this were not so, one could not simply recall hearing someone say 'damn' rather than 'mad'. (2) From this it follows that one can simply recall that X preceded Y if one can recall a continuous sequence of happenings starting with X and ending with Y. If, without the aid of specifically relevant causal considerations, I can recall hearing C♯ before G♯, hearing G♯ before G♮, hearing G♮ before B♯,....etc., then without their aid I can recall hearing C♯ before the final note of the melody.[2] (3) One may simply recall that X preceded Y by recalling a time when one experienced Y while recalling X.

But these counter-examples to Kant's thesis cover only a small fragment of all the temporal orderings we wish to establish. If I am asked 'Did you clean your shoes before or after you went for a walk?', I may be able—in the manner of (1)—to recall the moment when I straightened my back from shoe-cleaning, put down the brush and strode off into the street; or (2) to relive the detail of my day from the shoe-cleaning episode through to the walk two hours later; or (3) to recall thinking, while on my walk, that it had been a mistake to clean my shoes before going out into the mud. But it is far more likely that my answer will have to be based on my recollection that I cleaned my shoes while the sun rose and walked as it was setting, or that I heard the one o'clock news while cleaning my shoes and arranged to go for a walk at three o'clock, or something else equally dependent for its relevance upon the truth of law-like statements about the objective realm. It would be—to put it mildly—a queer personal history which could be ordered solely in the manner of (1), (2) and (3).

Even if those three classes of exceptions did not exist at all, however, the ordering argument would not prove the second Analogy in its full strictness. For one can know that X must have preceded Y without also knowing that X and Y were completely causally determined: the causal or objective considerations which assure me that I saw a certain street-accident between leaving New Zealand and reaching England do not suffice to assure me that the accident was completely subsumable under causal laws. Still, the ordering argument does bring out one more way in which the appeal to objectivity is necessarily involved even in our talk about our own inner states.

Reverting to the way the ordering argument relates to Kant's text: what I have treated as versions of the object/process argument, interrupted and distorted by hints of the ordering argument, might be argued to be the ordering argument pure and simple. For I have taken 'objective' to mean 'other than oneself', counting one's past intuitions as subjective; but Kant may not, at this stage in the *Critique*, be drawing the subjective/objective line in that way. He may instead be taking as 'objective' any matter which admits of the distinction between what seems to be and what really is the case, which admits of error and correction of error, reasonable hesitancy in giving an answer, adducing of additional evidence and so on; and *all* questions about one's past states are 'objective' in that sense. The passages I have quoted could largely be read in that way; but I should not care to insist that Kant explicitly took this, or any other, view of the matter.

NOTES

PAGE 4

1 Views about geometrical method: A 712–38 = B 740–66.
2 'we shall have to treat': A 708 = B 736.
3 All quotations within this paragraph are from A 7 = B 11.

PAGE 7

1 'I must not restrict': A 718 = B 746.
2 'The concept of the sum': B 15.
3 'That the straight line': B 16.

PAGE 8

1 'No doubt the concept': A 43 = B 61.

PAGE 9

1 'Necessity and strict universality': B 4.
2 W. V. Quine, *From a Logical Point of View* (Cambridge, Mass., 1953), chh. ii and iii.
3 Ludwig Wittgenstein, *Philosophical Investigations* (Oxford, 1953) §§ 185–95; *Remarks on the Foundations of Mathematics* (Oxford, 1956), Pt. I §§ 1–5, 113–41.

PAGE 11

1 His most famous formulation: *Prolegomena to any Future Metaphysics*, §4; B 19.
2 Kant raises the question: A 7–10 = B 11–14.
3 'the connection of the predicate': A 7 = B 10.

PAGE 15

1 One queer remark: A 23 = B 37.
2 'Whatever the origin': A 98–9.

PAGE 17

1 'referred to something outside me': A 23 = B 38.

PAGE 18

1 'it should not obtain favour': A 46 = B 63.
2 'not merely possible': A 48–9 = B 66.
3 'Since the propositions of geometry': A 46–7 = B 64; cf. B xvii.
4 'If we have a proposition': B 3.

PAGE 19

1 'If, then, a judgment': B 4.
2 'Since these sciences': B 20.

1 Other versions of the causal theory: e.g. that of H. P. Grice, 'The Causal Theory of Perception', *Aristotelian Society Supplementary Volume*, XXXV (1961).
2 'If I turn my eyes': Locke, *An Essay Concerning Human Understanding*, IV. xi. 5.

1 G. E. Moore's hands: G. E. Moore, *Philosophical Papers* (London, 1959), pp. 145–6.
2 Kant on transcendental/empirical realism: A 369–72; cf. A 490–2 = B518–21.
3 'I must never presume': A 822 = B 850.

1 'It is...this transcendental': A 369.
2 'The transcendental idealist': A 370.
3 'A question as to the constitution': A 479 n. = B 507 n.

1 Chapter on phenomena/noumena: A 235–60 = B 294–315.
2 'landed in the absurd conclusion': B xxvi–xxvii.
3 'The true correlate': B 45.
4 'A priori knowledge...': B xx; cf. A 108–9, A 249–53, B 308–9.
5 Kant has been said to argue: A. C. Ewing, *A Short Commentary on Kant's Critique of Pure Reason* (London, 1938), p. 191.
6 Kant does sanction: A 494 = B 522.

1 the argument of §7: see top of B 219.

1 Kant has been congratulated: G. Martin, *Kant's Metaphysics and Theory of Science* (Manchester, 1955), pp. 18 ff.
2 Hume on geometry: Hume, *A Treatise of Human Nature*, I. ii. 1–5.

1 '*extremely* thin coloured pictures': J. Wisdom, *Philosophy and Psychoanalysis* (Oxford, 1953), p. 40.

1 'Our sight informs us not': Hume, *op. cit.* I. iv. 2.
2 The most rational philosopher: Berkeley, *A New Theory of Vision*, §§41 ff.; *Principles of Human Knowledge*, §§42–4.

PAGE 31

1 'I must admit': A. C. Ewing, *A Short Commentary*, p. 46.

PAGE 32

1 'In very recent years': A. Grünbaum, *Philosophical Problems of Space and Time* (London, 1964), p. 154.

PAGE 33

1 Strawson's chapter: P. F. Strawson, *Individuals* (London, 1959), ch. 2.

PAGE 35

1 'the crucial idea': *ibid.* pp. 73–4.

PAGE 36

1 Strawson invents an opponent: *ibid.* pp. 78–9.

PAGE 37

1 Birth and death of sound-sequences: *ibid.* p. 76.

PAGE 38

1 Identity of indiscernibles: A 283–5 = B 339–41; Leibniz, *New Essays Concerning Human Understanding*, II. xxvii. 1–3.

PAGE 39

1 Quine on conceptual efficiency: W. V. Quine, *From a Logical Point of View*, pp. 42–6.

PAGE 41

1 The hearer's concept of 'I': Strawson, *op. cit.* pp. 81–5.

PAGE 43

1 A priori brute facts: see the sentence on B 145–6.

PAGE 45

1 The inner-sense theory: A 34 = B 50–1.

PAGE 47

1 'Proposition' is a theoretical term: A. Church, *Introduction to Mathematical Logic* (Princeton, 1956), §04.

PAGE 49

1 True for all humans: A 42 = B 59; B 72.

PAGE 50

1 'We deny to time': A 35–6 = B 52.
2 'Against [my] theory': A 36–7 = B 53.

PAGE 51

1 'immediately evident through consciousness': A 38 = B 55.
2 'It is...solely': A 26-7 = B 42-3.

PAGE 52

1 Time and arithmetic: A 242 = B 300; *Prolegomena* § 10.
2 'Time has only one dimension': A 31 = B 47.

PAGE 53

1 'There are two stems': A 15 = B 29.

PAGE 54

1 'Sensibility alone yields us': A 19 = B 33.
2 Wittgenstein on concepts: L. Wittgenstein, *Philosophical Investigations*, §§ 1-37, 191-9.
3 Kant's use of 'representation': e.g. on A 68 = B 93.
4 Wittgensteinian use of 'concept': A 51-2 = B 75; A 67-9 = B 92-4.

PAGE 55

1 Thinking and sensing: Descartes, *Principles of Philosophy*, I. ix, xxx-xxxii. Locke, *Essay*, II. xi. 8-9. Spinoza, *Ethics*, II. xl. note II. Hume, *Treatise*, I. i. I.
2 'Leibniz *intellectualized* appearances': A 271 = B 327; cf. A 44 = B 61-2.
3 Differing not at all: Berkeley, *Principles*, Introduction, §§ 22, 25.
4 Like Berkeley before him: Berkeley, *op. cit.* §§ 28-9.
5 Activity and passivity: A 19 = B 33; A 51 = B 75; A 68 = B 93; B 150.

PAGE 56

1 Kant emphasizes: B 149.
2 'The concept of a noumenon': A 255 = B 310-11.

PAGE 57

1 When he makes it best: B 307; A 287-8 = B 344; A 288-9 = B 344-5.

PAGE 58

1 A graver mistake: A 248-50 (seven paragraphs); B 305-9 (four paragraphs).
2 'we cannot comprehend': B 307.
3 'an understanding which [would] know': A 256 = B 311-12.
4 Two major Kantian emphases: B 145.

PAGE 59

1 'If we abstract': A 34 = B 51.
2 'If the senses represent': A 249-50.
3 We 'distinguish the mode': B 306.
4 'The concept of a *noumenon*': A 254 = B 310.
5 'Appearances, so far as': A 248-9.

PAGE 60

1 'absolutely objective reality'; A 249.

PAGE 61

1 'the concepts of space and time': A 89 = B 121.
2 'do not represent the conditions': A 89 = B 122.
3 'Everything might be in such confusion': A 90-1 = B 123.

PAGE 62

1 We do have concepts of space and time: A 85-6 = B 118; A 89 = B 121.
2 'The original representation': B 40.

PAGE 63

1 Kant permits us to define: A 24-5 = B 39.

PAGE 64

1 Ambiguity of '...are intuitions': B 73.
2 'from mere concepts': A 47 = B 64-5.
3 'Pure intuition...contains': A 50-1 = B 74-5.
4 Quinton's argument: A. M. Quinton, 'Spaces and Times', *Philosophy*, vol. 37 (1962).

PAGE 66

1 Quinton himself shows: *ibid.* pp. 144-7.
2 Space is necessarily infinite: B 39-40.

PAGE 67

1 Ambiguity of 'curved': E. Whittaker, *From Euclid to Eddington* (New York, 1958), §17.
2 Time is necessarily infinite: A 32 = B 47-8.

PAGE 71

1 One passing remark: B 159.
2 'gone through in a certain way': A 77 = B 102.

PAGE 76

1 'In Aristotle's doctrine': G. Ryle, 'Categories', in A. G. N. Flew (ed.), *Logic and Language*, second series (Oxford, 1955), p. 73.

PAGE 77

1 'If we abstract': A 70 = B 95.
2 One remark of Kant's: B 110-11.

PAGE 78

1 Non-mortal and immortal: cf. G. Bird, *Kant's Theory of Knowledge* (London, 1962), p. 107 n.
2 Explanation of the modality-features: A 74–6 = B 99–101.

PAGE 79

1 Tradition has been cogently attacked: C. H. Whiteley, 'The Idea of Logical Form', *Mind*, vol. 60 (1951).

PAGE 80

1 'specify the understanding': A 79 = B 105.

PAGE 83

1 'as little capable of further explanation': B 146.

PAGE 84

1 'A concept is a recognitional capacity': H. H. Price, *Thinking and Experience* (London, 1953), p. 355.

PAGE 85

1 Much stressed by Moore: G. E. Moore, *Some Main Problems of Philosophy* (London, 1953), pp. 61, 109.

PAGE 86

1 'I shall, therefore': G. E. Moore, *Principia Ethica* (Cambridge, 1951), p. 6.
2 'If I am asked': *ibid.* pp. 6–7.

PAGE 87

1 I discuss this distinction: J. Bennett, *Rationality* (London, 1964), §§9–11.

PAGE 89

1 I have argued for this: *ibid.* §8.
2 Quine's proposal: W. V. Quine, *Methods of Logic* (London, 1952), §37.

PAGE 90

1 Strawson's reply: P. F. Strawson, 'Singular Terms, Ontology and Identity', *Mind*, vol. 65 (1956).
2 'the empiricist premise': *ibid.* pp. 445–6.
3 Pointing is linguistic: *ibid.* p. 451 n.

PAGE 91

1 'Some universal terms': *ibid.* p. 446.

PAGE 93

1 Kant's boast: A 80–1 = B 106–7.

1 'there arise precisely': A 79–80 = B 105.
2 His declared intention: A 136 = B 175; A 148 = B 187–8. Cf. A 161 = B 200.
3 'explanations of the [modal categories]': A 219 = B 266.

1 '*de facto* mode of origination': A 85 = B 117.
2 A priori 'origin' or 'source': A 56 = B 80; A 158–9 = B 197–8.
3 'Those who would assert': Hume, *Enquiry Concerning the Human Understanding*, section II.
4 When the detail is filled in: see A. Flew, *Hume's Philosophy of Belief* (London, 1961), ch. 2.

1 Utterly at variance: E. R. Hilgard and D. G. Marquis, *Conditioning and Learning* (New York, 1961), pp. 2–3, 9–10.
2 Hume's account: Hume, *Treatise*, I. i. 7.
3 Locke's comparable story: Locke, *Essay*, II. xi. 9.

1 Always have a surrealist air: P. Geach, *Mental Acts* (London, 1957), §7.
2 Locke seems to have argued: Locke, *Essay*, I. i. 23 and *passim*.
3 Leibniz apparently saw: Leibniz, *New Essays*, Preface and I. i.
4 '...except the mind itself': *ibid*. II. i. 2.

1 The 'patchwork theory': N. Kemp Smith, *A Commentary to Kant's Critique of Pure Reason* (London, 1923), pp. 202–34. R. P. Wolff, *Kant's Theory of Mental Activity* (Cambridge, Mass., 1963), ch. II.
2 Hume vis-à-vis Locke and Berkeley: Hume, *Treatise*, I. iv. 2, especially last two paragraphs.

1 'they would mean nothing': A 240 = B 299.

1 'Thoughts without content': A 51–2 = B 75–6.
2 The central argument: A 106–7, 110–11, 115–17, 121–6; B 129–39.
3 'The...unity of consciousness': B 138.

1 The extraordinary suggestion: C. D. Broad, *Examination of McTaggart's Philosophy* (Cambridge, 1933), vol. I, p. 174.
2 'It must be possible': B 131–2.

PAGE 105

1 '[If I had the mentality...]': quoted in N. Kemp Smith, *op. cit.* pp. xlix–l.

PAGE 106

1 The mind of a Neanderthal man: William Golding, *The Inheritors* (London, 1959).

PAGE 107

1 'The supreme principle': B 136–7.

PAGE 109

1 'so constantly, and so quick': Locke, *Essay*, II. ix. 9.
2 'that self-consciousness which': B 132; cf. A 116–17.
3 *abgeleitet*...which has been suggested: by Goldschmidt; see the edition of the *Critique* by R. Schmidt (Hamburg, 1956).

PAGE 111

1 'The manifold to be intuited': B 145.

PAGE 112

1 'I am conscious to myself': B 135–6.
2 'To this act the general title': B 130.
3 'taking place a priori': B 151.
4 'nothing but the faculty of combining': B 135.
5 'that act of the understanding': B 143; see also B 138–9.

PAGE 113

1 'If this manifold is to be known': A 77–8 = B 102–3.

PAGE 114

1 Kant's account of combination: B 129–31.
2 'The manifold of representations': B 129–30.

PAGE 115

1 Several passages which show this: A 116; A 121–2.
2 'The thought that the representations': B 134.

PAGE 117

1 'This thoroughgoing identity': B 133.

PAGE 120

1 Following Quine: W. V. Quine, *From a Logical Point of View*, ch. iv.

PAGE 121

1 'the same consciousness': Locke, *Essay*, II. xxvii. 9–10 (given in A. C. Fraser's edition (London, 1959) as II. xxvii. 11–10).
2 Grice's article: H. P. Grice, 'Personal Identity', *Mind*, vol. 50 (1941).

PAGE 123

1 'Each representation, in so far as': A 99.
2 'The word "concept"': A 103.

PAGE 125

1 'Everything might be in such confusion': A 90 = B 123.
2 'All possible appearances': A 113–14.

PAGE 126

1 Kant on objectivity: A 104–6; A 128–30; B 140–2.
2 'the object is viewed': A 104–5.

PAGE 127

1 'We have to deal only': A 105; cf. A 108–10.
2 Kemp Smith's *Commentary*: N. Kemp Smith, *op. cit.* pp. 204 ff.
3 Wolff's *Kant's Theory*: R. P. Wolff, *op. cit.* ch. ii.
4 Equally regressive hints: A 85 = B 117; A 88 = B 120.
5 Berkeley on objects: Berkeley, *Principles*, §§ 1, 4.
6 'objects are nothing but representations': A 371.

PAGE 128

1 Hume on objects: Hume, *Treatise*, I. iv. 2.

PAGE 129

1 'can be a rule for intuitions': A 106.
2 'There can be no *it*': S. Körner, *Kant* (Penguin Books, 1955), p. 62.
3 'Since a mere modification': A 129.

PAGE 130

1 'A judgment is nothing': B 141.
2 'What solipsism *means*': L. Wittgenstein, *Tractatus Logico-Philosophicus* (London, 1922), 5.62.
3 Even the best of them: A 108; B 162–3.

PAGE 131

1 'the unity of consciousness': B 138.
2 'Everything, every representation': A 189–90 = B 234–5.
3 'this unity of possible consciousness': A 129.

PAGE 132

1 'constitutes a formal a priori knowledge': A 129–30.
2 'The concept of body': A 106.
3 'To say "The body is heavy"': B 142.

PAGE 133

1 A similar mistake: *Prolegomena*, §20, footnote.
2 misuse of experience/perception distinction: B 140–2.
3 'a *judgment*, that is': B 142.
4 'experience is knowledge': B 161; cf. B 218–19, B 234, B 275.
5 'The a priori conditions': A 111.

PAGE 134

1 'All experience does indeed contain': A 93 = B 126.
2 'All representations have': A 108.
3 'Since every appearance contains': A 120.

PAGE 135

1 'some third thing': A 138 = B 177.
2 'the two extremes': A 124.
3 'It is one and the same': B 162 n.; cf. sentence on B 153–4.
4 'There are three original sources': A 94.
5 'This spontaneity': A 97.

PAGE 136

1 'If we were not conscious': A 103.
2 'When I seek to...represent': A 102.
3 'If, in counting': A 103.

PAGE 137

1 'For the concept of the number': A 103.
2 'The unity of apperception in': A 119.
3 '[1] *Sense* represents appearances': A 115.
4 'There must...exist in us': A 120.
5 '[2a] There exists a subjective ground': A 121.

PAGE 138

1 '[2b] If, however, representations': A 121.
2 'apperception which must be added': A 124.

PAGE 141

1 'representation of a universal procedure': A 140 = B 179–80.
2 'a rule according to which my imagination': A 141 = B 180.
3 A difficulty which is fatal: A 140–1 = B 180.

1 Construction *v.* recognition in mathematics: A 140 = B 179, A 713–14 = B 741–2.
2 'This schematism of our understanding': A 141 = B 180–1.
3 'so constantly and so quick': Locke, *Essay*, II. ix. 9.

1 Colour-samples in our heads: L. Wittgenstein, *The Blue and Brown Books* (Oxford, 1964), pp. 3–5.
2 Understanding and judgment: A 132–4 = B 171–4.

1 '[If we] sought to give': A 133 = B 172.
2 Kant tries to square this: A 135–6 = B 174–5.
3 Referential rules: S. Körner, *Kant*, p. 71.

1 'understanding'/'judgment'—the three versions: A 69 = B 94; A 126; A 132–3 = B 171–2.
2 'illegitimately separating the application': G. J. Warnock, 'Concepts and Schematism', *Analysis*, vol. 9 (1948–9), p. 80.
3 'the higher faculties of knowledge': A 130 = B 169.
4 Wittgenstein's fertile treatment: L. Wittgenstein, *Philosophical Investigations*, §§172–97, 292; *Remarks on the Foundations of Mathematics*, Pt. I §§1–5, 113–41.

1 Two features...which he often stresses: see B 151–2.
2 (iii) as having noticed the difference: cf. B 154–5.

1 'the representation of the object': A 137 = B 176.
2 'the concepts through which': A 138 = B 177.

1 'In all subsumptions of an object': A 137 = B 176.
2 'I think Kant's point is': G. J. Warnock, *op. cit.* pp. 80–1.
3 '" This is the cause"': *ibid.* p. 81.

1 'mediate the subsumption': A 139 = B 178.
2 '[it] is so far homogeneous': A 138–9 = B 177–8.

1 'In the principle itself': A 181 = B 224.

PAGE 152

1 'The categories have this peculiar feature': A 244–5.

PAGE 153

1 'the concept of a cause involves': A 112.
2 'The schema of cause': A 144 = B 183.
3 'While Kant insists': S. Körner, *Kant*, p. 74.

PAGE 154

1 'the mind has a great propensity': Hume, *Treatise*, I. iii. 14.
2 'The concept of cause': B 168.
3 Empirical counter-examples: A. C. Ewing, 'A Defence of Causality', *Proceedings of the Aristotelian Society*, vol. 33 (1932–3). W. Kneale, 'Natural Laws and Contrary-to-Fact Conditionals', *Analysis*, vol. 10 (1950).

PAGE 155

1 'the very concept of a cause': B 5.
2 Kant sometimes seems to identify: see the sentence on A 195–6 = B 241.
3 'Kant is emphatically not saying': W. H. Walsh, *Reason and Experience* (Oxford, 1947), p. 153.

PAGE 156

1 Hume discussed the two together: Hume, *Treatise*, I. iii. 3.
2 'An understanding...through whose': B 139.
3 'The order and regularity': A 125.

PAGE 157

1 'That nature should direct itself': A 114.
2 Imposition...in other passages too: A 92 = B 124–5, B xv–xviii, B 164, A 196 = B 241.
3 'the lawgiver of nature': A 126.
4 'new mode of thought': B xv–xviii.
5 'Since he could not explain': B 127.
6 'However exaggerated and absurd': A 127.
7 'The question...arises': B 163.

PAGE 158

1 'Pure understanding is not': B 165.
2 Thoroughly ambiguous passage: A 92 = B 125.
3 'All empirical laws': A 127–8.
4 'special determinations': A 126.
5 'The laws of nature': A 159 = B 198.
6 Hume was wrong in inferring: A 766 = B 794.
7 Familiar to readers of Popper: K. Popper, *The Logic of Scientific Discovery* (London, 1959), ch. 1.

PAGE 159

1 'Reason has insight': B xiii.

PAGE 160

1 'If we [were to say] that experience': A 91–2 = B 123–4.

PAGE 161

1 No warrant in the German: cf. J. Bennett, 'The Status of Determinism', *The British Journal for the Philosophy of Science*, vol. 14 (1963), p. 111.
2 'inseparable from one another': B 4.
3 Like Berkeley before him: Berkeley, *New Theory of Vision and Other Writings* (London, 1960), p. 237; cf. 'see with your eyes', on p. 236.
4 'Experience never confers': B 3–4.

PAGE 163

1 I have argued elsewhere: J. Bennett, 'The Status of Determinism'.

PAGE 164

1 'division of the concept of *nothing*': A 291 = B 348.

PAGE 165

1 Kant's defence of 'Analogies': A 179–80 = B 222–3.
2 His use of 'Anticipations': A 167 = B 209.
3 'There are no axioms': A 164 = B 204; see also A 733 = B 761.
4 'the mathematics of appearances': A 165 = B 206.
5 'the concept of a *number*': B 111.

PAGE 166

1 'the principles of modality': A 219 = B 266.
2 Kant's explanations of the modal categories: A 218 = B 265–6.
3 Kant's account of 'actuality': A 225–6 = B 272–4.
4 Not a category itself but something narrower: A 146–7 = B 186.
5 'It is, indeed, a necessary': A 220 = B 267–8.

PAGE 167

1 'the third postulate': A 226 = B 279.
2 Schemas of actuality and necessity: A 145 = B 184.
3 'permanence of the real in time': A 144 (wrongly given in most editions as A 143) = B 183.
4 'permanence (which is existence...)': A 242 = B 300.
5 'All intuitions are extensive magnitudes': B 202; cf. A 162.

PAGE 168

1 'the representation of its parts': A 162 = B 203.

PAGE 169

1 'I cannot represent to myself': A 162–3 = B 203–4.
2 'The synthesis of the manifold parts': A 412 = B 439.
3 'occupies only an instant': A 167–8 = B 209–10.

PAGE 170

1 'as the [element of] pure intuition': A 163 = B 203–4.
2 'matters which do not come': A 149 = B 188.
3 'transcendental principle of the mathematics': A 165 = B 206; cf. A 178 = B 221.
4 One of his dreadful appeals: A 165 = B 206.
5 'apprehended only as unity': A 168 = B 210.

PAGE 171

1 Mention of infinite divisibility: A 165 = B 206.
2 'property of magnitudes': A 169 = B 211.
3 'intensive magnitude, that is, a degree': A 166; cf. B 207.

PAGE 172

1 'In all appearances': A 166; cf. B 207.
2 'forestall experience precisely in that': A 167 = B 209.
3 'Every sensation...is capable': A 168 = B 209–10.

PAGE 173

1 'Even if the whole intuition': A 172–3 = B 214.
2 Descartes...would have benefited: Descartes, *Principles of Philosophy*, II. vi.

PAGE 174

1 'Almost all natural philosophers': A 173–4 = B 215–16.
2 'I do not at all intend': A 174–5 = B 216.

PAGE 175

1 'The proof of an empty space': A 172 = B 214; cf. A 213–14 = B 260–1.

PAGE 176

1 'If space were only a line': Leibniz, *New Essays*, II. xv. 11.
2 He rightly infers: A 172 = B 214.

PAGE 178

1 'that which is bound up': A 218 = B 266.
2 Mendelssohn's argument: B 413–15.
3 '[Mendelssohn] failed to observe': B 414.
4 'there would be no time': B 414.

1 Kant makes just these moves: A 207–9 = B 253–4.
2 'all smaller degrees': A 208 = B 254.
3 'The question...arises': A 208 = B 253.
4 'In the [field of] appearance': A 209 = B 254.
5 Elsewhere Kant does better: A 171 = B 212–13.

1 'All substances, in so far': B 256; cf. A 211.
2 'Experience is possible': B 218; cf. A 176–7.
3 'All appearances are': A 176–7.
4 'the determination of the existence': B 219.

1 Time is even invoked to explain: A 215 = B 262.
2 'The three modes of time': A 177 = B 219.
3 An illuminating paper by Kneale: W. C. Kneale, 'The Notion of a Substance', *Proceedings of the Aristotelian Society*, vol. 40 (1939–40).

1 'All appearances contain': A 182.
2 Permanence (*Beharrlichkeit*): A 185 = B 228–9.
3 'The proposition that substance': A 184 = B 227.
4 'In all change of appearances': B 224.
5 The category of 'Inherence and Subsistence': A 80 = B 106.
6 Kant sometimes says, of 'substance': A 144 = B 183.
7 'something which can be thought of': A 147 = B 186.

1 'the sensible determination of permanence': A 147 = B 186.
2 A confusion about 'substance': for detailed references to Locke and Berkeley,
see J. Bennett, 'Substance, Reality and Primary Qualities', *American Philosophical Quarterly*, vol. 2 (1965).

1 Many passages wither under scrutiny: Berkeley, *Principles*, §§16, 17, 37, 74,
76.
2 Sometimes Berkeley says something useful: *ibid.* §§18–20, 49.

1 'Qualities are nothing but *sensations*': *ibid.* §78.
2 A famous defence of phenomenalism: A. J. Ayer, *Language, Truth and Logic*
(London, 1949), p. 42.

1 Phenomenal *and objective*: see A 191 = B 236.

1 'All that alters *persists*': A 187 = B 230-1.

1 He does deny that physical things: B 277-8.

1 'A coming to be': A 188 = B 231.

1 'If the sentence': G. J. Warnock, *Berkeley* (Penguin Books, 1953), pp. 181-2.

1 Criteria for *our* distinctions: A 147 = B 186-7, A 242-3 = B 300-1.

1 'If I leave out permanence': A 242-3 = B 300-1.
2 Existence-statements and quantifiers: W. V. Quine, 'Designation and Existence', in H. Feigl and W. Sellars (eds.), *Readings in Philosophical Analysis* (New York, 1949).

1 Pioneered by Kant in the Dialectic: A 592-602 = B 620-30.
2 Kant thinks that he has given an answer: B 232-3.

1 'We have nothing permanent': B 278.
2 'its quantum in nature': B 224.
3 Conservation of matter: A 185 = B 228.

1 Passages which I have ignored: A 144 = B 183, A 182-4 = B 224-7.
2 'Kant's argument amounts to this': H. J. Paton, *Kant's Metaphysic of Experience* (London, 1951), vol. 2, p. 201.
3 'Therefore, to apprehend': H. A. Prichard, *Kant's Theory of Knowledge* (Oxford, 1909), p. 272.
4 Other commentators: A. C. Ewing, *Short Commentary*, p. 153; T. D. Weldon, *Kant's Critique of Pure Reason*, 2nd edn. (Oxford, 1958), p. 312; W. H. Walsh, *Reason and Experience*, p. 147; S. Körner, *Kant*, p. 84.

PAGE 202

1 'Refutation of Idealism': B 274–9.
2 'the only addition': B xxxix n.
3 'I am conscious': B 275.
4 Most commentators have taken Kant at his word: see T. D. Weldon, *op. cit.* p. 312.

PAGE 203

1 'The mere, but empirically': B 275.
2 'In the above proof': B 276–7.

PAGE 204

1 'I am conscious': B 275, as modified on B xxxix n.

PAGE 205

1 'The mere, but empirically determined': B 275.
2 'that outer experience is really': B 276–7.
3 'The existence of outer things': B 278.

PAGE 206

1 Ayer has tried: A. J. Ayer, 'Can there be a Private Language?', *Aristotelian Society Proceedings Supplementary Volume* 28 (1954). 'Professor Malcolm on Dreams', *The Journal of Philosophy*, vol. 57 (1960).
2 'Justification consists in': L. Wittgenstein, *Philosophical Investigations*, §265.
3 'In the present case': *ibid.* §258.

PAGE 209

1 'There [could not] be an empirical synthesis': A 101.

PAGE 210

1 Wittgenstein also assumes: L. Wittgenstein, *op. cit.* §258.

PAGE 211

1 Wittgenstein's 'private': see *ibid.* §§244–316.
2 'If the argument were valid': cf. P. F. Strawson, review of *Philosophical Investigations*, *Mind*, vol. 63 (1954), pp. 84–5.
3 'The argument rules out': cf. N. Malcolm, *Knowledge and Certainty* (Englewood Cliffs, N.J., 1963), pp. 97, 124.

PAGE 213

1 'it is not possible to obey': L. Wittgenstein, *op. cit.* §202; cf. §258.
2 'On the private-language hypothesis': N. Malcolm, *op. cit.* p. 103.

PAGE 214

1 '"Imagine a person"': L. Wittgenstein, *op. cit.* §271.

PAGE 215

1 Kant refutes Descartes: A 366–80, A 490–2 = B 518–21.
2 'In order to arrive': A 371.

PAGE 216

1 'If the existence of outer things': B 418.
2 He tries to reconcile these two claims: B 274–5.
3 Objectivity statements as permanently corrigible: see C. I. Lewis, *An Analysis of Knowledge and Valuation* (La Salle, Ill., 1946), pp. 185–90.
4 Good reasons have been given: J. L. Austin, *Philosophical Papers* (Oxford, 1961), pp. 54–7. N. Malcolm, *op. cit.* pp. 1–57.

PAGE 217

1 The realism argument does not guarantee: B 278–9.
2 'In order to determine': B xli n.
3 'The transcendental idealist': A 371.

PAGE 219

1 'All alterations take place': B 232; cf. A 189.
2 A sequence of six arguments: H. J. Paton, *op. cit.* vol. 2, p. 224.
3 A single argument: T. D. Weldon, *op. cit.* pp. 312–13.
4 'If we enquire': A 197 = B 242.

PAGE 220

1 Prefaced by a paragraph: A 189–91 = B 234–6.

PAGE 221

1 'In the perception': A 193 = B 238–9.
2 Kant wrongly takes it to be relevant: A 211 = B 258.

PAGE 222

1 Weldon on the second Analogy: T. D. Weldon, *op. cit.* pp. 309–10.

PAGE 223

1 'Let us suppose': A 194 = B 239.

PAGE 224

1 'In this case, therefore': A 193 = B 238.

PAGE 225

1 'I perceive that appearances': B 233–4.

NOTES

PAGE 226

1 'The death of Julius Caesar': H. J. Paton, *op. cit.* vol. 2, p. 228.
2 'Since absolute time': A 200 = B 245.

PAGE 227

1 'All empirical knowledge': A 201 = B 246.

PAGE 228

1 All quotations in this paragraph are from passages quoted earlier in this section.
2 The melody: the adagio theme in the slow movement of Bruckner's seventh symphony.

INDEX

INDEX

time *(cont.)*
  objective/subjective, 51 f., §53
  temporal order, §54
Transcendental Deduction, §§28–34, 170, 181
  purpose of, 71, 100–3, 124 f., 130 f.
transcendental idealism, 23 f., 50–2, 64, 101 f., 126–9, 166, 178, 193 f., §52, 220

understanding, §17, 61 f., §34, 144–6
  as active, 55 f., 58 f., 135, 143
  inventory of its powers, 80–3

Vaihinger, H., 100, 138

Walsh, W. H., 155, 201 n.
Warnock, G. J., 146, 149 f., 194–6
Weldon, T. D., 201 n., 202 n., 219, 222 f.
Whiteley, C. H., 79 n.
Whittaker, E., 67 n.
Wisdom, J., 29
Wittgenstein, L., 9 f., 54, 97, 130, 144, 146, 204–6, 209–14
Wolff, R. P., 100 n., 127

Sonata # 3 in A min for Harpsichord + violin (3rd Allegro movement)